Migration, Modernity and Transnationalism in the Work of Joseph Conrad

Migration, Modernity and Transnationalism in the Work of Joseph Conrad

Edited by Kim Salmons and Tania Zulli

BLOOMSBURY ACADEMIC
LONDON • NEW YORK • OXFORD • NEW DELHI • SYDNEY

BLOOMSBURY ACADEMIC
Bloomsbury Publishing Plc
50 Bedford Square, London, WC1B 3DP, UK
1385 Broadway, New York, NY 10018, USA
29 Earlsfort Terrace, Dublin 2, Ireland

BLOOMSBURY, BLOOMSBURY ACADEMIC and the Diana logo are trademarks of Bloomsbury Publishing Plc

First published in Great Britain 2021
This paperback edition published 2023

For legal purposes the Acknowledgements on p. xiii constitute an extension of this copyright page.

Cover design by Namkwan Cho
Cover image © Alexandra Boardman

A catalogue record for this book is available from the British Library.

A catalog record for this book is available from the British Library.

ISBN: HB: 978-1-3501-6892-3
PB: 978-1-3502-5552-4
ePDF: 978-1-3501-6893-0
eBook: 978-1-3501-6894-7

Typeset by Integra Software Services Pvt. Ltd.

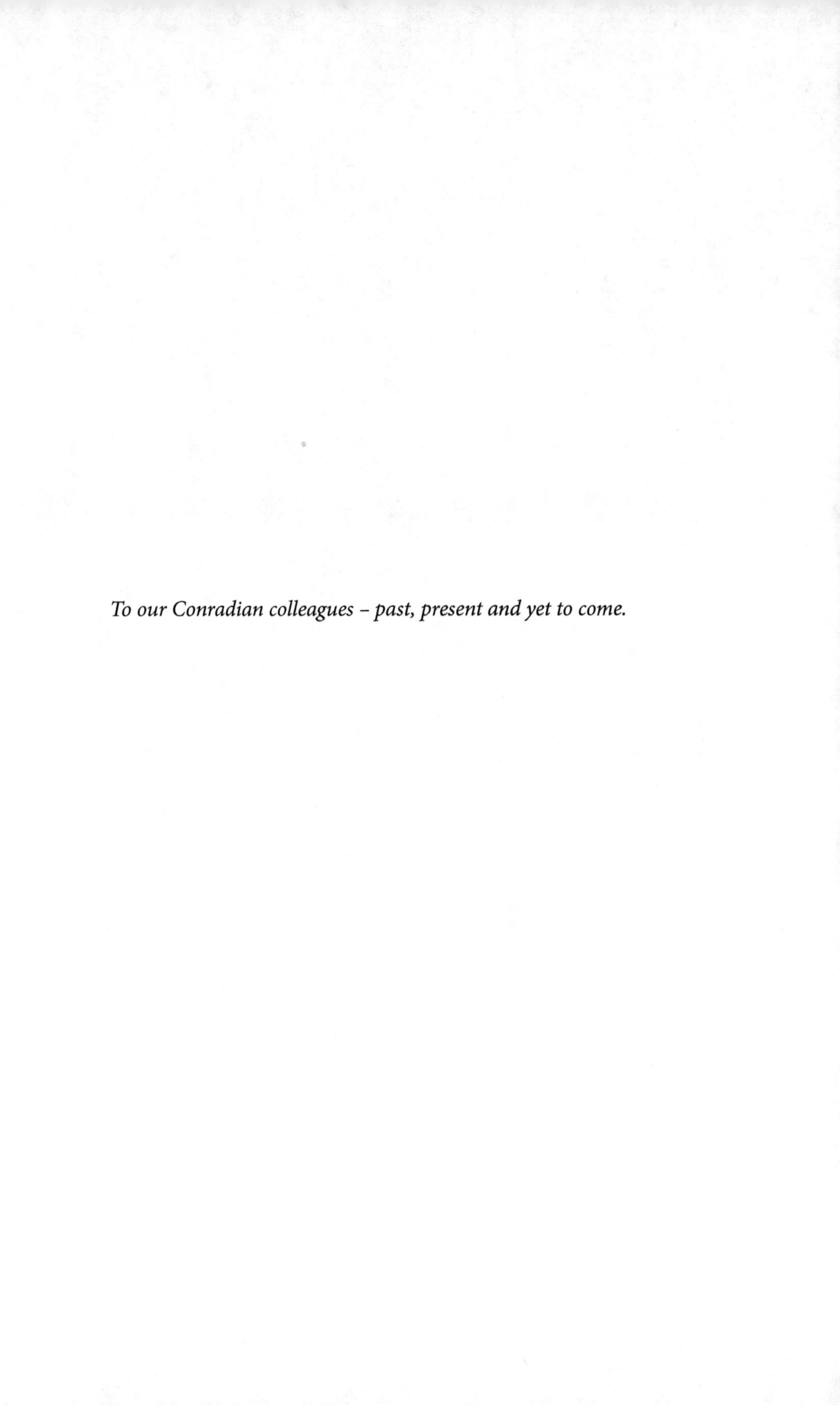

To our Conradian colleagues – past, present and yet to come.

Contents

Figures

Chapter 3

Chapter 8

Contributors

Agnieszka Adamowicz-Pośpiech is Associate Professor of English Literature and Translation Studies at the University of Silesia (Poland) in the Literary Studies Department. Her research interests focus on British modernism, contemporary drama, descriptive translation studies and visual cultural studies. She has published articles on J. Conrad, T. S. Eliot, R. Browning, W. Golding, G. B. Shaw, H. Pinter and J. Verma. Her most recent book is *Travels with Conrad* (2016). She is currently involved in the project *The Transcultural Conrad.*

William Atkinson, Professor in the English Department at Appalachian State University, North Carolina, teaches world literature and mythology, with a principal scholarly interest in animal studies. His publications include essays on Conrad, Synge and Beckett, the most recent being 'Yet Again, Achebe and *Heart of Darkness*: Updating the Horror' in *The Conradian*, Autumn 2018.

Katherine Isobel Baxter is Professor of English Literature at Northumbria University. Her research engages with colonial and postcolonial literatures, and focuses on issues of law and literature, literary multilingualism, trauma and transnationalism. She has published extensively on Joseph Conrad including *Joseph Conrad and the Swan Song of Romance* (2010) and *Conrad and Language* (edited with Robert Hampson, 2016). Her most recent book is *Imagined States: Law and Literature in Nigeria, 1900–1966* (2019).

Riccardo Capoferro teaches English Literature at Sapienza Università di Roma. He has published books and articles on the British eighteenth century, focusing on the relation between epistemological change and the emergence of new narrative genres. His research interests currently focus on the work of Joseph Conrad and its impact in a transmedial world.

Laurence Davies is Visiting Senior Research Fellow at King's College London. With a roster of colleagues he edited the nine-volume *Collected Letters of Joseph Conrad* and also the *Selected Letters.* He serves on the boards of the Cambridge Edition of Conrad's works and the Oxford Edition of Ford Madox Ford's. His other interests include speculative fiction, literature and science, millenarianism, international modernisms, and the Scottish author and radical campaigner R. B. Cunninghame Graham. Conrad, Ford and Graham aside, he has also published in recent years on Katharine Burdekin, James Baldwin, Hawthorne, Poe, Guillermo del Toro, Atwood, Zamyatin and the perils of Gothic hostelries.

Andrew Francis is an independent scholar based in Cambridge. A member of the Executive Committee of The Joseph Conrad Society (UK), he gained his PhD from the University of Cambridge following a career in commerce. His *Culture and Commerce in Conrad's Asian Fiction* (Cambridge University Press) was published in 2015. With interests in Dutch and British colonial fiction, his research and publications are concerned particularly with Conrad's Asian fiction, especially in the context of Dutch East Indies culture and history. He is currently finishing editing and co-translating essays in Dutch and Indonesian on Conrad by the Indonesian scholar G. J. Resink.

Chris GoGwilt is Professor of English and Comparative Literature at Fordham University, New York. He is the author of *The Passage of Literature: Genealogies of Modernism in Conrad, Rhys, and Pramoedya* (2011), *The Fiction of Geopolitics* (2000) and *The Invention of the West: Joseph Conrad and the Double-Mapping of Europe and Empire* (1995); and co-editor of *Mocking Bird Technologies* (2018) and *Conradian Crosscurrents: Creativity and Critique*, a recent special issue of *Conradiana*.

Robert Hampson FEA, FRSA is Professor Emeritus at Royal Holloway, University of London; Visiting Professor at the University of Northumbria and a research fellow at the University of London Institute for English Studies. He is the author of *Joseph Conrad: Betrayal and Identity*, *Cross-Cultural Encounters in Joseph Conrad's Malay Fiction* and *Conrad's Secrets*, and he co-edited *Conrad and Language* with Katherine Isobel Baxter. He has a research interest in Conrad, borders, cosmopolitanism and transnationalism, and he has just completed a critical biography of Conrad. He is currently chair of the Joseph Conrad Society (UK).

Yael Levin is Associate Professor in English at the Hebrew University of Jerusalem and Second Vice President of the Joseph Conrad Society of America. She is author of *Tracing the Aesthetic Principle in Conrad's Novels* and *Joseph Conrad: Slow Modernism*. Her work on modernism, postmodernism, narratology, the subject and disability has appeared in *The Conradian*, *Conradiana*, *Partial*

Answers, Twentieth-Century Literature, Journal of Modern Literature and *Journal of Beckett Studies*, and in a number of edited collections.

Richard Niland has been a tutor/lecturer in literature for over fifteen years and has published on Joseph Conrad and a range of other nineteenth- and twentieth-century writers. The author of *Conrad and History* (2010) and editor of the Norton Critical Edition of *The Secret Agent* (2016), he currently teaches at Imperial College and the City Literary Institute in London.

Kim Salmons is Associate Professor in Humanities & Liberal Arts at St Mary's University, London, in the Institute of Theology & Liberal Arts. She is also the Conference Secretary for the Joseph Conrad Society (UK) and the Book Review Editor for *Joseph Conrad Today*. Her research interests focus on the social and political history of food in modern literature. Her most recent publications include *Food in the Novels of Joseph Conrad: Eating as Narrative* and *Food in the Novels of Thomas Hardy: Production & Consumption*. She is also published in *The Conradian* and in RSV, Journal of Victorian Studies.

Tania Zulli is Professor of English at 'G. d'Annunzio' University of Chieti-Pescara. Her research interests focus on translation studies and the stylistic analysis of literary texts. She has published on colonial and postcolonial literature and language, transnational language theory and cross-cultural pragmatics. Her most recent books are a translation of Conrad's short story 'Amy Foster' (Marsilio 2018), the volume *Joseph Conrad, Language and Transnationalism* (Solfanelli 2019), and a collection on Conrad's fiction edited with Fausto Ciompi (*Joseph Conrad: linee d'ombra*, 2019). She is a founding member of the AISC (Associazione Italiana di Studi Conradiani).

Acknowledgements

This book is the result of shared research interests in Joseph Conrad by the two editors. The themes of migration and transnationalism have been chosen for two reasons. First, we have followed our scholarly interest in issues that are central to today's political, social and cultural world. Second, and on a more personal note, while researching on these topics, we have realized that the theme of the transnational, with all its cultural implications, characterizes the relationships shared between Conradian colleagues. The members of the Joseph Conrad Society (UK), the Associazione Italiana di Studi Conradiani (Italy), and the Joseph Conrad Society of America have not only supplied stimuli and ideas on the project, but also contributed to bring about a rich diversity of perspectives. The authors hail from many different countries – Israel, Italy, Poland, the United Kingdom, the United States – making this work, in its essence, transnational.

For this reason, we would first and foremost like to thank the contributors for their knowledge, expertise and generosity in making this volume possible. Our fellow Conradian scholars have demonstrated a level of support and understanding that has made the experience of putting together this collection a joyful and enlightening one. It is this generosity of knowledge and spirit which underpins the Conrad community and ensures that the 'invincible conviction of solidarity' which lies at the heart of Conrad's work lives on and continues to speak to new generations of scholars who discover his fiction.

We would especially like to thank Hugh Epstein for his advice, comments and scrupulous reading of many of the essays in this volume. His depth of critical understanding and insight has been invaluable. We would also like to thank Robert Hampson and Laurence Davies, who have not only contributed to the volume with their own essays, but provided support during various phases of the project. Our thanks go to Linda Dryden for advice and encouragement, to Alexandra Boardman for the use of her beautiful painting on the cover, and to Lucy Brown and Ben Doyle at Bloomsbury for their support in the preparation of the manuscript.

Finally, we would like to acknowledge each other's debt of gratitude in such a fruitful cooperation. Friendship, sincerity, scholarship and humour have characterized this collaboration.

Abbreviations

CL	*Collected Letters of Joseph Conrad*
Narcissus	*The Nigger of the 'Narcissus'*
NLL	*Notes on Life and Letters*
Record	*A Personal Record*

Introduction

Kim Salmons and Tania Zulli

> We are in the epoch of simultaneity: we are in the epoch of juxtaposition, the epoch of the near and far, of the side-by-side, of the dispersed. We are at a moment, I believe, when our experience of the world is less that of a long life developing through time than that of a network that connects points and intersects with its own skein. One could perhaps say that certain ideological conflicts animating present-day polemics oppose the pious descendents [*sic*] of time and the determined inhabitants of space.

With these words, pronounced at a lecture given to a group of architectural students in 1967,[1] Michel Foucault described the twentieth century as an 'epoch of simultaneity' and 'juxtaposition' by depicting the world as a network connecting economies, societies and cultures in which the very concept of space is seen in relation to time, as well as social and cultural forces. This sense of variety, intersection and contradiction which began to shape economic and social relations at the beginning of the twentieth century has later been adopted to describe the concept of 'literary' or 'critical' transnationalism animating current debates about world literature. The focus of literary transnationalism is the result of a dynamic encounter between people across national boundaries and, if on the one hand it concerns those 'forms of cultural production that take place in the liminal spaces between real and imagined borders' (Jay 2010: 1), on the other, one cannot deny that such borders (either real or imagined) are essential to the understanding of a literary national identity.

Transnationalism has often been regarded as a product of today's increasingly globalized world, and the consequence of closer interactions brought about by the breaking of geographical, economic and cultural barriers which have resulted in 'a fluidity of constructed styles, social institutions and everyday practices' (Vertovec 1999: 6). It is, therefore, a relatively recent concept, originating from the development of advancing means of transport and communication. However, in its literary declination and in its intellectual and narrative forms, as the expression of global relations articulating the interaction of cultures and ideas through scholarly thought and fictional representations, transnationalism is a much earlier concept. Joseph Conrad described the world as 'in a state of transition' (Conrad 1926: 130), a perception that was not confined to geographical movement, but instead encompassed the philosophical, psychological and political changes that populate his fiction. In his essay 'Travel', first published in December 1922 as a Preface to Richard Curle's *Into the East: Notes on Burma and Malaya*, Conrad affirmed that travelling had changed since, he said, 'this earth [is] girt about with cables, with an atmosphere made restless by the waves of ether, lighted by that sun of the twentieth century under which there is nothing new left now, and but very little of what may still be called obscure' (Conrad 1926: 128).[2] There was no place in the world that had not been explored or was not known. Modern travelling had lost the charm and the spirit of adventure; it could not light up imagination anymore. And yet, in Conrad's opinion, the traveller – and the writer – should continue to be 'sensitive, meditative, with delicate perceptions and a gift for expression' (Conrad 1926: 134).

Perceptions and expressions of migration and transnationalism

Perceptions and expressions lie at the heart of this volume in that each contributor has perceived and expressed their own interpretation of migration and transnationalism and how the characters within Conrad's novels are positioned as 'migrants', 'immigrants' or *emigrés*. Where modernity is situated at the end of the nineteenth and the first half of the twentieth centuries, the terms 'migrant' and 'immigrant' – although in some incidents used interchangeably – express the impermanent and permanent nature of movements of people and cultures within this historical moment. If the noun 'migrant' implies a person in continuous movement, 'immigrant' designates an identity imposed on the outsider by the native. In contrast, *emigré* suggests the self-perception of a transnational individual, with 'trans' meaning to go across, to go beyond and even to overcome; qualities that are witnessed in Conrad's characters as they move between geographical, cultural, moral and social boundaries; and on a more philosophical level, the boundaries between the real and the imagined and that of life and death.

To compartmentalize perceptions and expressions of transnationalism is short-sighted. There are many borders, margins and crossings that Conrad experiences in his own life, not only as an immigrant to England – examined closely in the following chapters – but in the perception of his own work. When writing *Under Western Eyes* (1911) the novel that famously resulted in Conrad experiencing a nervous breakdown, the author slips in and out of the conscious and unconscious world: '[Conrad] lives mixed up in the scenes and holds converse with the characters [from *Under Western Eyes*]', writes his wife Jessie (Blackburn 1958: 192). She describes how '[h]is mind was evidently back in the past' imagining that as he was moved from the chair to his bed, Conrad connected that movement with 'his terrible transportation to the African Coast when he was taken ill on the Congo River' (Jessie Conrad 1935: 143). Existing in a liminal space in which time and place overlap and linguistic boundaries dissolve, Jessie recalls how Conrad 'spoke all the time in Polish, but for a few sentences against poor J. B. Pinker' (Jessie Conrad 1935: 143); while he repeated – in English – the burial service from the *Book of Common Prayer* for those who die at sea.

The breakdown that Conrad suffered on completion of *Under Western Eyes* is, claims Bernard C. Meyer, attributed to his 'hidden sense of identification [with the Russians] expressing a fundamental Slavic unity' (in Najder 2007: 411). As such, this slippage in his transnational identity as a Pole and as an English author reveals itself through a mental struggle that he cannot reconcile. The 'dramatic confrontation', as Najder describes it (2007: 412) – and that Conrad posits in *Under Western Eyes* as the only future for Russia and therefore Poland – is in the five lines that Razumov writes on a scrap of paper before taking a penknife and stabbing the paper to the wall at the end of his bed. The first line reads 'History not Theory', while the second demands 'Patriotism not Internationalism'. The act reflects Conrad's own conflicting thoughts, feelings and impulses as he agonizes over his transnational status and his position as an internationalist, most clearly articulated in his essay 'Autocracy and War' (1905), in which he envisages a Europe with 'no frontiers' (1924: 103). Najder's assertion that 'it has barely been noticed that Conrad held an idea of Europe as a potential *political* entity based, implicitly, on shared elements of civilization and culture' (1997: 169) goes someway to explaining the author's moral issue with reconciling patriotism and internationalism. His transnational conflict is not just a state of being but a state of mind, with the word 'state' completing the irony of his geographical and psychological struggle.

This ability to cross the boundaries of the real and the imagined questions the tangibility and reality of national borders. This tension is played out in

Nostromo (1904), the only one of Conrad's novels to be set in a fictional country, Costaguana, and inhabited by an imagined community of immigrants. As J. Hillis Miller suggests, *Nostromo* is a novel that 'appears' to be about the 'nation building of an imaginary South American republic' (Peters and Lothe 2017: 209). This 'imagined community' is made up of various races and ethnicities, but the myriad of languages and the inequality of status based on ethnic origin creates a space that is a '(non)-community' and demonstrates the 'dissolution, the dislocation, or the conflagration of community' (213).

The transnational nature of the character of the title, Nostromo, is evident from the 'Author's Note' in which Conrad claims that he is an Italian and was based on 'Dominic, the Padrone of the Tremolino' (Conrad 2007: 452). Dominic Cervoni was a Corsican, originating from the Caporali families who 'date back to the twelfth century' (Conrad 2008: 153).[3] This provenance is a complicated one with the history of Corsica – like the history of Costaguana – going through various national transitions from Greek, to Roman, and then settling under the control of Pisa and Genoa as City States, before coming under French rule during the eighteenth century. At the time that Conrad was writing *Nostromo*, Corsica was a French nation. Cervoni's family-line suggests a transnational identity and, despite claiming him as an Italian, Conrad quotes Cervoni in his 'Author's Note' as speaking in French: 'Vous autres gentilshommes!' (Conrad 2007: 452). This linguistic transnationalism is apparent too in *Nostromo* in that, as J. Hillis Miller points out, 'bits of three languages exist in the novel' with Nostromo – unlike Cervoni – speaking Italian.

Unlike *Under Western Eyes* where Conrad was trapped and conflicted by the real political history and oppression of his homeland, *Nostromo* offers an opportunity to create his own imagined history and political tensions and when, as he explains in his 'Author's Note' to the novel, he had 'thought' himself 'to a standstill over the tangled-up affairs of the Republic' he would 'pack' his 'bag, rush away from Sulaco for a change of air, and write a few pages of the *Mirror of the Sea*' (Conrad 2007: 451). This act of mental migration – in which it seems Dominic Cervoni accompanied Conrad – forces the reader to question the concept of nation and nationality whether based on linguistics, geography or shared interests (material or otherwise).

Transnationalism and migration when explored within the context of Conrad's literature – and within a modern world that operates against the legalities of geographical demarcation – have no boundaries. The terms not only defy their own categorizations but undermine the 'imagined communities' they attempt to transcend.

Conrad, migration and transnationalism in critical context

Transnational fiction extends beyond the boundaries of a writer's physical or geographical location to encompass literatures written in a second language or those that deal with themes that engage with the voice or perspective of another culture (Ashcroft, Griffiths and Tiffin 2000: 214). By extension these literatures often have a direct link to migration, either being written by authors who are migrants, or introducing topics that invariably concern the encounter and connection between different cultures. As Steven Vertovec explains in his essay 'Conceiving and Researching Transnationalism' (1999), the term is inextricably tied to the sociocultural expressions of diaspora and migration and, as a consequence, individual migrations and migrating communities play a crucial role in the definition and re-definition of the transnational in the modern period. This is true for economic, social and political activities, as well as for the cultural and literary interactions generated by transnational relations.

Despite covering a wide range of meanings, transnationalism and migration prove to be two crucial notions able to magnify the literary stature and fictional production of an author such as Joseph Conrad. Reading Conrad's work as a contribution to topical discourses on transnationalism, migration and modernity demands a consideration of those more direct aspects of his cosmopolitanism and multiculturalism as well as an acknowledgement of the presence of cross-cultural themes in his works. This recognition brings into focus the capacity of his writing to reflect such interactions through experiments with genres, forms, languages and literary traditions. Several contemporary studies on Conrad's fiction underline its value in expressing the modern phenomenon of globalization, highlighting how his novels '[grapple] with the ramifications of living in a global world: the moral and material impact of dislocation, the tension and opportunity of multiethnic societies, the disruption wrought by technological change' (Jasanoff 2017: 9). Previous publications have variously focused on the cosmopolitan, cross-cultural qualities of Conrad's narrative, while highlighting the ability to 'travel across' the works of authors from different countries. But Conrad's transnationalism goes beyond the ethical realm, demanding to be considered in terms of his artistic choices, his intellectual identity and the studies of his works performed by critics. As far as Conradian criticism is concerned, the fashioning of a European Conrad – which took shape in a significant number of critical works across the world – can be traced back to the middle of the twentieth century. In 1935, Emilio Cecchi inaugurated a critical tradition in Italy which would recognize Conrad as a European novelist who took advantage of an international literary context which expanded and enriched his status as a British writer and placed him as a model for his contemporaries in Italy (see Ambrosini 2019: 9). Such recognition has been followed by studies focusing on Conrad's personal and intellectual relationships with Polish, French, British and colonial culture, all acting as an anticipatory reflection on the transnational quality of his fiction. Reading Conrad's work in relation to other literatures (and other authors) invites the reader to consider a redefinition of his poetics in the light of wider cultural perspectives.

In 2011, a comparative study on Joseph Conrad and Witold Gombrowicz published by George Z. Gasyna (*Polish, Hybrid and Otherwise: Exilic Discourse in Joseph Conrad and Witold Gombrowicz*) set the author's life of exile at the core of 'the layering of identity that is precipitated by the experience of cultural rupture' (Gasyna 2011: 2). A few years later, the volumes included in the series *Joseph Conrad: Eastern and Western Perspectives* made an important contribution to the role played by Conradian fiction in relation to other literatures. For example, articles contained in *From Szlachta Culture to the 21st Century, Between East and West: New Essays on Joseph Conrad's Polishness* (2013, ed. Wieslaw Krajka) re-examine the boundaries of Conrad's Polish identity while also analysing the relations of his works with other European authors through biographical, historical and literary contextualization. Both publications focus on Conrad as a Polish writer, and on the way in which his Polish identity emerged through the comparison with other European literatures. In addition, Conrad's Polishness is enriched by the confrontation with his 'other souls'; his French education and British citizenship made him an author whose position extends beyond the figure of an English writer with Polish origins, as he has long been defined.

The critical debate on Conrad's transnationalism over the past ten years has taken shape outside the borders of Poland. In a 2013 issue of the journal *Studia Neophilologica* (*Transnational Conrad*) the reader of 'Conrad's multifocal and multilayered novels and stories' was invited to 'parse their geographical location, protagonists, frame narrative, and, beyond all these, the voice of the author himself, within a matrix of conflicting and overlapping national perspectives, prejudices, and languages' (Donovan 2013: 2). In the same volume, Conrad's transnationality was recognized as a quality he brought to English literature, a sign of his intellectual originality that allowed him to manipulate forms and literary conventions (Ambrosini 2013: 6). More recently, two volumes of *L'Époque Conradienne*, the Journal of the French Conrad Society, entitled *Transnational Conrad*[4] (2017–18), have shown how a cross-cultural approach can shed new light on the author's writing by underlying the variety of traditions, cultures, languages and narrative modes in his fiction and by addressing questions of national identity, language, the impact of Conrad's writing on imperial and postcolonial topics, as well as his influence on contemporary literature.[5]

Border crossings and rites of entry

The chapters of this volume examine 'rites of entry' and 'barriers to belonging' within the life and work of Conrad through the multicultural and transnational characters that comprise his fiction, while locating the author as a subject of the Russian state whose provenance is Polish, but whose identity is that of a merchant sailor and English country gentleman. Although a 'rite of entry' suggests a distinct place to enter, in Conrad's fiction such places are indeterminate: liminal spaces and the negotiation and exploration of boundaries shape and coincide with his own redefinition and realignment not least of the protocols and codes of Englishness. Despite this, Conrad's characters are often marked by crossings – changes of nation, changes of culture, changes of identity – which refract the author's own cultural transitions. These crossings subjectivize the experience of the migrant not only through cross-cultural encounters of food and language, but also through the modern complexities of technology and speed. Conrad's work writes across historical, political and ethnic borders speaking to a transnational reality (and unreality) that continues to have relevance today. The study of migration, modernity and transnationalism in Conradian narratives allows an insight into his biographical and fictional world which carries an understanding of the intersections and boundaries that mark the personal experience from the public rendering. In some respects, this allows the reader to separate the life from the art; but at the same time allows a glimpse into the transactions that take place between Conrad's personal life and his fiction.

Robert Hampson's opening chapter sets the scene of the migrant condition by considering the role of documentation or the lack of it in rites of entry to a new nationality. As Hampson points out, Conrad's admission into British nationality is widely described in his works, starting from the author's first visit to London in 'Poland Revisited'. Hampson deals with 'incomplete rites of passage' (26) such as that in 'Amy Foster' by analysing Yanko Goorall's paperless entry into Kent before extending his study beyond entries into nationalities exploring the migrant's re-entry into his native society and culture, as analysed in 'Poland Revisited' and *The Rover*. Continuing this theme, William Atkinson's chapter introduces key elements of the volume by positioning 'rites of entry' alongside borderlands in Conrad's life and fiction. After investigating crucial rites of passage in Conrad's life, such as the three examinations for second mate, first mate, and master described in *A Personal Record*, he analyses how 'rites of entry' and 'rites of passage' are performed in Conrad's fiction, spanning from *Heart of Darkness* to *Nostromo*, 'The Secret Sharer' and 'The Shadow-Line'. The indeterminacy of places entered by Conrad's characters is initially linked to the author's own place of birth, Ukraine; the nomenclature defining a lack of territorial specificity in that its etymology, as Atkinson points out, means 'frontier' or 'borderland'.

This lack of definiteness is the subject of Agnieszka Adamowicz-Pośpiech chapter which traces Conrad's international nature back to both his land of origin and migratory life. The exploration of *A Personal Record* proves that Conrad's real and imaginary journeys provide a definition of the concepts of migration and dislocation which is inextricably linked to his own memories. The resulting image is that of the writer as an 'intellectual nomad' whose work (*A Personal Record* in particular) can be viewed as an 'auto-bio-atlas', a literary, geopolitical map featuring real and cultural spaces across national borders.

Border crossings and cultural transitions, from both a geographical and an aesthetic point of view, are explored by Riccardo Capoferro. In his chapter, Capoferro reads *A Personal Record* as the fictionalized story of a professional vocation and considers Conrad's crossing to the British Empire and, more specifically, to British literature, as the result of a lifelong fascination. Within this fictionalized story, Conrad articulates 'an aesthetic agenda that questions national boundaries and is meant to nourish a far-reaching sense of communal identity' (73). In performing his self-representation as a writer, Conrad steps outside the boundaries of a British identity infused with the sense of a moral superiority. Consequently, he introduces in *A Personal Record* elements of his Polish and European heredity concretizing his status as a transnational artist.

A similar process of transition can be also detected in Conrad's first collection of short stories, *Tales of Unrest* (1898). As Richard Niland makes clear, these tales mark the author's transition from professional sailor into professional novelist and allow him to form and articulate the narrative techniques which establish his place as a writer of modernist fiction. These tales with their geographical and thematic range provided Conrad with the opportunity to use and negotiate liminal spaces and to explore the boundaries that shaped and coincided with his own process of redefinition and realignment, not least the protocols and codes of Englishness. The range of 'crossings' that articulate Conrad's 'duplex' nature is evident in the perspectives and sources of inspiration.

Conrad's cosmopolitan literary identity does not only emerge from a study of his life and writing career but also finds its expression in the themes and structures of his novels. As Kim Salmons demonstrates, cultural barriers to belonging can be revealed, for example, through the study of migratory food practices in his fiction, which determine the bridge between Europe and the East. Through the analysis of *Almayer's Folly*, Salmons examines food as a conveyor of impediments to integration and acceptance, while in *The Secret Agent* she explores the process of entering the colonial world by adapting and hybridizing native food practices. If food in *Almayer's Folly* creates cultural division, in *The Secret Agent* it epitomizes the process of the migrant's adaptation allowing for the loss of authenticity.

Tania Zulli's chapter develops the discussion on rites of entry through the use of language in literary texts, by drawing on the value of communication and speech acts in social and cultural contexts. The speech of some of Conrad's expatriate characters discloses different attitudes to their condition as outcasts. This is the case with the two protagonists of *Almayer's Folly* and 'Amy Foster', Almayer and Yanko Goorall, whose speech acts reveal forms of ambiguity enriching the very concepts of 'migration' and 'transnationalism'. Eventually, Conrad's dialogues unveil an important feature of his own writing, that of making formal structures advocate his theory of the novel. In such terms, the author's artistic philosophy leads to a re-evaluation of his position as a transnational writer.

Further problematization on the idea of the 'transnational' is introduced by looking at the historical context of migration in the British and Dutch colonies. Andrew Francis contends that Conrad's representation of peoples – Arab, Chinese, European, Indian, Buginese and other Malays – suggests an extended history of migration leading to a more complex understanding of cultural relations. In this regard, Almayer's self-definition of 'settled resident', as Francis notes, invites rethinking on the nature of residency and to the status of residents who are not settled. The social and relational changes brought about by migration in Conrad's fiction cast new light on the concept of transnationalism as a condition to be reached in a dynamic confrontation of different identities.

Katherine Isobel Baxter's essay expands the analysis of globalization and Eastern power relationships in connection to migration by dealing with the mobility between East Asia and the Middle East in Conrad's fiction. These movements concerned and troubled European colonial powers such as that of the British and Dutch in the Malay Peninsula as well as the power struggles across the Levant and North Africa during the decline of the Ottoman Empire. This historical and political moment provides the context in which contemporary readers of Conrad would have considered the Arab and Muslim characters who appear in his novels.

Yael Levin's chapter extends the volume to consider how the shock of modernity impacted the migrant experience and influenced the history of migration, through a comparative analysis of Henryk Sienkiewicz's *After Bread*, Franz Kafka's *Amerika* and Conrad's short story 'Amy Foster'. In the first, Levin considers the migrant's ability to respond to the sensory overloads of the city as a measure of their successful transition from one culture to another; while in the latter she focuses on the cultural and technological shocks experienced by Yanko Goorall as he journeys through the familiar landscape of his rural and agricultural homeland – a geographical rendering of his own identity – to the unfamiliar and unknown encounters such as the steam ship and train carriage that unsettle the perspective through which he understands himself.

The final chapter of the collection moves the discussion of transnationalism into a postcolonial context extending the analysis to authors who 'wrote back' to Conrad's handling of migration and transnationalism. By drawing on the legacy in transnational texts exploring the life and works of Conrad, Laurence Davies investigates literary genres which have been shaped by the experience of exile and migration through a consideration of place and time. The traces left by Conrad in the works of other authors establish his fiction as the ideal ground for intertextual analysis exploring narrative borderlands, revisiting imperial ideologies and strengthening the transnational relations of global literature.

Chris GoGwilt's 'Afterword' brings the volume into the present moment by examining with a forensic eye the implications of Conrad's work in a modern Western society that is coming to terms with its racist past. GoGwilt's challenging finale to the volume questions the place of Black lives within Conrad's fiction by asking how much they matter to Conrad. He argues that it is impossible to discuss issues of migration and transnationalism within the context of the modern world, without considering the issue of racism, which he acknowledges all the essays in the volume address. However, the 'Afterword' adds an important perspective to this issue by considering the place of Black characters in Conrad's 1899 novel, *Heart of Darkness*, and more specifically the role of James Wait in the 1897 novel, *The Nigger of the 'Narcissus'*. As GoGwilt suggests, 'the experience of migration and transnationalism [Wait's] character embodies has an important bearing nonetheless on the range of different perspectives each essay analyzes'

(219). Although arguments about race have populated critiques of Conrad's work since Chinua Achebe's 1975 lecture,[6] what this volume hopes to do is demonstrate Conrad's extraordinary capacity for articulating a transnational and migrant experience that is as relevant today as when he was writing. This volume does not claim to provide a comprehensive analysis of migration and transnationalism in Conrad's extensive canon but sets out instead to show that even in a modern world where technology connects us all, no matter which part of the globe we reside, his belief in that 'bond between us and that humanity so far away' remains at the heart of Conradian studies.

Notes

1 The lecture was later published with the title 'Des Espaces Autres' ('Of Other Spaces') in the journal *Architecture/Mouvement/Continuité* (October 1984). The English version, translated by Jay Miskowiec, is available at: https://web.mit.edu/allanmc/www/foucault1.pdf (accessed 13 July 2020).

2 The perception of modernity as a cultural force shaping the world, as well as the way of crossing it and describing it, envisaged a reconsideration of the people performing those crossings, be they exiles, migrants or simple travellers. See T. Eagleton, *Exiles and Emigrés; Studies in Modern Literature* (New York: Schocken Books, 1970); E. Said, *Reflections on Exile and Other Essays* (Cambridge, MA: Harvard University Press, 2002).

3 '*Dominic the padrone of the Tremolino*: Dominique-André Cervoni (1834–90), born in Luri Corsica, appears in *The Mirror of the Sea* as the *padrone* (the boss) of the Tremolino, in which Conrad claimed he was engaged in arms-smuggling for the supporters of Don Carlos of Bourbon, pretender to the Spanish throne. Conrad sailed with Cervoni, who was first mate in the *Saint-Antoine* when she sailed for the West Indies in 1876. Conrad repeatedly hinted that on this voyage as well he smuggled arms for the conservative rebels in Colombia. No evidence substantiates either claim' (Pauly 2007: 455 n. 10).

4 The two issues of *L'Époque Conradienne*, n. 41 (2017–18) and n. 42 (2019), collect the papers of the International Conference 'Transnational Conrad: between Texts and Theory' held in Limoges (France) on 21–22 September 2017.

5 The literature on Conrad's transnationalism and migration is very wide, and only the major volumes published on this topic have been mentioned. However, among the studies featuring the question of migration and the transnational in the works of Conrad, the following may also be of interest: Andrea White, 'Writing from Within: Autobiography and Immigrant Subjectivity in The Mirror of the

Sea', in Carola M. Kaplan, Peter Lancelot Mallios, Andrea White (eds), *Conrad in the Twenty-First Century: Contemporary Approaches and Perspectives* (New York: Routledge, 2005), 241–50; Scott A. Cohen, '"Get Out!": Empire Migration and Human Traffic in *Lord Jim*', *NOVEL: A Forum on Fiction* 36 (3), Modernisms (Summer, 2003): 374–97; Stephen Clingman, *The Grammar of Identity: Transnational Fiction and the Nature of the Boundary* (Oxford: Oxford University Press, 2009); Tamas Juhasz, *Conradian Contracts: Exchange and Identity in the Immigrant Imagination* (Lanham, MD: Lexington Books, 2011); Robert Hampson, 'Conrad, the "Polish Problem" and Transnational Activism', *Conradiana*, 46 (1–2), 2015: 21–38; Robert Hampson, 'Crossing Borders: National and Transnational Loyalties', *The Conradian*, 42 (2), 2017: 35–54.

6 Achebe's second Chancellor's Lecture, given at the University of Massachusetts Amherst in February 1975, was later published with the title 'An Image of Africa: Racism in Conrad's Heart of Darkness' and included in his 1988 collection, *Hopes and Impediments. Selected Essays, 1965–1987.*

Works Cited

Ambrosini, R. (2013), 'Reconceptualizing Conrad as a Transnational Novelist: A Research Programme', *Studia Neophilologica*, 85: 1–12.

Ambrosini, R. (2019), *Le storie di Conrad. Biografia intellettuale di un romanziere*, Roma: Carocci.

Ashcroft, B., Griffiths, G., and Tiffin, H. (2000), *Post-Colonial Studies: The Key Concepts*, London and New York: Routledge.

Blackburn, W. (1958), *Joseph Conrad's Letters to William Blackwood and David S. Meldrum*, Durham: Duke University Press.

Conrad, Jessie. (1935), *Joseph Conrad and His Circle*, London: Jarrold's Publishers.

Conrad, Joseph. (1924), *Notes on Life and Letters*, London and Toronto: Dent.

Conrad, J. (1926), *Last Essays*, London and Toronto: Dent.

Conrad, J. (2007), *Nostromo*, London: Penguin.

Conrad, J. (2008), *The Mirror of the Sea & A Personal Record*, ed. Keith Carabine, Hertfordshire: Wordsworth.

Donovan, S. (2013), 'Introduction: Conrad under the Sign of the Transnational', *Studia Neophilologica*, 85: 1–4.

Foucault, M. (1984), 'Des Espaces Autres' ('Of Other Spaces') *Architecture/Mouvement/Continuité* (October), Eng. Trans. Jay Miskowiec. Available online: https://web.mit.edu/allanmc/www/foucault1.pdf (accessed 13 July 2020).

Gasyna, G. Z. (2011), *Polish, Hybrid and Otherwise: Exilic Discourse in Joseph Conrad and Witold Gombrowicz*, London: Bloomsbury.

Jasanoff, M. (2017), *The Dawn Watch: Joseph Conrad in a Global World*, London: Penguin.

Jay, P. (2010), *Global Matters: The Transnational Turn in Literary Studies*, New York: Cornell University Press.

Martinière, N., ed. (2017–18), *Transnational Conrad. L'Epoque Conradienne. Journal of the French Conrad Society*, 41.

Martinière, N., ed. (2019), *Transnational Conrad. L'Epoque Conradienne. Journal of the French Conrad Society*, 42.

Meyers, J. (1990), 'Conrad's Influence on Modern Writers', *Twentieth Century Literature*, 36 (2): 186–206.

Morgan, P. (2017), 'Literary Transnationalism: A Europeanist's Perspective', *Journal of European Studies*, 47 (1): 3–20.

Najder, Z. (1997), *Conrad in Perspective: Essays on Art and Fidelity*, New York: Cambridge University Press.

Najder, Z. (2007), *Joseph Conrad: A Life*, Rochester & New York: Camden House.

Pauly, V. (2007), 'Introduction and Notes' to *Nostromo*, London: Penguin.

Peters, J. G. and Lothe, J., eds. (2017), *Reading Conrad: J. Hillis Miller*, Columbus: Ohio State University Press.

Vertovec, S. (1999), 'Conceiving and Researching Transnationalism', *Ethnic and Racial Studies*, 22 (2): 445–62.

Part One

Crossing borders

1

Conrad's rites of entry and return

Robert Hampson
University of London

Conrad begins *The Mirror of the Sea*, his first published act of extended reminiscence, with the observation 'Landfall and Departure mark the rhythmical swing of a seaman's life and of a ship's career' (1906: 3). He then proceeds to define the two terms and to rescue them from the misconceptions of 'landsmen'. Landfall is the 'more easily understood': 'you fall in with the land, and it is a matter of a quick eye and of a clear atmosphere'. The departure, by comparison, is not so much 'a sea event as a definite act entailing a process – the precise observation of certain landmarks by means of the compass card'. The landfall 'you meet at first with a single glance', whereas the departure 'is distinctly a ceremony of navigation' (Conrad 1906: 3). However, as the final part of *The Nigger of the 'Narcissus'* makes clear, arrival is a much longer process than merely making landfall. The section that follows will focus on Conrad's descriptions of arrivals and consider, in particular, the complications involved in these acts of entry and re-entry. It will trace Conrad's own entry into British nationality, and the various rites it involved. Subsequent sections will explore rites of passage in other Conrad texts and will foreground the failure of such rites to produce complete incorporation.

Arrival

In 'Poland Revisited', Conrad describes his first entry into London in 1878 by train from Lowestoft, navigating the streets around Liverpool Street Station with part of a map in his hand 'with something of the feeling of a traveller penetrating into a vast and unexplored wilderness' (Conrad 1924: 150). Although he emphasizes his sense of isolation ('No explorer could have been more lonely' [Conrad 1924: 150]), this is obviously no 'unexplored wilderness', since he carries not just a map but also 'a cutting from a newspaper, containing the address of an obscure shipping agent' (Conrad 1924: 151). These two bits of paper are the first documents in what will prove a long paper trail in the course of his two careers. As we will see, although landfall is a simple event, entry, like departure, is distinctly a process with its own ceremonies of navigation. Papers and documents, for obvious reasons, are an important component of that process.

One of the early stages in Conrad's process of naturalization was the series of professional examinations he took for promotion in the Merchant Marine with the resulting pieces of 'ass's hide'. His uncle, Tadeusz Bobrowski, clearly saw these examinations in the light of a progression through the naval hierarchy ('the first step is taken' [Najder 1964: 65]) with naturalization as the final outcome ('concentrate on your examinations and get yourself naturalized' [Najder 1964: 89]). However, he also responded to the news of Conrad's passing the examination for second mate with a different set of considerations. First, it signified that Conrad had proved 'to [his] country and [his] own people that he had not "eaten [his] bread in the world for four years in vain"' (Najder 1964: 64). It was also the opportunity for an improving moral lesson: "the duty not only of feeling gratitude" (to the "good people" who had helped him,' but also of acquiring 'a general love of people and of helping others who need your help' (Najder 1964: 64). The prospect of Conrad's passing the first mate's examination prompted a different response: 'I should prefer to see your face … as that of a free citizen of a free country, rather than … still as that of a citizen of the world' (Najder 1964: 88). This proved to be a false opposition. As this essay will demonstrate, although Conrad became a British subject (not quite a 'free citizen'), he never ceased to be 'a citizen of the world'.

Conrad presents these Board of Trade examinations that were stages in his progress towards naturalization as a rite of passage in anecdotal form in *A Personal Record* and in fictional form in *Chance*. In the opening chapter of *Chance*, young Powell recalls his examination for second mate. He notes that he had 'the hottest time of his life with Captain R ——, the most dreaded of the three seamanship Examiners who at the time were responsible for the merchant service officers qualifying in the Port of London' (Conrad 1913: 5). Of the examination itself, he reports only that 'He kept me for an hour and a half in the torture chamber and behaved as though he hated me. He kept his eyes shaded with one of his hands. Suddenly he let it drop saying, "You will do!"' (Conrad 1913: 5). Conrad gives a fuller account of his own experience of these examinations towards the end of *A Personal Record.* He begins by praising 'That august academical body of the Marine Department of the Board of Trade', before observing that he had been 'face to face at various times with all the examiners of the Port of London': 'Three of them were examiners in seamanship, and it was my fate to be delivered into the hands of each of them at proper intervals of sea service' (Conrad 1912: 112). Conrad passed his second mate's examination in May 1880. He sat for his first mate's examination in November 1884, but failed – a fact not mentioned in *A Personal Record.* He passed on his second attempt a month later. In July 1886, he similarly failed his master's examination on the first attempt, but passed it on the second attempt in November.

This narrative is tidied up in *A Personal Record.* Here he describes three successful examinations in terms of the character of the examiner in each case. The first examination lasts so long that Conrad imagines himself as a kind of Rip van Winkle, 'coming out of this room into the world of men a stranger, friendless, forgotten by my very landlady' (Conrad 1912: 113). Conrad's second examination experience is given in much more detail. The Examiner, unsurprisingly, seems to have been the same as young Powell's. At least, Conrad describes him in very similar terms (Conrad 1912: 114). What follows is an almost comic account of an examination process based on a succession of nautical disasters. As Conrad puts it, that 'imaginary ship seemed to labour under a most comprehensive curse' (Conrad 1912: 115), as the Examiner kept piling on further problems. The third examination is of a different character altogether. In the course of the examination with this easy-going and somewhat garrulous examiner, Conrad hears 'an instructive anecdote bearing upon a point of stowage' (Conrad 1912: 117), learns about a jury-rudder the Examiner had invented some years before and also details about the transport service at the time of the Crimean War. What Conrad derives from this experience is a sense of 'the continuity of that sea-life into which I had stepped' (Conrad 1912: 118). With this conclusion, passing these examinations is presented as an induction into a tradition and a family.

The Nigger of the 'Narcissus'

The two rites of passage described in *The Nigger of the 'Narcissus'* present a less positive picture. The first is the roll-call at the start of the narrative. As the ship prepares to leave Bombay, Mr Baker, the chief mate, musters the crew:

> As the chief mate read out a name, one of the men would answer: 'Yes, sir!' or 'Here!' and, detaching himself from the shadowy mob of heads visible above the blackness of starboard bulwarks, would step bare-footed into the circle of light, and in two noiseless strides pass into the shadows on the port side of the quarter-deck. (Conrad 1897: 15–16)

In effect, each is briefly called into being before stepping out of the light into the collective identity of the crew. This collective identity is evident when the ship's passage begins:

> The men had shaken into their places, and the half-hourly voice of the bells ruled their life of unceasing care. Night and day the head and shoulders of a seaman could be seen aft by the wheel, outlined high against sunshine or starlight, very steady above the stir of revolving spokes. The faces changed, passing in rotation. Youthful faces, bearded faces, dark faces … but all akin with the brotherhood of the sea. (Conrad 1897: 30)

Although they are serving under a British flag, they are united in a multinational community of labour, which is dedicated to the care of the ship and, at the same time, marked by the cares this dedication brings. We can compare this with the description of the young captain's experience, in *The Shadow-Line*, when he sits for the first time in the captain's chair in the ship's saloon: 'A succession of men had sat in that chair. I became aware of that thought suddenly, vividly, … as if a sort of composite soul, the soul of command, had whispered suddenly to mine of long days at sea and of anxious moments' (Conrad 1917: 52–3). Where the crew join a temporary community in a specific place for a limited period of time, the captain feels the support of a continuing community that exists across time.

The second rite of passage occurs at the end of the narrative: the detailed (and fictional) account of the *Narcissus*' journey up the Thames and its arrival at St Katherine's Dock. The account of the ship's arrival and docking prepares us for the final impression we are given of the sailors ashore as men out of their element. For example, there are the various voices which greet them. The first of these voices is that of the waiting woman who 'screamed at the silent ship, "Hallo, Jack!" without looking at any one in particular, and all hands looked at her from the forecastle head' (Conrad 1897: 164). In its way, this is as disturbing as the French gun-ship firing into the bush in *Heart of Darkness*. There is a disconnect between the woman, who looks at no one in particular, and the men who each looks attentively at her as if addressed personally. What initially sounds like a familiar greeting, the interpellation of a particular man, known to the speaker, dissolves into something depersonalized and generic. The Jack she addresses is 'Jack Tar', the prey of prostitutes, publicans and boarding-house-keepers. As Hallie Rubenhold observes, prostitutes, pimps and procuresses 'kept abreast of when vessels were due into port' (2019: 320).[1] She quotes the social reformer Edward W. Thomas: 'when a ship arrives in the docks, so many of the women who are disengaged go down to the entrance, and there and then endeavour to enveigle the seamen' (1879: 36). This single figure in Conrad's narrative stands in for a bustling world of activity beyond the dock-gates, much of this designed to separate the returning sailor from his wages. Her generic salutation stands in contrast to the ritual of naming with which the voyage began: it anticipates the disintegration of the collective of the crew into separate individuals.

The next voices we hear are the cries of the dock men, calling out 'Stand clear of that rope!' (Conrad 1897: 164). After all their experience of ropes involved in sailing the *Narcissus* to this point, at the docks the crew's expertise and agency is set at nought.[2] They are reduced to passive spectators. And once the *Narcissus* comes to her berth, 'a swarm of strange men, clambering up her sides, took possession of her in the name of the sordid earth' (Conrad 1897: 165). This dispossession of the *Narcissus* is continued in the following paragraph as other figures appear on deck: 'a 'toff in a black coat and high hat'; a lady, 'a real lady in a black dress and with a parasol'; and then 'an underhand-looking lot of seedy-looking chaps with shifty eyes wandered in and out of the forecastle looking for a job' – or something to steal (Conrad 1897: 165). The first two apparitions, who are identified as the second mate's brother and the captain's wife, have an almost surreal quality in their unexpectedness after the more elemental concerns of the voyage. They are a reminder of the class divisions in shore society, as a result of which the able chief mate, Mr Baker, who conducted the initial muster, has no chance of becoming captain (unlike the 'gentlemanly' Mr Creighton with his 'swell friends', who will 'get on' [Conrad 1897: 20, 167]). The captain's wife and the second mate's brother, along with their comic counterpart, Charley's mother, also introduce the shore life of familial units, which shows up the lack of family of other members of the crew, like Baker: 'Mother dead; father and two brothers, Yarmouth fishermen, drowned together on the Dogger Bank; sister married and unfriendly' (Conrad 1897: 166). Meanwhile, the 'chaps with shifty eyes' are a reminder of the poverty that characterizes the community around the docks.

The formal disintegration of the crew is marked by another ritual: the re-assembling of the scattered crew in the shipping office to receive their pay. At the end of the voyage, one of the Board of Trade officials makes the announcement that 'The *Narcissus* pays off'. Another oversees the payments with the Captain. The narrator offers the following description of the shipping office:

> The room was large, white-washed, and bare, a counter surmounted by a brass-wire grating fenced off a third of the dusty space, and behind the grating a pasty-faced clerk, with his hair parted in the middle, had the quick glittering eyes and the vivacious jerky movements of a caged bird. Poor Captain Allistoun, also in there, and sitting before a little table with piles of gold and notes on it, appeared subdued by his captivity. (Conrad 1897: 167–8)

The powerful and impressive Captain Allistoun is now reduced to this caged figure. The members of the crew are also diminished. This is most evident in the responses of the Board of Trade official to them. For example, the narrator describes the different ways in which the sailors receive 'the wages of their glorious and obscure toil' as they go up, one by one, to the pay-table: 'They swept the money with care into broad palms, rammed it trustfully into trouser pockets, or, turning their backs on the table, reckoned with difficulty in the hollow of their stiff hands' (Conrad 1897: 168). This last group is treated impatiently by the Board of Trade clerk: 'Money right? Sign the release. There – there … How stupid these sailors are!' (Conrad 1897: 168). When the 'venerable', 'patriarchal seaman', old Singleton reveals that he can't write, the clerk is shocked, and, after Singleton 'painfully sketched in a heavy cross', he mutters: 'What a disgusting old brute' (Conrad 1897: 169). By contrast, Donkin, who leaves the ship with 'a bad discharge', is regarded by the clerk as 'an intelligent man' (Conrad 1897: 169). As the crew disperses and loses its collective identity, the narrator reinforces this sense of a shift between land and sea values, when he observes that Donkin 'had better clothes, had an easy air, appeared more at home than any of us' (Conrad 1897: 169). Where Donkin has found his place in a more congenial shore society, the remaining sailors seem lost in this society and markedly homeless.

One significant absence from this final ritual, of course, is James Wait. As the captain explains to Belfast, Wait's effects have been 'locked and sealed' and given up to the Board of Trade (Conrad 1897: 169). Belfast had wanted 'something of his' (Conrad 1897: 169) as a memento for his private ritual of mourning. Belfast's emotional attachment to his dead shipmate contrasts with the business-like processes of the Board of Trade: 'James Wait – deceased – found no papers of any kind – no relations – no trace – the Office must hold his wages' (Conrad 1897: 169). Indeed, Belfast's continuing evident emotional distress also separates him from his other colleagues: he confides to Marlow ('You were his chum, too') that he 'couldn't go' to the pub with the rest of the crew (Conrad 1897: 171). Wait, himself, has already gone through another ritual of departure. Earlier in the narrative, Conrad provides a detailed account of his burial at sea. This begins with the disintegration of the community of sailors after his death; the wrapping of the body in a white blanket; Belfast's sorrowful vigil; and the stitching of the body into a piece of sailcloth. Belfast's tearful assistance to the sailmaker in this process ends in the sailmaker's rebuke to him ('What makes you take on so?'). As a lesson for Belfast, the sailmaker recalls an incident on the 'West India Station', when he 'sewed in twenty men a week' without thinking about it, and these were 'Portsmouth-Devonport men – townies – knew their fathers, mothers, sisters', whereas 'these niggers like this one – you don't know where it comes from' (Conrad 1897: 158). The sailmaker's racist language and attitude, his dehumanizing and depersonalizing of Wait, are rejected by the mournful Belfast, who insists on Wait's importance to himself, and, implicitly, by the narrator, who describes how 'James Wait' was carried aft by four men 'under the folds of the Union Jack' (Conrad 1897: 158). For the extended description of the ceremony that follows, the narrator restores Wait's name and identity and invokes the common bond of this temporary international community 'under the folds of the Union Jack'.

If this part of the narrative raises questions about the nature of this community and the schisms within it, it is interesting that the novella has already supplied an answer to the sailmaker's challenge 'Who will miss him?' (Conrad 1897: 158). On his deathbed, Wait had already returned, in his imagination, to the cosmopolitan London that he knows: 'He was swaggering up the East India Dock Road; saying kindly, "Come along for a treat," pushing glass swing-doors, posing with superb assurance in the gaslight above a mahogany counter' (Conrad 1897: 149). He thinks fondly of his 'Canton Street girl' and the oysters she cooks for him (Conrad 1897: 149).[3] Wait's memories provide the most vivid evocation of the London life of Britain's merchant sailors: like Donkin, he, too, has a certain place within shore society.

Rites of passage

In *The Rites of Passage* (1909), Arnold van Gennep drew attention to the ceremonies or rituals by which an individual moves from one sub-group in a society to another. These rituals related to such life-events as births, marriages, deaths and the transition from childhood to adulthood – but might also include the crossing of borders or the transition from one sub-group to another. Van Gennep discussed such rites of passage in terms of three phases: separation, liminality and incorporation. It would be possible to read the opening of *The Nigger of the 'Narcissus'* in these terms. The crossing of Bombay Harbour 'in shore-boats rowed by white-clad Asiatics' (Conrad 1897: 4) marks the separation from shore life; the noisy conversations in the forecastle as the 'new hands' (Conrad 1897: 4) arrive are a credible liminal phase; and the muster is the ceremony of incorporation by which the diverse multinational crew becomes a temporary community. By contrast, however, the ritual at the end of the voyage – although it involves separation from the *Narcissus* and a liminal period ashore before the 'paying off' ceremony – does not involve incorporation into shore society. Or, rather, some members of the crew are incorporated into sub-groups ashore (Allistoun, Creighton, Donkin), but the impression is that the majority of the crew disappear into an atomized and predatory shore society.

Marlow in *Heart of Darkness* goes through a similarly disrupted or incomplete process of incorporation both on his entry into Africa and on his return to Europe. When he seeks to join the Company, he undergoes the expected rituals of separation, the interview and the medical examination, and then experiences a period of liminality marked by his voyage down the coast and his overland journey, but there is no subsequent incorporation either at the Central Station or at the Inner Station. At the Central Station, he encounters an individualistic society characterized by 'backbiting and intriguing' in pursuit of wealth and power (Conrad 1902: 78). At the Inner Station, he makes his 'choice of nightmares' and allies himself with Kurtz, who has set up his own rituals of incorporation. However, after he has seen the heads on poles around Kurtz's house, Marlow has no wish 'to know anything of the ceremonies used when approaching' him (Conrad 1902: 131).

Marlow's return to Europe similarly involves a period of liminality ('a period of time which I remember mistily, with a shuddering wonder, like a passage through some inconceivable world that had no hope in it and no desire' [Conrad 1902: 152]), and his re-entry into Europe also entails certain ceremonies – a visit from a representative of the Company; a visit from 'Kurtz's cousin' (who is given 'some family letters and memoranda without importance' (Conrad 1902: 153); a visit from a journalist (who takes away Kurtz's report on the 'Suppression of Savage Customs' (without the postscript); and Marlow's own visit to Kurtz's Intended 'with a slim packet of letters and the girl's portrait' (Conrad 1902: 154). His meetings with the Company representative, the journalist and perhaps even the 'cousin' are not part of a process of incorporation after his return, but rather part of the system designed to protect Leopold's extraction of wealth from the Congo by ensuring that no information about his practices escaped into the public domain. Adam Hochschild provides ample evidence of Leopold's use of lawyers and the press to prevent or discredit any criticism.[4]

Up to this point, Marlow has suffered from reverse culture shock: 'I found myself back in the sepulchral city resenting the sight of people hurrying through the streets to filch a little money from each other, to devour their infamous cookery, to gulp their unwholesome beer, to dream their insignificant and silly dreams' (Conrad 1902: 152). Now, just as the prospect of meeting Kurtz had held out some kind of hope of explanation or understanding during his time in Africa ('The point was in his being a gifted creature, and that of all his gifts the one that stood preeminently … was his ability to talk, his words – the gift of expression' [Conrad 1902: 113]), the meeting with the Intended is invested with various hopes and desires based on Marlow's reading of the studio portrait: 'She seemed ready to listen without mental reservation, without suspicion, without a thought for herself' (Conrad 1902: 155). The woman he meets, however, is very different from this projection. The encounter offers him initiation into 'cruel and absurd mysteries' (Conrad 1902: 157) as she reveals herself not at all 'ready to listen', but, on the contrary, traps Marlow within her coercive discourse. And, far from being 'without a thought for herself', she asserts not only her own knowledge of Kurtz ('no-one knew him so well as I'), but also her pride in that knowledge ('to know I understood him better than anyone on earth') (Conrad 1902: 158). Whatever Marlow's 'other feeling' (Conrad 1902: 155) might have been prior to his meeting with the Intended, the encounter does not serve to further his incorporation back into European society. Instead, the question emerges whether contemporary European society actually constitutes a community in which he can be incorporated. This is reinforced by his relations with his auditors on board the *Nellie*, which are not the same as those he had with the same group in 'Youth'. In the earlier story, he was sharing memories with a group of like-minded middle-aged men, all linked by 'the strong bond of the sea' (Conrad 1902: 3); in *Heart of Darkness*, he is aware of his difference from his listeners ('each moored with two good addresses, like a hulk with two anchors' [Conrad 1902: 114]), and he has to be reminded to 'be civil' (Conrad 1902: 94).

A similar question is raised by *The Secret Agent*. Verloc's visit to the unidentified embassy in Chesham Square covertly encodes Conrad's own visits to the Russian Embassy there for release from Russian subjecthood. However, just as the end of *Heart of Darkness* presents Marlow's alienated experience of a European capital city, *The Secret Agent* presents London as an atomized and alienating environment. The Assistant Commissioner is a particularly interesting case. Like Marlow (and Peyrol later), he is one of Conrad's returnees. He has returned to England from 'a tropical country', where he had been in the colonial police, a job he had enjoyed: 'He had been very successful in tracking and breaking up certain nefarious secret societies amongst the natives' (Conrad 1907: 99). More importantly, this work 'had the saving character of an irregular sort of warfare or at least the risk and excitement of open-air sport', which appealed to his 'adventurous disposition' (Conrad 1907: 113). When he married, he had expected to return to this work, but his wife had 'formed an unfavourable opinion of the colonial climate on hearsay evidence' (Conrad 1907: 99). Through her 'influential connections', presumably, he has become Assistant Commissioner in the Metropolitan Police, but he takes no pleasure in the work. He hates the English spring with its 'rough east winds', 'raw fog' and 'cold rain', and the 'futility of office work especially appalled him' (Conrad 1907: 100). He seizes on the Greenwich bombing as an opportunity for some real 'police work' (Conrad 1907: 99), an outlet for 'his considerable gifts for the detection of incriminating truth' (Conrad 1907: 117). Nevertheless, despite his sexually unsatisfying marriage and his sense of being 'chained to a desk' (Conrad 1907: 113), with his well-connected wife and his early evenings at his gentlemen's club, he gives every appearance, at least, of being comfortably settled.[5]

The most extreme experience of a disrupted or incomplete rite of passage is that of Yanko Goorall in 'Amy Foster'. His story begins with an appropriate ritual to mark his separation from his old life: 'before he left his home, he drove his mother in a wooden cart … to offer prayers and make a vow for his safety' (Conrad 1903: 115). This Christian narrative is shadowed by another narrative with its own ritual of separation, the folk-tale with its 'bargaining away of the paternal cow' (Conrad 1903: 117) as the precursor to the quest for gold.[6] After these two very different rituals of separation, Yanko's story also includes a clear and extended period of liminality. The first stage of this is the journey via Berlin and Hamburg to the Kent coast. The first part of this journey involves his experience of estrangement presented to the reader through a series of defamiliarized descriptions: the long journey 'on the iron track'; the 'house of bricks' with its high 'glass roof' and the 'steam machines' which 'rolled in at one end and out at the other'; and then the 'thing like a great house on the water' with 'bare trees in the shape of crosses' growing from its roof (Conrad 1903: 114–15). The second stage, once he takes his place in 'the bottom of that ship', is 'a period of blank ignorance'; it is an experience in which he is taken completely 'out of his knowledge' (Conrad 1903: 116, 117, 118). The third stage of liminality occurs after he has been shipwrecked off the Kent coast. He seems to have come ashore by clinging to a hencoop (Conrad 1903: 123), and for a long time he is associated with various non-human animals. He begins his new life by 'crawling' over the sea-wall, rolling into a dyke, and then making his way 'on all fours' until he finds himself 'among some sheep huddled close under the lee of a hedge' (Conrad 1903: 112). He is subsequently found 'hiding in Hammond's pig-pound' (Conrad 1903: 118) and then amongst the loose straw in Smith's stockyard 'swinging ... to and fro like a bear in a cage' (Conrad 1903: 120).

For Yanko himself, when he first comes ashore after his disorienting journey, 'England was an undiscovered country' (Conrad 1903: 112). This recalls Conrad's later account, in 'Poland Revisited', of his arrival in London and his navigation of the streets around Liverpool Street Station (Conrad 1924: 150). However, Yanko's welcome is vastly different from Conrad's. As a castaway on an unknown shore, he fears 'death from starvation on a barren coast', 'violent death or else slavery' (Conrad 1903: 113). The treatment he experiences from the natives casts him in a range of socially marginal roles: as a 'gypsy', a 'tramp', a drunk, 'an escaped lunatic', a 'beggar' or simply as a 'horrid-looking man' (Conrad 1903: 118, 119, 120, 124, 118). Accordingly, he is greeted with 'rough angry tones' by the fishermen of West Colebrook, when he knocks against the walls of their cottages (Conrad 1903: 118); he is 'lashed' with a whip across the face, when he tries to stop Mr Bradley's milk-cart; he is pelted with stones by schoolboys; he is hit over the head with an umbrella by Mrs Finn; and finally locked into the wood-lodge by Smith. If the natives are acting out of 'the dread of an inexplicable strangeness' (Conrad 1903: 120), the narrator's judgement on Yanko's plight presents the other's perspective: 'It is indeed hard upon a man to find himself a lost stranger, helpless, incomprehensible, and of a mysterious origin' (Conrad 1903: 113). And, here, Yanko's experience speaks to the general condition of the migrant and the refugee – and to the specific position of Conrad himself. Yanko's liminal position might also be discussed in terms of Agamben's 'bare life that is more and more driven to the margins of the nation-states' (Agamben 1998: 133). In the account of his arrival on shore, he is imagistically positioned on the 'threshold of articulation between nature and culture' (Agamben 1998: 181); and, in his exclusion from the local community, he is exposed to various forms of violent treatment.

The process of incorporation begins with what might be seen as another ritual act: Amy Foster's offering of half a loaf of bread to the starving Yanko. As the narrator observes, 'Through this act of impulsive pity he was brought back again within the pale of human relations' (Conrad 1903: 125). The stages of this move towards incorporation are marked by food, work and even, eventually, wages. He is given food and shelter by the Swaffers, even if the food is given him 'at the back-door' to be carried off in his hands to the outhouse (Conrad

1903: 128) – literally signifying his liminal position. They discover that 'he could use a spade' (Conrad 1903: 127). More than that, 'he could help at the ploughing, could milk the cows, feed the bullocks in the cattle-yard, and was of some use with the sheep' (Conrad 1903: 130). However, it is only after his rescue of Swaffer's granddaughter from drowning that Yanko has his meals laid out 'on the kitchen table' and is paid a wage (Conrad 1903: 131). This suggests a gradual process of incorporation through successive, incremental stages. However, full incorporation never happens: 'His foreignness had a peculiar and indelible stamp' (Conrad 1903: 131–20). Not only does he dress differently, but he likes to sing and dance, and his 'lithe' and 'supple' body movements mark him out from the local men, 'slow, unsmiling, with downcast eyes … uncouth in body and as leaden of gait as if their very hearts were loaded with chains' (Conrad 1903: 110–11).

The crisis arises from his continuing connection to his own language and culture. To begin with, his wife is alienated by his desire to sing to his son 'a song such as the mothers sing to babies in the mountains', to teach him the prayers he had been taught by his father, to talk with him 'in that language that to our ears sounded so disturbing' (Conrad 1903: 137). Just as the returned Assistant Commissioner is to some degree distanced from his successful London life by his memories of his colonial experiences, Yanko Goorall's otherness (and the responses to it from the natives) prevents his full incorporation. His wife's panicked response to his fevered demand for water epitomizes the latent potential for rejection within that continuing perception of otherness. His 'passionate remonstrances' in that 'disturbing' language turn him back from being her husband to 'that strange man' who came ashore from the shipwreck (Conrad 1903: 140). From Yanko's perspective, this is the migrant's nightmare fear of slipping back unconsciously into the mother tongue, under conditions of stress or illness, and ceasing to be comprehensible. From Amy's perspective, it is an instance of what Kennedy described as 'the dread of an inexplicable strangeness' (Conrad 1903: 120). Kennedy sees in her eyes 'the spectre of the fear which had hunted her on that night three miles and a half to the door of Foster's cottage' (Conrad 1903: 140). This fear drives Amy back to the shelter of her father's house; while her abandonment of her husband returns Yanko to that earlier marginalized, non-human animal state ('a bird caught in a snare'. 'a wild creature under the net' [Conrad 1903: 141]). In this 'exposure in the relation of abandonment', Yanko returns to that condition of 'residual and irreducible bare life … excluded and exposed to a death that no rite and no sacrifice can redeem' (Agamben 1998: 83, 100).

Return

In July 1914, Conrad set out on his first visit to Poland since 1893. By the time the Conrad family reached Cracow, Austria-Hungary had declared war on Serbia and the mobilization of Austrian forces had begun. In his essay 'Poland Revisited', Conrad recalls how sightseeing in Cracow was interrupted by the appearance of 'the men of the *Landwehr* corps, that passed through Cracow to reinforce the Austrian army in Eastern Galicia' (Conrad 1924: 157). Once the war had started, the pattern of alliances created particular problems for Poles. In a letter to Cunninghame Graham, Conrad described the 'mental and nervous strain' he experienced seeing 'the sheer despair' of his Polish friends, since they could foresee 'nothing but ruin and ultimate extinction whatever would happen' (*CL* 1996: 446). As he put it in another letter, the Triple Entente, the alliance of Britain and France with Russia at the outbreak of the war, produced 'the bewildered despair of a people robbed suddenly of its hereditary hopes of support' from France (*CL* 1996: 456).[7] Since Napoleon's time, many Poles had looked to France for liberation from Austrian, Prussian and Russian domination. The particular bind in which the Poles (and Conrad) found themselves now was, if Britain and France were victorious (as they would have hoped), the alliance meant that Russia would extend its control over Poland. If they lost, Austria and Germany would do the same.

In 'Poland Revisited', Conrad shows how the return to Cracow meant a confrontation with memories of his last few months with his dying father and his father's funeral. It also meant a more general confrontation with that 'store of memories … with which I was to break violently by throwing myself into an unrelated existence' (Conrad 1924: 145). In this context, the public recognition of the 'ardent fidelity' of his father's life (Conrad 1924: 169) stands as a challenge to him. At the same time, that violent break 'into an unrelated existence' means that, while his moonlit walk in the Square is haunted by ghosts (including the memory of himself 'as a small boy of eleven' (Conrad 1924: 167), he also feels ghost-like (Conrad 1924: 164), a revenant. This is comparable to the narrator's experience, at the end of 'Karain', of two competing realities: his present location in the vibrant life of the Strand in London and the remembered world of Karain. The start of the essay also acknowledges other loyalties: in his exchanges with the Germanophile captain of the cross-channel ferry, he is accused of being a Frenchman (Conrad 1924: 159). He also acknowledges the 'very strong hold' his neighbourhood in Kent has on him (Conrad 1924: 149). Conrad works through this set of complications in *The Rover*.

Conrad described *The Rover* as 'a seaman's return' (*CL* 2008: 318). It begins in Toulon in 1796 with Jean Peyrol's return to France after a lifetime spent at sea. As he views the mass of people gathered to view his ship dock, he 'felt like a navigator about to land on a newly discovered shore', and realizes that 'he had grown a stranger to his native country' (Conrad 1923: 2). His disembarking is accompanied by two rituals. First, there is a private ritual of shaving and dressing to prepare himself for the official encounter with the port authorities. The clothes he puts on (the white shirt; the short, blue jacket; the red bandana) are the colours of the new Republic: through this process, he transforms himself into 'Citizen Peyrol' (Conrad 1923: 11). Secondly, there is the public ritual of presenting himself to the officials in the Port Office: 'here he was; and there were his ship's papers and his own papers and everything in order' (Conrad 1923: 3). Nevertheless, once he has his discharge, he doesn't stay in Toulon, but makes his way to the Giens peninsula where he grew up.

Through Peyrol's return home after such a long absence, Conrad articulates two aspects of the returnee's situation. On the one hand, as Peyrol readily understands, his past life is unknown to those around him: 'Nobody could know what his forty years or more of sea-life had been, unless he told them himself' (Conrad 1923: 5). He is a stranger in the place where he was born since his activities for the last forty years are completely unknown there. On the other hand, from observation of those around him, he also has a sense of what he might have been like had he stayed (Conrad 1923: 10, 16). Thus, he is a stranger here in a second sense in that his experiences abroad have made him unlike those who have stayed at home. At the same time, as Conrad experienced in Cracow, the countryside he returns to has 'a sort of strange familiarity' (Conrad 1923: 6), the oxymoron catching precisely the ambivalence of the experience.

In the novel's conclusion, Conrad returns to the complex loyalties of the returnee that he had intimated in 'Poland Revisited'. Peyrol undertakes an action which proves him 'a good Frenchman', but that action draws on the skills he has learned away from France and elicits the appreciation of the English enemy ('There is a clever seaman aboard that tartane' [Conrad 1923: 262]). The mutual appreciation of Peyrol and Captain Vincent overrides the national hostility that is its context.[8] In this final action, in which Peyrol takes the place of the young naval officer, Réal, in order to place fake documents in the hands of the English, the resolution of his complex loyalties is accompanied by the suggestion of another ritual.[9] Arlette was earlier described as being 'like the scapegoat charged with all the murders and blasphemies of the Revolution' (Conrad 1923: 232). J. G. Frazer describes the series of substitutions that are involved in certain scapegoating rituals (Frazer 1922: 573–4).[10] A similar series of substitutions takes place in *The Rover*. While Arlette is described as the scapegoat, it is that other victim of the Revolution, Réal, who seems destined to be sacrificed for the benefit of France. When Peyrol takes his place, he not only sacrifices himself, but also takes with him the tartane with its bloody secrets and another relic of the Revolution, the Jacobin Scevola.

This act of self-sacrifice is also an action ultimately based on love. When Peyrol first sees Arlette, her oval face and the whiteness of her throat 'forced from the Citizen Peyrol a slight hiss through his clenched teeth' (Conrad 1923: 21). The narrator encourages us to explore this response by observing that it represented 'a feeling that was no longer surprise or curiosity, but seemed to be lodged in his very breast' (Conrad 1923: 21–2). This description recalls Marlow's account of his response to the portrait of the Intended: 'Curiosity? Yes; and also some other feeling perhaps' (Conrad 1902: 155). In Peyrol's case, another hint is offered, when, after Arlette fingers his coat as 'a child might have done', Peyrol experiences 'a soft indefinite emotion' (Conrad 1923: 23). In Chapter VII, this 'indefinite emotion' is further clarified: after noting Peyrol's sense of Arlette as a 'lovable creature', the narrator observes that she 'aroused a kind of intimate emotion which he had not known before to exist by itself in a man' (Conrad 1923: 88). What Peyrol experiences now is not desire, but a quasi-parental, protective love. A similar emotional attentiveness is present in his response to Lieutenant Réal. In his first reported conversation with Réal, Peyrol claims that his insight into the young officer's 'heart' prevented him from killing him (Conrad 1923: 44). In the conclusion, Peyrol draws on these emotional insights and sacrifices himself to enable the marriage of the young couple and the corresponding regeneration of the community. In doing so, he also achieves a form of survival for himself: 'they talked of him openly, as though he had come back to live again amongst them' (Conrad 1923: 284). *The Rover* begins with Peyrol's return to what Conrad calls with reference to himself 'that corner of the earth' where his 'boyhood had received its earliest independent impressions' (Conrad 1924: 146), and it ends with this second return as a memory, as part of the emotional life of the young couple. The final sentence operates in the mode of haunting, of what Yael Levin calls 'the otherwise present', as it evokes the presence of the absent Peyrol asleep at noonday in the shade of the mulberry tree (Levin 2009: 1–10).

As noted earlier, when Conrad passed the examination for second mate, Bobrowski had advised him to cultivate 'a general love of people and of helping others who need your help' (Najder 1964: 64). In his Preface to *The Nigger of the 'Narcissus'*, this was rephrased as: 'the latent feeling of fellowship with all creation … the subtle but invincible conviction of solidarity that knits together the loneliness of innumerable hearts' (Conrad 1897: viii). Peyrol seems to have learned the same lessons through his years in the strange household at the Escampobar farm. As mentioned earlier, in 'Poland Revisited', Conrad's account of his own 'sailor's return', the hauntings by ghosts of the past and the exploration of the various feelings involved, which we would expect from such a narrative, is preceded by brief references to two other experiences of place. The first is his visit to Sheffield, where he felt himself 'a stranger in a strange city' (Conrad 1924: 141). This might suggest his anxieties about his return to Cracow, but, as we have seen, his experience of return was more complex and more nuanced than this. The second reference is a brief evocation of 'the most peaceful nook in Kent', where he has made his home, and the acknowledgement that this Kent countryside 'had a very strong hold' on him. The full quotation reads: 'it was dear to me not as an inheritance, but as an acquisition, as a conquest in the sense in which a woman is conquered – by love, which is a sort of surrender' (Conrad 1924: 148). The image of love as a conquest and involving an acquisition is obviously problematic. However, the distinction between two different ways of belonging to a place – historically by inheritance or emotionally through acquisition and surrender – remains valid. What is also important is that affirmation of love – for people, for a place. This is also what is intimated through the story of Peyrol's final self-sacrifice.

Notes

1 Rubenhold's account of these five lives gives an insight into the precarious lives of single women in the docklands of the 1880s.

2 Even their language is taken from them with the nautical terms 'sheets' and 'lines' being replaced by the landsman's term 'ropes'.

3 The East India Dock Road and Canton Street are part of Limehouse, which was thought of as 'China Town', though most of the Chinese there were sailors between ships.

4 Adam Hochschild, *King Leopold's Ghost: A Story of Greed, Terror and Heroism in Colonial Africa* (London: Pan Books, 2002). See, for example, his account of Leopold's funding of favourable accounts of his doings in French and American newspapers (80, 82) or his account of Leopold's newspaper campaign to discredit the Black American historian and journalist George Washington Williams, who, in 1890, published an *Open Letter* to Leopold as a pamphlet and also *A Report upon the Congo State*, exposing all the human rights abuses perpetrated by Leopold's colonial regime (108–13).

5 We are told that 'he considered himself the victim of an ironic fate – the same. No doubt, which had brought about his marriage with a woman exceptionally sensitive in the matter of colonial climate, besides other limitations testifying to the delicacy of her nature – and her tastes' (SA 113).

6 In 'Jack and the Beanstalk', for example, Jack trades the family cow for a handful of beans, from which the beanstalk grows.

7 For the Polish political investment in Napoleon, see Richard Niland, *Conrad and History* (Oxford: Oxford University Press, 2010), 183.

8 For a fuller discussion of this conclusion, see Robert Hampson '"Not a Bad Frenchman": Conrad and National Identity', in Paul Goring, Domhnall Mitchell and Jakob Lothe (eds), *Each Other's Yarns: Essays on Narrative and Critical Method for Jeremy Hawthorn* (Oslo: Novus Press, 2012), 279–89.

9 For a discussion of the use of myth and ritual as 'a form of thought' (17) in modernist fiction, see Thomas J. Cousineau, *Ritual Unbound: Reading Sacrifice in Modernist Fiction* (Newark: University of Delaware Press, 2004). Cousineau pays particular attention to the modernist revaluation of scapegoating.

10 See Robert Hampson, 'Frazer, Conrad and the "Truth of Primitive Passion"', in Robert Fraser (ed.), *Sir James Frazer and the Literary Imagination* (London: Macmillan, 1990), 172–91.

Works Cited

Agamben, G. (1998), *Homo Sacer: Sovereign Power and Bare Life*, trans. Daniel Heller-Roazen, Stanford: Stanford University Press.

Conrad, J. ([1897] 1923), *The Nigger of the 'Narcissus'*, London: J. M. Dent.

Conrad, J. ([1902] 1923), *Youth, Heart of Darkness and The End of the Tether*, London: J. M. Dent.

Conrad, J. ([1903] 1923), *Typhoon; and Other Stories*, London: J. M. Dent.

Conrad, J. ([1906] 1923), *The Mirror of the Sea and A Personal Record*, London: J. M. Dent.

Conrad, J. ([1907] 1923), *The Secret Agent*, London: J. M. Dent.

Conrad, J. ([1912] 1923), *The Mirror of the Sea and A Personal Record*, London: J. M. Dent.

Conrad, J. ([1913] 1923), *Chance: A Tale in Two Parts*, London: J. M. Dent.

Conrad, J. ([1917] 1923), *The Shadow-Line*, London: J. M. Dent.

Conrad, J. (1923), *The Rover*, London: J. M. Dent.

Conrad, J. (1924), *Notes on Life and Letters*, London: J. M. Dent.

Conrad, J. (2008), *The Collected Letters of Joseph Conrad, Volume 8*, ed. F. R. Karl and L. Davies, Cambridge: Cambridge University Press.

Cousineau, T. J. (2004), *Ritual Unbound: Reading Sacrifice in Modernist Fiction*, Newark: University of Delaware Press.

Frazer, J. G. (1922), *The Golden Bough*, London: Macmillan.

Hampson, R. (1990), 'Frazer, Conrad and the "Truth of Primitive Passion"', in Robert Fraser (ed.), *Sir James Frazer and the Literary Imagination*. London: Macmillan, 172–91.

Hampson, R. (2012), '"Not a Bad Frenchman": Conrad and National Identity', in Paul Goring, Domhnall Mitchell and Jakob Lothe (eds), *Each Other's Yarns: Essays on Narrative and Critical Method for Jeremy Hawthorn*, Oslo: Novus Press, 279–89.

Hochschild, A. (2002), *King Leopold's Ghost: A Story of Greed, Terror and Heroism in Colonial Africa*, London: Pan Books.

Levin, Y. (2009), *Tracing the Aesthetic Principle in Conrad's Novels*, London: Palgrave Macmillan.

Najder, Z., ed. (1964), *Conrad's Polish Background: Letters to and from Polish Friends*, London: Oxford University Press.

Niland, R. (2010), *Conrad and History*, Oxford: Oxford University Press.

Rubenhold, H. (2019), *The Five: The Untold Lives of the Women Killed by Jack the Ripper*, London: Doubleday.

Thomas, E. W. (1879), *Twenty-five Years Labour among the Friendless and Fallen*, London: R. K. Burt and Co.

2

Back in (the) Ukraine: Rites of passage and rites of entry

William Atkinson
Appalachian State University, North Carolina

1

Joseph Conrad was born in Ukraine. While this statement may seem uncontentious enough, it in fact warrants close examination. There is no question that Conrad's birthplace – Berdychiv – lies within the territory of the modern state of Ukraine. But Zdzisław Najder tells that in Conrad's time, Ukraine meant, 'and not just in Polish, only the Kiev province, and especially its western part (the "right bank")' [of the Dnieper]. And 'Neither Podolia, from where the Korzeniowski family came, nor Volhynia with its capital Źitomierz (Zhytomyr), where Conrad lived with his parents, was called "Ukraine"' (1998: 45). Yet, in 1912, Conrad himself wrote, 'I was unpacking my luggage after a journey from London into Ukraine' (2008: 47). The eleventh edition of *Encyclopædia Britannica* (1911), under *Ukraine*, provides the following: '("frontier"), the name formerly given to a district of European Russia, now comprising the governments of Kharkov, Kiev, Podolia, and Poltava' (vol. 27, 564). 'Frontier' is the key term and represents the standard understanding of the word, which is of Slavic origin, derived from the Indo-European root *krei 'to cut'. The secondary meaning of *krei is edge, from which comes the Ukrainian and Polish *ukraïna* or *ukrajina*, or the Polish word *kresy*. *Ukraïna* is first attested in documents copied in the fifteenth century referring to events that took place two or three centuries earlier. In none of these documents, writes Paul R. Magocsi, is the word 'ever used in reference to a specific territory. Rather, when it is used, ukraïna simply means an undefined borderland' (2010: 189). Adam Zamoyski confirms this reading from a Polish perspective: 'from the forests and lakes of Mazuria to the wild plains of Podolia rolling away into the distance, which the Poles referred to as "Ukraina", meaning "margin" or "edge"' (1987: 105).

There is a distinction between *borderland* (a *margin*) and *frontier* (or *edge*). The former suggests a territory of some extent. If it borders two or more polities, to which does it belong? It may be continually contested, or it may belong to neither and simply be a politically undetermined region. *Frontier*, on the other hand, derives from *front* and is where one determinate territory abuts onto another. Strictly speaking, a frontier is a line without substance; it is simply where one territory ends and another begins. It is a cut or an edge rather than an area. When frontier does to refer to an area, it tends to refer to the space behind the frontier line. Thus, the Polish frontier would be the area immediately behind the demarcating line, within Poland.[1]

Poland annexed much of what is now Ukraine in 1569. The Poles acknowledged that there had been a high level of culture in the region during the period of Kievan Rus' – a medieval confederation of East Slavic peoples beginning in the later ninth century. But Kievan Rus' had fallen into decline and was destroyed by the Mongol invasions of the 1240s. So Ukrajina[2] was a borderland between the Polish heartland and what was on the other side. The area was not significantly Polonized, and when the Ukrainian lands passed to Russia in 1793, the peasantry were speaking various eastern Slav dialects, which were closer to Russian than to Polish, and they had not adopted Latin Christianity. Even in 1795, Poles made up only 10 per cent of the population, and the census of 1897 shows that only 3.5 per cent of the right (west) bank provinces – Kiev, Volhynia and Podolia – was Polish (Magocsi 334). Nonetheless, the Polish gentry continued to dominate the socio-economic and cultural life of the area (Magocsi 2010: 365), which they called Ruthenia (Najder 1998: 52). The word Ruthenia, like Russia, derives from Rus'. The etymology of Rus' itself is controversial, but the contemporary states of Russia, Belorussia and Ukraine all claim Kievan Rus' as their cultural progenitor.

In the nineteenth century, Russians and the majority of the people of what later became Ukraine referred to the area as Little Russia, and they spoke Little Russian. In the first half of the century, there was something of a vogue for Little Russian. It was considered chic, and people began to publish in it. Polish intellectuals were worried that Ukrainianism was being used to de-Polonize the provinces on the west bank of the Dnieper. But attitudes in St. Petersburg changed in the second half of the century as provincial governors in 'Little Russia' began to receive reports of Ukrainian leaders who wanted 'to separate Ukraine from Russia' (Magocsi 2010: 268). One response was a ministerial decree that 'the

Little Russian language has not, does not, and cannot exist' (370). In 1876, from the spa at Ems, in Germany, Emperor Alexander II issued a decree (the Ems Ukase) that set about putting an end to all ideas of Ukrainian nationalism and separatism. It proscribed the publication or importation of Ukrainian-language books and banned all theatrical performances in Ukrainian; even Ukrainian songs were forbidden (Plokhy 2015: 167).

Ruthenia had been for the Poles a borderland, the ukraine between Poland and the other side. For the Russians it was also a borderland rather than a linear frontier. Little Russia – lesser Russia – was an intermediary region that functioned to distinguish between Russia and not-Russia. Thus, the territory and the people were included within Russia and at the same time excluded from it. Ukraine was in Russia but not of it. Ruthenians/Little Russians were slowly coming to regard themselves as Ukrainians. Ukraine as borderland is an identity forced upon it from somewhere else. In the first half of the twentieth century, Ukrainian linguistic scholars began to argue that (in Ukrainian) *ukraine* does not mean borderland but native land, its own country (Pivtorak). Accordingly, Ukraine has lost its definite article because it is not *the* borderland or *the* frontier of anywhere else. It is itself.

Conrad's earliest surviving holograph makes his own sense of identity absolutely clear. In the dedication on the back of a photograph taken when he was six years old, he describes himself as 'Grandson, *Polak-Katolic* [Pole-Catholic], and *szlachcic* [gentleman], Konrad' (Stape 2007: 14). He would not have thought of himself as Ukrainian,[3] but the term is so very appropriate because wherever he was born,[4] it was not strictly speaking in Poland. Indeed, Poland did not exist as an independent polity between 1795 and 1918. During those years, it was a temporal borderland – a ukraine – existing only in relation to when it had existed and to when it would again exist. Whoever lives in a ukraine cannot but be aware of the presence both of here and of there, of then and of now. This dislocation, a sense of being here and now and yet not, is reiterated throughout Conrad's work.

2

Apropos of a collection on crossings, one or two of my fellow contributors use the term 'rites of entry'. For this particular chapter, I need to distinguish *rites of entry* from the more familiar *rites of passage* because the latter are usually also the former, but the reverse is not the case. Arnold van Gennep in *Rites of Passage*

(1909), his classic study of the subject, writes of their 'over-all goal – to insure a change of condition or a passage from one magico-religious or secular group to another' (1960: 11). He subdivides such rites into three: 'rites of separation, transition rites, and rites of incorporation' and acknowledges that 'these three subcategories are not developed to the same extent by all peoples or in every ceremonial pattern' (11). A rite of passage that enables right of entry is, in effect, also a rite of entry. But while rites of passage bring about a change of condition (from spinster to wife, from lay person to priest, from civilian to soldier), rites of entry do not necessarily do so. When I enter a foreign country, there is a rite of entry to undergo – passport and customs – but once past these barriers and afforded right of entry, I am not fundamentally changed. I would need to undergo the rite of citizenship, which is a rite of passage, for that to happen.

There are rites of passage in Conrad's work, but on the whole, the initiand either fails or the rite is not entirely effective: the three examinations – for second mate, first mate and master – that he describes in *A Personal Record* (1912) are undoubtedly rites of passage in that they effect his incorporation into the officer group. After both examinations for mate, once released from the building, Conrad walks 'on air along Tower Hill' (Conrad 2008: 103, 105). After the third and final examination, 'I did not walk on air', even though 'I was now a British master mariner beyond a doubt' (107). Conrad has undergone the rite of passage, but it has not taken effect; it is no more than a rite of entry. He thus finds himself in an indeterminate position, *in* but not *of*. To return to the ontology of ukraine: is he in a border*land*, or is he pinned at the cut between two states or conditions, about to jump?

Conrad's explanation for his dispiritedness at his success is oblique. He recalls the resistance he encountered to his teenage desire to go to sea and concludes, 'I verily believe mine was the only case of a boy of my nationality and antecedents taking a, so to speak, standing jump out of his racial surroundings and associations' (Conrad 2008: 108). Such a jump was evidently to be a transition from one state to another. But Conrad offers no suggestion of what as a boy he was hoping to jump into. 'The truth is that what I had in view was not a naval career, but the sea' (108), the sea, to which anyone and everyone has the right of entry, and which is itself a huge marginal space between countries. So the jump was to be into an indeterminacy, a watery ukraine.

The Master's examination is more like a conversation with an equal than an ordeal. The examiner 'offered me his hand and wished me well. He even made a few steps towards the door with me' (Conrad 2008: 107). The gesture indicates that Conrad is now 'one of us'. He has landed; he is no longer in his birthplace, no longer in ukraine. At another level, he is being pushed across a frontier. The examiner's last words are, 'If I were you, I would go into steam' (107). Conrad mostly represents sailing ships as the norm and steam ships as being rather new-fangled and certainly beneath the dignity of a real sailor. Yet by the time he first went to sea, in 1874, 'steamships had never been so profitable, so comfortable, or so numerous. The tea races under sail ended in 1873; within ten years, steamships carried more international cargo than sail' (Jasanoff 2017: 95–6). Conrad's sea life was a fading reality from the start; he was indeed a Pole at sea in that his profession was being reduced year by year much as Poland was reduced piece by piece from 1772 to 1795. At the end of the examination, the old mariner acknowledges Conrad as a fellow master. But the counsel to go into steam means that the fellowship into which Conrad has been inducted is no longer what he had believed it to be. Of course, Conrad knew all about steam, but the advice coming from his sponsor brings the reality home: while he has undergone a rite of passage, there is nothing for him to enter into. Like a Pole without a state, he is a sailor without sails.

A Personal Record is about his second great standing jump, not from sailing to steam but to the life of a writer of fiction.[5] Conrad represents the motives for his jumping ship as entirely mysterious: 'The necessity which impelled me was a hidden obscure necessity, a completely masked and unaccountable phenomenon' (Conrad 2008: 69). Hidden necessities became central to the narratives of much of his fiction. On the morning when he began *Almayer's Folly*, 'I was not at all certain that I wanted to write, or that I meant to write, or that I had anything to write about' (70).[6] Just like a man of the days of sail, he sits down and waits for a wind. The narratives of his novels proceed like a sailing ship, tacking back and forth, now taking the story forward, now going back across to catch the wind from a better angle; and they are often completely becalmed. They are so very different from the steamship narratives of H. G. Wells, for example, which, once loaded, follow their course firmly and deliberately.

3

Marlow's steamboat in *Heart of Darkness* (1899, 1902) is most un-Wellsian. It is wallowing in the river when he first comes across it, and even when he has his rivets, the vessel can no more than crawl, beetlelike, towards the inner station and Marlow's encounter with Kurtz; it seems to be carrying him across the borderland to where he will learn the truth about Leopold's Congo. The journey can be read as the first phase of a rite of passage, of separation: 'cut off for ever from everything you had known once – somewhere – far away – in another existence perhaps' (Conrad 2010: 77).

Leopoldian propaganda was making all sorts of claims about how the company would enable the people of central Africa to cross over into the modern world. Marlow's aunt is enthusiastic for the work of improvement, but Marlow dismisses it as a lot of rot and ventures to point out that the company is established to make a profit (Conrad 2010: 53). Once in Africa, he hears more about this philanthropy and the sarcastic phrase 'gang of virtue' is used to denigrate such work by those who are suspicious of it all (68). Thus, Marlow's own scepticism makes him bedfellow to the egregious manager and his henchman, the brick maker. We are, perhaps, to understand that while the latter two are motivated entirely by self-interest, Marlow has reached his position after disinterested and realistic consideration. He understands that Kurtz came out to Africa meaning to do good for the people of the river and to profit for himself at the same time. Marlow does not indicate that he believes Kurtz acted initially in anything but good faith. He describes the famous report to the Association for the Suppression of Savage Customs as moving and well written (95). With the exception of the Accountant, all the white men whom Marlow encounters impress him as incompetent and motivated by nothing other than shallow self-interest. Everything he hears about Kurtz suggests that here was a much more substantial man than the Manager or any of the traders. He wants to meet him in order to see what a superior man with a developed ethical sense would do. He discovers that Kurtz's superiority manifests itself as an exceptional ruthlessness. His current activities – raiding the country for ivory, getting himself adored – follow from the judgement of the postscript, 'Exterminate all the brutes' (95), and indicate that Kurtz has lost all interest in the project for which he came out. 'Exploit all the brutes' would have more accurately indicated Kurtz's final position.

Standard readings of the novella tell us that Kurtz himself lacked the key quality of restraint; therefore, he succumbs to the wilderness (Conrad 2010: 96, 114). In the absence of the restraints of nineteenth-century life, of public opinion and the policeman around the corner (94), Kurtz reveals himself to be what he really is, to be all too human. This reading is perhaps ultimately Augustinian: man is naturally sinful. The church is replaced by the various carrots and sticks of late nineteenth-century urban life, which are not intrinsically different from those of the twenty-first century. There are many instances in Conrad's corpus where characters behave much like Kurtz once they are no longer embedded in modern life: Gentleman Brown, Mr Jones and Ricardo, Falk; Guzmán Bento and General Montero in Costaguana have no restraints because they have absolute power.

Marlow is represented as being deeply sceptical of the Company's philanthropic claims. There cannot but be an element of 20/20 hindsight here because Conrad was writing almost ten years after he saw what he saw on the river. He had had, in addition, the opportunity to read various periodical publications on central Africa that showed Leopold's Congo as it truly was. However, it would still have been possible to say that the circumstances on the ground were the problem, that the absence of the restraints of European practice, custom and law was the reason for the horror. We now know, and the work of Edmund Morel and the Congo Reform Association was making it increasing clear in the first years of the twentieth century, that what went on in central Africa was policy directed from Brussels. Those deserving extermination were not in Africa but in Europe. The horror was not a function of the unrestrained life of the equatorial forest but of the paved streets and solid buildings of the imperial centre. *Heart of Darkness* does not say any of this directly.[7] It seems to present itself as a story of the periphery, about practices possible only at the periphery. But in closing in Brussels, in the Intended's house, it figuratively and literally brings the narrative back to its home. At best, the Leopoldian regime lacked restraint enough to restrain its servants in central Africa; at worst, Kurtz's horror is the regime. And the fact that Marlow's crew, 'the cannibals', has restraint (Conrad 2010: 85) proves that neither being in Africa nor being African is a factor.

Marlow has gone halfway round the world and crossed various political frontiers to undergo apparently a rite of passage. He experienced separation, and then what Victor Turner characterizes as 'margin' or 'limen' (threshold), during which the subject 'passes through a cultural realm that has few or none of the attributes of the past or coming state' (1969: 94). 'Liminal entities', Turner tells us, 'are neither here nor there; they are betwixt and between' – ukrainian. Liminality is 'frequently liked to death' (95). Kurtz dies and is buried in a muddy hole. 'And then they very nearly buried me' (Conrad 2010: 117). Marlow's wrestle with death took place 'in an impalpable greyness with nothing under foot, with nothing around, without spectators, without clamour, without glory, without the great desire of victory, without the great fear of defeat, in a sickly atmosphere of tepid skepticism, without much belief in your own right and still less in that of your adversary'. His final judgement on his own rite of passage is that 'if such is the form of ultimate wisdom then life is a greater riddle than some of us think it to be' (118). If the novella indeed is an account of a rite of passage, this judgement is the third and final phase, 'aggregation' (Turner 1969: 94) or 'incorporation' (van Gennep 1960: 11); Marlow seems to have moved from one indeterminate state to another, from ukraine to ukraine. It was, as the narrator says at the beginning of the narrative, 'one of Marlow's inconclusive experiences' (Conrad 2010: 47).

At the political level, however, Marlow's experience is entirely apposite. He did not need to cross any oceans to find the heart of darkness. He did not even need to cross the Channel. There was no border to cross; it had already been crossed both temporally and topographically. He points out at the very beginning of his narrative, 'And this also has been one of the dark places of the earth' (Conrad 2010: 45). And it still is. There is no borderland between here and there. Darkness was always already here.

4

Nostromo (1904) is an exacting text: it has been noted that one cannot read the novel until one has read it – and read it more than once. Were *Nostromo* designed to make an argument, it would be arranged otherwise, in such a way that the reader could apprehend the argument's development. The novel would have a teleology, a conclusion towards which it would be moving in an orderly manner. But the novel's chronology undermines a clear sense of sequentiality. The second chapter, for example, describing the port of Sulaco tells us:

> The only sign of commercial activity within the harbour, visible from the beach of the Great Isabel, is the square blunt end of the wooden jetty which the Oceanic Steam Navigation Company (the O.S.N. of familiar speech) had thrown over the shallow part of the bay soon after they had resolved to make of Sulaco one of their ports of call for the Republic of Costaguana. The state possesses several harbours on its long seaboard. (Conrad 1930: 9)

The present tense marks the description as indicating the present time, but when we reach Captain Mitchell's tour of Sulaco, twenty-four chapters later, the town is described as the capital of the Occidental Republic rather than a port of call in Costaguana, and the augmentation of the O.S.N. Company's establishment, 'with its crowds of clerks, an office in town, the old office in the harbor, the division into departments-passenger, cargo, lighterage, and so on' (473), requires (would have required) far more construction than the blunt end of a wooden jetty. Furthermore, Captain Mitchell's account is (will be) all in the past tense referring the Sulaco described in Chapter 2. By the end of the text, the narrative is looking back on events that took place long after the 'now' of the opening description, a 'now' that placed (places) those past events in the future. We can understand the story only when we have a vision of its temporal totality, a folding together of past, present and future that renders all the events coeval. The text does not settle on any single time-being. Costaguana, the Occidental Province or Sulaco exists only in relation to when it had existed and to when it will exist. It is – they are – in a multi-temporal borderland; all is becoming, unsettled and without predetermination.

Don Carlos Gould – namesake of King Carlos IV, whose statue used to stand at the entrance to the Alameda – is known in the capital of Costaguana as 'the King of Sulaco' (Conrad 1930: 69), and the San Tomé mine is an 'Imperium in imperio'; the phrase is repeated several times. It originates with Don José Avellanos, who evidently feels ambivalent about the whole idea. He speaks the words 'with an air of profound self-satisfaction, which, somehow, in a curious way seemed to contain a queer admixture of bodily discomfort' (111). And well it might. An empire within an empire: imperial power is absolute, so how can there be imperial power subject to such power? Can one cross the border from imperium to imperio? Clearly one of them is not a true imperium. The logic – the illogic of the phrase – will lead to the Occidental province's successful war of secession.

Imperium in imperio is generally understood to refer to entities within a polity which do not appear to answer to the formal ruler. An embedded imperium is often a way for the formal ruler to sanction activities which for moral or political reasons may not be acknowledged. One thinks of intelligence agencies that act without the formal authorization of the ruler but nonetheless act in accordance with the ruler's true, yet unacknowledged, desires. The idea is manifest in the Janus quality of the word *sanction*: the ruler may secretly sanction such activities but would have to sanction them were they to become public. Should the imperium in imperio regularly act against the will of the formal ruler, there will ultimately be an overt power struggle of some kind. When General Montero declared himself Emperor of Costaguana, he was claiming imperium over the whole country. But less than a month later, he was shot dead (Conrad 1930: 487). The shot was fired by a young artillery officer, but at several removes behind him was the King of Sulaco. In this case the king trumps the emperor who was no true ruler and was shot from within. Gould was the true imperator beneath the emperor – and above him or within him or without him.

In *Heart of Darkness*, restraint is the key word: Kurtz in Africa lacks it; the Company in Europe lacks it; only the African crew, in Africa, have it. *Nostromo*'s indispensable marker is 'material interests'. The mine of the Gould Concession is the material heart of the Occidental Province and of Costaguana, but during the 'fifty years of misrule' it produced nothing other than the money extorted from Charles Gould's father. The son raised money from abroad to make the mine once again a going concern, and as such it again became a matter of interest beyond the Occidental Province. The Montero brothers cast greedy and distinctly materialistic eyes on it. The question for Gould and his backers is how to maintain the political, social and economic stability that is required for the mine to flourish, how to counteract the disorder and misrule that has characterized Costaguana for so long. Gould's material interests are his backers abroad as opposed to the material interest of the Monteros and their like. 'Only let the material interests once get a firm footing', Gould tells his wife, 'and they are bound to impose the conditions on which alone they can continue to exist. That's how your money-making is justified here in the face of lawlessness and disorder' (Conrad 1930: 84). These widely quoted sentences are an extraordinarily deft account of the ideology behind global capitalism. Law and order are not founded on any moral or ethical legal grounds. Once the material-interests machine takes over, it is bound by the logic of its own system to maintain order. However, the analysis assumes a gap, a border period, between disorder and the stability brought by material interests. This bordertime is the text of *Nostromo*.

'I pin my faith in material interests' (Conrad 1930: 84), declares Gould. The text assures us that Gould 'had no illusions' (85), yet the material interests require faith and therefore must be abstract. One cannot see or touch a material interest in itself. 'A Dane, a couple of Frenchmen, a discreet fat German, smiling with downcast eyes', these are 'the representatives of those material interests that had got a footing in Sulaco under the protecting might of the San Tomé mine' (192). Material interests have representatives. The interests themselves are not present in Costaguana, 'firm footing' notwithstanding. The fact of their absence is made quietly explicit on the day when Don Vincente comes to Sulaco to inaugurate the national railway. The people take the opportunity for a public holiday, with feasting, music and horse racing. Charles Gould points out to his wife that the land on which it takes place now belongs to the Railway Company. 'There will be no more popular feasts held here', he says (123). What had been a place held in common by the people of Sulaco, no doubt many of them Indians, is now private property, owned by interests far across the sea. 'Countries and populations altogether beyond your understanding' (104) as Father Román explains to the

Indian mineworkers. It is appropriate that a priest should be telling of such transcendental ownership.

The centre of the material interests, to the extent that they have one, is in a tall building in San Francisco, where Holroyd, the mine's principal investor, has his being. But this is just a manner of speaking. The centre is everywhere and nowhere. Towards the end of the novel, Dr Monygham presents Mrs Gould a withering account of her husband's beloved material interests:

> There is no peace and rest in the development of material interests. They have their law and their justice. But it is founded on expediency, and it is inhuman; it is without rectitude, without the continuity and the force that can be found only in a moral principle. Mrs Gould, the time approaches when all that the Gould Concession stands for shall weigh as heavily upon the people as the barbarism, cruelty, and misrule of a few years back. (511)

Just as Marlow found the heart of darkness on the Thames, Dr Monygham sees continuity with the fifty years of misrule. The Occidental Province will remain a province even when independent, its border no more than notional, because it will be truly ruled by external interests far across the sea who have no more than material interest in the welfare of its citizens. There is no border-line to step across. Elsewhere is a shadow of *here*, and *here* casts its shadow *there*.

5

In this final section, I want to return to the sail-steam dichotomy set up in *A Personal Record* and to follow a few more shadows. In the Author's Note to *The Shadow-Line* (1917), Conrad tells us that he had held the story in mind for a long time, under the title of *First Command* (Conrad 2013: 6), and acknowledged that 'it *is* personal experience' (6). He goes on to write that he held the command for two years, and his resignation marked the beginning of the 'terminal phase' of his seaman's life (7).

'For no reason on which a sensible person could put a finger I threw up my job – chucked my birth – left a ship of which the worst that could be said was that she was steamship' (Conrad 2013: 11–12). Thus, the narrator of *The Shadow-Line* begins his story. Two or three pages later we get an intimation of what that worst might have been. Although his year and a half aboard had been 'full of new and varied experience', all that experience under steam power 'appeared a dreary, prosaic waste of days', from which 'no truth' was to be got (14). The kind of truth that interests the narrator is associated with sail; only a sailing ship is worthy of 'blind loyalty' (12), of faith like Charles Gould's faith in distant material interests, or we might even suggest, a Pole's loyalty to a state that no longer existed. Accordingly, when he discovers that the captaincy of a sailing ship is available and that he is considered the best man available, he accepts the position. Emerging from the Harbour Master's office, like the earlier Conrad walking on air after his first two examinations, the narrator experiences a sense of 'deep detachment from the forms and colours of this world' by mere thought of his new command (34). The text could not be more explicit: the story to follow is not quite of *this* world.

Some of the 'truth' of sailing ships lies in their beauty, seeming more natural than manmade. In port, one is compared to a bird 'folding her white wings for a rest' (Conrad 2013: 31), and the narrator's own ship is 'a creature of high breed' (45). But for the most part, they are 'true' because they are of the past and not of this present world. 'She was there waiting for me', declares the narrator, 'spellbound, unable to move, to live, to get out into the world (till I came), like an enchanted princess' (38). As Frederic Jameson observes: 'It is historically unsurprising that, in the context of an emerging mass culture, nostalgia for older forms should express itself in their revival and imitation as high-art products' (2020: 29). Conrad has the narrator describe the ship herself in terms of art: 'That illusion of life and character which charms one in men's finest handiwork radiated from her' (Conrad 2013: 45).

There was nothing wrong with the earlier ship except that she was a steamship. 'One day I was perfectly right and the next everything was gone, glamour, flavour, interest, contentment – everything' (Conrad 2013: 12). The 'green sickness of late youth' (12), the green of 'an enchanted garden' (11), is the problem.[8] 'One goes on. And the time goes on – till one perceives ahead a shadow-line warning one that the region of early youth too must be left behind' (11). The garden need not be understood as Eden but simply as the garden where enchanted princesses are to be found – or shall we say, wherever princesses are still enchanted and enchanting? The shadow-line indicates the garden is becoming a borderland between *then* and what is to come. The line's presence denies the possibility of being fully present in the garden any more because the future is now present. Thus, the line condemns the narrator to an experience of no actual time at all, to being locked in a constant liminality, or what I have already called a ukraine.

Another way to understand a shadow-line is as the edge of a figurative shadow or where the shadow becomes distinct. If the shadow-line is ahead, presumably the shadow is cast by oneself and the light is coming from behind, from the sun moving down towards the horizon. But a body, particularly a moving body, does not cast *a* shadow-line. Some pages later, the figure is repeated: 'And I was still young enough, still too much on this side of the shadow-line, to be surprised and indignant at such things' (Conrad 2013: 36). Here, the line appears to be clear and singular, and but again, it is not apparent what is casting the shadow. It would seem to be something solid either behind the writer or beyond him on the far side of the line. But whoever is experiencing a shadow-line cannot really know very much about his situation and himself until he can determine what is casting the shadow, and he cannot do that until he has crossed the line into a different condition. In other words, he cannot make sense of his situation until he has moved beyond it to a place and time when he can look back. The present cannot be understood until the future, by which time it is the past.[9]

The narrator's command is cursed by a plague of tropical fever. The ship's store of quinine very soon runs out and the vessel is becalmed for many days in the Gulf of Siam. Although only one crewman dies, all succumb to fever except the Captain-narrator and the steward, whose strength is compromised by a heart condition. When a stiff breeze finally blows up and the ship gets under way, these two and the convalescing Mate are the only three men able to sail it to down to Singapore. In his journal, written at sea, fifteen days after leaving Bangkok, the narrator had written, 'It seems to me that all my life before that momentous day is infinitely remote, a fading memory of light-hearted youth; something on the other side of a shadow' (86). The narrator's season with death, like Marlow's on his journey back from the heart of darkness, is a rite of passage. It is a time of separation from this world. He describes it as 'an ordeal which had been maturing and tempering my character – though I did not know it' (102). His experiences on the voyage have pulled or pushed him across the shadow-line from youth to maturity. By the end of the text, he is the disenchanted man who, at its beginning, did not understand that he only came to take the position of captain of the sailing vessel because he was still 'green' enough, far enough on 'this side of the shadow-line', to find the prospect sufficiently enchanting.

On his return to Singapore, the narrator meets again Captain Giles, who had been instrumental in his getting the captaincy. Their conversation, captain to captain, marks the final integrational phase of the rite. The narrator begins the conversation with a rather puzzling phrase: 'I want you to know exactly what you have let me in for' (Conrad 2013: 104). The present, 'you have', indicates that although the action of *letting* is completed, the condition continues. Captain Giles lets the narrator in for something, but that something has not yet happened or is not yet finished. Yet the worst is surely over now: the ship is safely in port, a new crew has been found, and the medicine cabinet has been restocked. So the standard English form would be, 'I want you to know exactly what you let me in for'. Even though Conrad had been writing in English for more than thirty years, the phrase as written is very probably an interference from French, in which present perfect for carries a preterite meaning. But the sentence as written knows best and indicates that the narrator is still in a liminal state. 'You let me in for' means that the story is over; 'you have let me in for' means that it is not. If the narrator has crossed a shadow-line, it is not to anywhere else. His rite of passage is a rite of re-entry into ukraine.

Notes

1 The English term *march* covers similar semantic and political ground to *ukraine*. The Welsh Marches refer to that part of England that borders on Wales, within the English polity. *March* was borrowed from French and is clearly cognate with the Germanic *mark* (see Denmark and Finnmark), *mearc* in Old English. The *OED* tells us that most Indo-European languages have a cognate derived from some undetermined IE origin. While it does seem to be clear that while this putative word meant boundary, the word was not *krei.

2 Magocsi uses Ukraïna when transliterating from Cyrillic. Ukrajina indicates that he is referring to Polish usage. However, Ukrajina is also widely used as a transliteration from Cyrillic (Ukrainian and Russian).

3 Najder writes that the Polish insurgents of 1863 'were ready to recognize a separate Ruthenian or Ukrainian nationality' (1998: 47). Later in the same article, he reiterates the point, 'The essence of the programme of the radicals to whom Apollo Korzeniowski [Conrad's father] belonged was to extend the traditional privileges and obligations of the *szlachta* to other classes of Polish society. When they advocated this principle also with regard to Ruthenians, their programme amounted to making the latter legally and politically equal to Poles' (1998: 51). If Poles and Ruthenians in Ruthenia/Ukraïna/Little Russia should be equal and if it is the Great Russians who are stopping them, then the legal and political equality derives from their living in the same land. So Conrad's father was easing himself towards some kind of Ukrainian identity.

4 Even Conrad's birth is temporally and spatially in doubt. Najder notes 'that he was born and baptized without a certificate', probably because he was baptized by a monk rather than a priest. His certificate of ceremonial baptism was issued in Zhytomyr in 1862. He was either in Warsaw or in exile with his parents in northern Russia throughout 1862. Thus, he was provided with 'a certificate of official baptism without himself having been present at the ceremony' ('Conrad and Ukraine' 48).

5 Frederic Jameson conjectures that the transition to steam 'surely played a part in his change of profession, his abandonment of maritime commerce for the perilous new métier of writing for a living' (2020: 29).

6 Compare this from Samuel Beckett, another writer of indeterminacy and failure: in his dialogue on Tal Coat, he insists that relevant art will devote itself to 'the expression that there is nothing to express, nothing with which to express, nothing from which to express, no power to express, no desire to express, together with the obligation to express' ('Three Dialogues' 139).

7 *The Inheritors* says it rather less indirectly, and in 'Geography and Some Explorers', Conrad himself says it directly: 'the vilest scramble for loot that ever disfigured the history of human conscience and geographical exploration' (2011: 14).

8 For 'green sickness', the Cambridge edition of *The Shadow-Line* suggests that in this context the term implies 'inertia, capriciousness and moodiness – as characteristic of the pains of untested youth generally' (Conrad 2013: 266). Capriciousness, and possibly moodiness, may plausibly be associated with an enchanted garden that is losing its glamour.

9 See Hugh Epstein's discussion of 'delayed encoding'. He is working from Ramon Fernandez's insight that in Conrad, characters 'undergo' experiences 'before they can be defined' (2020: 34).

Works Cited

Beckett, S. (1983), 'Three Dialogues', in Ruby Cohn (ed.), *Disjecta: Miscellaneous Writings and a Dramatic Fragment*, 138–5, London: Calder.

Conrad, J. (1926), *Twixt Land and Sea*, Garden City: Doubleday.

Conrad, J. (1930), *Nostromo: A Tale of the Seaboard*, Garden City: Doubleday.

Conrad, J. (2008), *A Personal Record*, ed. Zdzisław Najder and J. H. Stape, Cambridge: Cambridge University Press.

Conrad, J. (2010), *Youth, Heart of Darkness, The End of the Tether*, ed. Owen Knowles, Cambridge: Cambridge University Press.

Conrad, J. (2011), 'Geography and Some Explorers', in Harold Ray Stevens and J. H. Stape (eds), *Last Essays*, 3–17, Cambridge: Cambridge University Press.

Conrad, J. (2013), *The Shadow-Line*, ed. J. H. Stape and Allan H. Simmons, Cambridge: Cambridge University Press.

Epstein, H. (2020), *Hardy, Conrad and the Senses*, Edinburgh: Edinburgh University Press.

Jameson, F. (2020), 'Time and the Sea'. *London Review of Books*, 42 (8) (16 April): 29–30.

Jasanoff, M. (2017), *The Dawn Watch: Joseph Conrad in a Global World*, New York: Penguin.

Magocsi, P. R. (2010), *A History of Ukraine: The Land and Its Peoples*, 2nd ed., Toronto: University of Toronto Press.

Najder, Z. (1983), *Joseph Conrad: A Chronicle*, New Brunswick: Rutgers University Press.

Najder, Z. (1998), 'Conrad and Ukraine: A Note', *The Conradian*, 23 (2): 45–54.

Pivtorak, G. P. *The Origin of Ukraine, Russia, Belarus, and Their Languages*, 'Ukraine Is Not a Margin'. Available online: http://litopys.org.ua/pivtorak/pivtorak.htm (accessed 26 April 2020).

Plokhy, S. (2015), *The Gates of Europe: A History of Ukraine*, New York: Basic Books.

Stape, J. (2007), *The Several Lives of Joseph Conrad*, New York: Pantheon.

Turner, V. (1969), 'Liminality and Communitas', in *The Ritual Process: Structure and Anti-Structure*, 94–130, Ithaca, NY: Cornell University Press.

van Gennep, A. (1960), *The Rites of Passage*, trans. Monika B. Vizedom and Gabrielle L. Caffee, Chicago: University of Chicago Press.

Zamoyski, A. (1987), *The Polish Way: A Thousand-year History of the Poles and Their Culture*, New York: Hippocrene Books.

3

From Berdyczów to Bishopsbourne: Conrad's real and imaginary journeys

Agnieszka Adamowicz-Pośpiech
University of Silesia, Poland

'I'm a *szlachcic* [nobleman] from the Ukraine' (*CL* 2: 323) – Conrad wrote to Józef Korzeniowski in 1901 almost thirty years after leaving the Ukraine. This is the place or rather places (Berdyczów, Terechowa, Żytomir, Nowochfastów) where his migratory life started. With his parents or on his own, moving from place to place (Warszawa, Vologda, Chernikhiv, Lwów, Przemyśl, Kraków) he never forgot where he came from. After years of travelling Conrad wrote a quasi-autobiographical volume mapping out his peregrinatory life. The aim of the chapter is not to verify to what extent *A Personal Record* is an autobiography – this has been done in profusion by a number of critics (Said 1966, Berthoud 1978, Tarnawski 1984: 104–10, Najder 1988, Pacukiewicz 2012)[1] – but rather to explore the reasons why Conrad processed his life as a journey and channelled it according to the modern categories of exile, migration and uprootedness. I wish to analyse his reminiscences through the optics of geopoetics and argue that in Conrad's nomadic vision constant movement, dislocation and instability constituted *conditio humana*. As Kenneth White, the proponent of geopoetics, explains, this approach consists in an integration of various aspects of different cultures in order to build 'new coherence' (White 2004a: 247, 1992).[2] Furthermore, my aim is to view Conrad's memoirs as a record of his spatial experiences and to demonstrate how some of them may constitute an auto-bio-atlas picturing his geographical, intellectual and imaginary (emotional) journeys. I propose to consider *A Personal Record* as a *waybook* (White's term)[3] sketching his presence in various places and to explore to what extend Conrad might represent an 'intellectual nomad' (White 2004b). Contrary to the *flâneur* (*Bauman*), the modern nomadic writer (subject) migrates to wild places where he can enjoy a close relationship with nature; he resigns from the position of cultural domination over other peoples, species as well as space. I wish to locate and interpret Conrad's real and imaginary journeys depicted in *A Personal Record* as a proof that the concepts of journey, migration and dislocation are the best prism through which one should approach Conrad's memories.

It seems to me that Conrad may serve as an example of an intellectual nomad whom White characterizes in the following way: 'an intellectual on the borders, a writer at the limits, moving fast over the territories, working at something outside the properties and proprieties that has no "rooted" name' (2004b: 8). An intellectual nomad is 'a pilgrim, a wanderer and his peregrination is as much an intellectual activity as it is a physical one' (White 2010b: 11). Wandering, dislocation and migration generate their own anamorphic mode of narration, not infrequently of autobiographic kind (e.g. W. Gombrowicz's *Dzienniki* [Memoirs] and G. Herling-Grudziński's *Dziennik pisany nocą* [The Journal Written by Night]) (Gasyna 2011). Conrad's *A Personal Record* is a case in point: it is characterized by an apparently chaotic and impressionistic structure (Kerzer 1974–5, Karl 1979: 661–2, GoGwilt 1995: 109–30, Adamowicz-Pośpiech 2009). Thus I wish to view the *Record* as an auto-bio-atlas (mapping significant places in the author's life) rather than an auto-bio-graphy (writing about oneself) (Lejeune 2001: 22–3). Drawing on the insights of recent work in human geography, and geopoetics, I will argue that the *Record* represents a literary cartography of significant locations for Conrad's migratory life. Furthermore, taking heed of the proposition by Richard Ambrosini (2018), I want to follow what Conrad 'chose to narrate, what he consigned to the memory of an internal narrator, and what he decided to leave wrapped in silence' (38)[4] and how he articulated it (since the mode of narration 'is Conrad's point of view as much as the subject matter' (Karl 1979: 661) rather than to pursue the elaborate interpretations of the critics (Morf 1930, Meyer 1967: 267–90). As GoGwilt aptly points out in the section 'The Geography of Writing' in the comingling of writing and geography Conrad addresses 'the relation between writing and the variety of cultural contexts in which and about which he has written' (113). Conrad's *Record* demonstrates that he was a transnational writer who was interested in cultural spaces which cross national borders (White's phrasing, 2010a, 24). Accordingly, the chapter consists of three sections in which Conrad's real and imaginary journeys in childhood, adolescence and adulthood are contextualized and discussed with reference mainly to *A Personal Record* and sporadically to other works and correspondence.

Polish years: Life in transit

Conrad as a man was formed by migration and constant translocation which was also his family heritage or rather burden (Brodsky 2016a). He was born in Berdyczów, and then changed locations from Terechowa (5.12.1857) to Derebczynka (1858), Żytomierz (1859) and Nowochfastów (1860–1) which he may not have remembered.[5] But after 1861 when he moved with his mother to Warszawa his memories became clearer as he recollected the meetings of the underground Central Committee[6] in the 'Author's Note' to the *Record*:

> [the meetings] were held in our Warsaw house, of which all I remember distinctly is one room, white and crimson, probably the drawing room. In one of its walls there was the lofties of all archways. Where it led to remains a mystery; but to this day I cannot get rid of the belief that all this was of enormous proportions, and that the people appearing and disappearing in that immense space were beyond the usual stature of mankind as I got to know it in later life. (Conrad 1994: 8)

Warszawa is the place he remembered well the whole of his life, most probably because of the traumatic experiences of waiting in front of the prison where his father was incarcerated: 'in the courtyard of this Citadel – characteristically for our nation – my childhood memories begin' (*CL* 1: 358).[7] For many generations of Poles the Citadel has been the symbol of Russian oppression,[8] transforming itself into *lieu de mémoire* evoking strong feelings of fear, humiliation and revolt (Nora 1989: 7).

After the court's verdict of exile Conrad spent numerous periods of time in different locations: Vologda, Chernikhiv, Nowochwastów (with his mother on her leave, then on vacation), Kiev (in hospital), Lwów (with his father, then in a boarding school), Przemyśl (with his father), Kraków (with his father, his grandmother, uncle and tutors). We get a glimpse of a few of these sojourns in the *Record* – bearing in mind Ambrosini's argument, let us explore which places Conrad shared with us in his auto-bio-atlas. One of such glimpses is Chernikhiv and the recollection of a grimy morning when he was caught by his father sitting at his desk and reading his manuscripts.

> It was during our exile in Russia and it must have been less than a year after my mother's death, because I remember myself in the black blouse with a white border of my heavy mourning. We were living together, quite alone, in a small house on the outskirts of the town of T—. That afternoon, instead of going out to play in the large yard which we shared with our landlord, I had lingered in the

> room in which my father generally wrote. What emboldened me to clamber into his chair I am sure I don't know, but a couple of hours afterwards he discovered me kneeling in it with my elbows on the table and my head held in both hands over the MS of loose pages. (Conrad 1994: 71–2)

What kind of existence did they lead if the father realized the absence of his son only after several hours? In between the lines we see a seven-year-old boy in deep mourning, left on his own, from time to time playing outside, but, if permitted or unnoticed, preferring to stay at home and read. Although Apollo was deeply immersed in his own loss, not paying heed to what his son was doing, he was seriously worried about the mental state of his child.[9]

This scene took place after the death of Ewa Korzeniowska, when they were living alone. It is worth noting that Conrad consistently portrays his relation with others through books, as if literature served as a filter enabling him not only to write about (and process) his past (when he was an adult)[10] but first and foremost survive those traumatic times (when he was a child). Similarly in Kraków, when his father was dying, to endure the excruciating days Konradek resorted to reading:

> I was rather indifferent to school troubles. I had a private gnawing worm of my own. This was the time of my Father's last illness. [...] I don't know what would have become of me if I had not been a reading boy. My prep. finished I would have had nothing to do but sit and watch the awful stillness of the sick room flow out through the closed white door and coldly enfold my scarred heart. *I suppose that in a futile childish way I would have gone crazy.* But I was a reading boy. (Conrad 2004: 133, emphasis added)

Conrad's sojourn in Chernikhiv was interrupted with several journeys to Nowochwastów. First in 1863 when his mother was granted the permission of a three-month leave from exile, then after the death of his mother he travelled there for vacation in May 1866, yet on return to Chernikhiv he fell ill, so he left for treatment to Kiev's hospital and on the doctors' advice he came back again to Nowochwastów (November 1866). The pattern of moving from place to place repeated itself several times: he was ill (December 1866), went to Kiev for medical treatment, returned to Nowochwastów, was ill again, went for treatment to Żytomierz and in the summer of 1867 he was taken for convalescence to Odessa by his uncle Tadeusz to return to Nowochwastów in autumn (Najder 2007: 23–31). This period from 1863 to 1867 emblematizes Konradek's life in transit. All those temporary stays in his uncle's estate were briefly described and conjoined to one visit:

> it was certainly in the year in which my mother obtained permission to travel south and visit her family [...]. I also remember, the great gathering of all the relations from near and far, [...] paying her the homage of respect and love in the house of her favourite brother [...]. *For me it seems the very happiest period of my existence.* There was my cousin, a delightful, quick-tempered little girl, some months younger than myself [...]. There were other children too, many of whom are dead now. (Conrad 1994: 34; emphasis added)

These were the moments of carefree play – rare ones, that would not get repeated (in Chernikhiv) only until later in the Taube family flat in Lwów or in Buszczyński's apartment in Kraków among his playmates. This stay in Nowochwastów must have been really a unique and happy moment of childish amusement since Conrad comes back to it in yet another reminiscence of the same visit in some other part of the *Record* recalling again his:

> little cousin in a short skirt of a tartan pattern with a deal of women of her own household: the head gouvernante, our dear, corpulent Francesca [...] and the good, ugly Mlle. Durand, the governess, with her black eyebrows [...] of all the eyes turned towards the carriage, her good-natured eyes were dropping tears, and it was her sobbing voice alone that broke the silence with an appeal to me: '*N'oublie pa ton français, mon chéri*'. In three months, simply by playing with us, she had taught me not only to speak French but to read it as well. She was indeed an excellent playmate. (Conrad 1994: 66)

However, the majority of his travels and stopovers at that time are wrapped in silence. One can trace Konradek's trajectory in the years 1867–74 only from the correspondence of his family (Najder 1964, 1983). Yet none of the places offered him the sense of rootedness for which children usually crave. After the death of his parents the feeling of dispossession must have grown even stronger; again the carousel of changing places began: Lwów, Kraków, Krynica, Odessa, Italy (Najder 2007: 29–46). It should come as no surprise then, that as a literary figure symbolizing his adolescence (and later life), Conrad chose the wandering knight – Don Quixote. The knight errant hovers above Conrad's Polish years as well as his trip through Europe referred to as 'holiday of travel' (1873). Together with his tutor Adam Pulman[11] they 'had seen Vienna, the Upper Danube, Munich, the Falls of the Rhine, the Lake of Constance [...]. [W]e had been tramping slowly up the Valley of the Reuss' (Conrad 1994: 40). Their 'route led over the Furca Pass towards the Rhone Glacier [...] and Häsli Valley' (47). Conrad in the *Record* chose Don Quixote as an emblematic figure of his life in transit linking his journeys in adolescent years (part II) with his mature wanderings (part VI)

(Adamowicz-Pośpiech 2011), as if, fundamentally, nothing was ever changing for him, the existential paradigm remained always the same: relocation and wandering, no matter if willed or not.

Imaginary journeys: Inspiration

A crucial factor that could have sharpened Conrad's perception of his life as continuous wandering was reading. As we know he was an avid reader not only of books[12] but also of journals such as *Wędrowiec* (*The Wanderer*). This periodical was mentioned twice in the recollections and letters to Conrad. Firstly, Jadwiga Kałuska (née Tokarska), Konradek's friend from Lwów,[13] recalls the sojourn of Konrad at their house in 1873: 'Konrad used to visit us often and our conversations were serious. He read a lot, mostly about travel. He wished to get to know the world. His favourite magazine was *Wędrowiec*, a weekly publication' (Najder 1983: 141). For the second time *Wędrowiec* is mentioned by Bobrowski in a letter to his nephew, but the hint is that the uncle referred to the magazine several times in earlier correspondence:

> As thank God you do not forget your Polish [...] and your writing is not bad, *I repeat what I have already written and said before* – you would do well to write contributions for *Wędrowiec* in Warsaw. We have few travellers, and even fewer genuine correspondents: the words of an eyewitness would be of great interest and in time would bring you in money. It would be an exercise in your native tongue – that thread which binds you to your country and countrymen, and finally a tribute to the memory of your father who always wanted to and did serve his country by his pen. Think about this, young man, collect some reminiscences from the voyage to Australia and send them as a sample [...]. Six reports sent from different parts of the world during the year would not take much of your time: they would bring you some benefit and provide you with a pleasant recreation while giving pleasure to others. (Najder 1964: 71–2; emphasis added)[14]

Najder poses the question why this appeal evoked no response (Najder 2007: 86). My contention is that it did trigger a reaction but delayed in time: namely, in the form of his constant 'scribbling' (Conrad 1994: 20) in his cabin, and finally in the chapters of *Almayer's Folly* written laboriously at various places all over the world.[15]

Indeed, Conrad must have read the journal many a time so that his friends and relatives do remember its title. *Wędrowiec* was a lively, well-edited magazine, published weekly in Warsaw since 1863 and subscribed widely in all three partitions (Kmiecik 1965: 142–59). It reprinted and translated a number of articles from the French travel journal *Le Tour du Monde. Nouveau journal des voyages* and generally it followed the French editorial and lay-out principles along with its elaborate engravings. It was targeted at a popular readership and described in detail most of the great expeditions which marked the turn of the century.[16] Usually on the cover there was a single engraving under the masthead that blocked half the page above twin columns of print, or very often the entire page. Another characteristic feature was the publication of the same travelogue in instalments over ten or more issues. According to the editors, W. L. Anczyc and later F. Sulimierski, it was 'a magazine publishing voyages and expeditions combined with descriptions of habits and customs of foreign peoples, lives of famous foreigners, stories and translations from foreign literature, news from the disciplines of natural science, industry and technology; varia, etc.'[17]

What did Conrad read about in *Wędrowiec* in the years 1866–74?[18] Strangely enough, the majority of the expeditions mentioned by Conrad, for example in his essay 'Geography and Some Explorers', were described in this journal. Let us briefly discuss the journal articles that Conrad read in Poland.[19] *Wędrowiec* covered almost all major expeditions from discovering the source of the Nile, to conquering the South Pole. Hence Konradek could bury himself in the direct reports of the expeditions to Africa, Asia, Australia and the polar region. Due to space considerations I wish to focus on the texts covering expeditions to Africa and the polar region since both of these topics stand out in some of Conrad's fiction. Conrad could have read the following travelogues describing the exploration of the Dark Continent: 'Brzegi Zambezy, z podróży dr. Livingstone'a' (The Banks of the Zambezi River, excerpts from dr Livingstone's Travel) (Figure 1), 'Dziennik podróży kupca Bolognesi do rzeki Gazell w Afryce' (Merchant Bolognesi's travelogue to the river Gazelle in Africa),[20] 'Podróżnik du Chaillu i jego dzieło o nieznanych dotąd krajach afrykańskich' (Traveller du Chaillu and his works on the so far unknown African countries),[21] 'Źródła Nilu. Dziennik podróży i odkryć kapitana Speke' (The sources of the Nile. Captain Speke's travelogue),[22] 'Żegluga na rzece Wami' (Navigation on the Wami river; based on the summary of Stanley's *How I found Livingstone*), 'Podróż po zachodnim Sudanie (1863–6) Pana Mage' (Mr Mage's travels in the Western Sudan),[23] 'Podróż Pana Tremeaux po wschodnim Sudanie. Podróż do środka Afryki' (Mr Tremeaux's Travels in the Eastern Sudan. Travel to the centre of Africa),[24] 'Podróże Aleksandryny Tinne' (Travels of A. Tinne; based on J. A. Tinne, *Geographical notes of expeditions in central Africa by three dutch* [sic] *ladies*),[25] 'Z dziedziny geografii' (On geography, based on the travels of Livingstone, Carlo Piagga, and H. M. Walmsley).[26] These are just several examples of more than a hundred texts on the exploration of and in Africa. One of the articles begins thus:

> On each map of Africa, even on the latest and most precise ones, we can see in the middle *a white and blank space*, stretching itself at a latitude of 15°, divided into two almost equal parts by the equator and equal in its area to the territory of half of European Russia. Who knows what kind of treasures for science and industry this area hides?[27]

Hence Conrad's recollection of the map-pointing scene reiterated several times in his fiction might not necessarily be totally fictitious as some critics believe it to be (Knowles 2010: 441–2, Brodsky 2005: 43). In his memoirs Conrad remembers how one day in 1868:

> when nine years old or thereabouts, that while looking at a map of Africa of the time and putting my finger on the blank space then representing the unsolved mystery of that continent, I said to myself with absolute assurance and an amazing audacity […]: 'When I grow up I will go *there*.' (Conrad 1994: 26)

I'd rather view this scene as a transformation of childhood memories so strong that they must have been channelled (and yes, partly fictionalized) into his autobiofiction. Still, as Ambrosini proposes let us note what Conrad wanted to share with us as a *memory*, even more so that he came back to that recollection several times. Since Conrad was accustomed to life in transit from his early childhood, it may reveal his will to continue it, and at the same time, as a textualized remembrance it may be interpreted as 'a sign of a willed identity of displacement' (GoGwilt 1995: 123) on the part of the adult writer. Najder's conclusion seems to be accurate: Konradek wanted to continue his peregrinatory life and going to sea offered such an opportunity; he did not want to become a mariner, though (Najder 2007: 45).

Another significant area covered comprehensively by *Wędrowiec* with which Conrad was fascinated was the account of the transnational competitive race to reach the North Pole as well as to explore the details of Arctic geography. Konradek must have been captivated by the descriptions of the sailors' perseverance and the will to sacrifice their lives on 'the altar of exploration'. He could read about such polar expeditions as, among others: 'Podróż M'Clintocka na Fox do bieguna północnego' (McClintock's Voyage on the Fox to the North Pole) (Figure 2),[28] 'Podróż podbiegunowa I. I. Hayes'a' (Northern Polar Voyage made by doctor I. I. Hayes, US maritime surgeon),[29] 'sprawozdanie z wyścigu polarnego G. Lamberta, A. Petermanna, Lamonta' (summary of the polar race of G. Lambert, A. Petermann, J. Lamont);[30] 'Z dziedziny geografii – strefy polarne'

Nr. 205. WĘDROWIEC. 1866 r.

Parowiec „Ma-Robert," na rzece Zambezie.

BRZEGI ZAMBEZY.

Z podróży Dra. Livingstone.

(Dalszy ciąg).

Sena posiada kilka dużych domów nowych, zwaliska kilku dawniejszych i krzyż, zniszczony przez czas, wzniesiony w miejscu gdzie niegdyś stał kościół. Wał obronny od strony rzeki, jest tak opuszczony, że krowy pasą się na nim.

Handel, można powiedzieć, że tu nie istnieje; kilku kupców wysyła zaufanych niewolników w głąb kraju na polowania na słonie i zakupywanie kości słoniowéj. Sena jest miejscem bardzo mało ożywionem i bardzo do snu usposabiającem; kto uniknął tu febry pierwszego dnia, ten można być pewnym że jéj dostanie nazajutrz.

Lecz Sena jest zarazem miejscem rodzinnem pana Ferrao, człowieka wielkiego serca, gościnnego, dobroczynnego i szlachetnego bez granic.

Biedni murzyni z oddalonych prowincyj, przechodzący przez to miasto, udają się wprost do niego i nie odchodzą nigdy nieopatrzeni. W czasie nieurodzajó pan Ferrao żywi krajowców. Setki swoich służących widzi tylko wtedy, gdy ci potrzebują jego pomocy, oni zaś mają go za swego patryarchę który godzi spory, dopomaga i chroni od głodu. Ojciec jego był gubernatorem Seny i posiadał ogromny obszar ziemi bardzo żyznéj, którą nabył sposobem uczciwym, lecz rząd kazał tę ziemię podzielić i rozdać pomiędzy emigrantów, tytułem wolnego ustępstwa, zachowując tylko obszar dwumilowy dla syna prawego właściciela i usprawiedliwiając ten czyn tem: „że nieprzystoi by poddany posiadał więcéj ziemi jak korona portugalska." Wkrótce potém przyszli landyowie i opanowali wszystko; tym sposobem zdziercy z kolei zostali obdarci.

Pan Ferrao zaprosił nas na śniadanie. Znaczniejsi obywatele miejscowi, którzy odwiedzili nas, zgadzali się w zdaniu, że krajowcy chętnieby uprawiali bawełnę w wielkich rozmiarach, gdyby mieli pewność zbytu. Niegdyś wysyłano ją ztąd do Maniki, a nawet i do Brazylii, jako produkt surowy, lub wyrobiony na tkaniny. „Odkąd ziemia do nich należy, mówili nam ci ludzie, godni wiary, krajowcy chętnie oddają się rolnictwu i handlowi. Gdy idzie o ich interes, murzyni są niezmordowani w pracy."

Tom VIII. 205.

Figure 1 Illustration on the *Wędrowiec* cover page to the excerpt from the account of Dr Livingstone's travels in Africa entitled 'Brzegi Zambezy' [The banks of the Zambezi River]. The caption: '*Ma-Robert* steamship on the Zambezi'.

(On Geography) – polar region explored by G. Lambert; 'Wyprawa do bieguna Polaris' ('Polaris' expedition to the North Pole). In one of the reports the author took for granted that the readers know the geography of the polar region by heart:

> We think that even without a map our readers are able to visualize the general outline of this area. From the Bellot strait, where McClintock spent winter, there spreads the Boothia Felix peninsula in the southern direction up to the American main land; together with the Adelaide peninsula it forms a deep bay, into which the Great Fish River flows. Among the islands within this bay there in Montreal. To the south-west from the Boothia Felix there is a strait called Ross's way, which leads to the King William Island. (*Wędrowiec* 1867–74: 194)

We can infer from this that the geography of the Arctic region constituted essential knowledge for the readers interested in the polar advancement. Conrad must have been one of them since he wrote of his own accord a two-page essay on 'the history of Arctic exploration' and knew Arctic geography well (Conrad 2004: 11).

Worth mentioning is the visual side of those texts. All the travelogues were lavishly illustrated since, according to the editor, it increased their value. The graphic material comprised engravings of maps, landscapes, portraits of the local inhabitants, depictions of plants and animals endemic to the area, hair-raising sketches of shipwrecks or fights with the locals. If one studies those articles in *Wędrowiec*, the idea of going to sea that the thirteen- or fourteen-year-old Konradek brought up seems less surprising.

How much of that did he remember? We cannot say but probably a good deal because he was able to draw maps from memory (Conrad 2010: 11)[31] and wrote the essay on polar expeditions, all of which were in the limelight at that time. Moreover he retold those stories of travel and exploration in a quasi-fictionalized form to his friends, as testified by Konstanty Buszczyński, his playmate from Kraków:

> What tales that boy [Konrad] told us ... Over on those steps we often sat, a group of us, while Conrad spun yarns ... They were weird and fantastic almost beyond belief, but in the way he told them they seemed to us actual happenings. The power of weaving tales – tales that literally seemed to live before one's eyes – was born in him. And also they were about the sea. Curious, that, for outside of Asia there probably is not a single other city so far from salt water as Cracow, and Conrad had never seen it. (Putnam 1990: 206)

Surely enough, Konradek had never seen those places he told stories about, but he had read about them in abundance, for example in *Wędrowiec.*

Nr. 245. WĘDROWIEC. 1867 r.

Statek *Fox* wśród lodów.

PODRÓŻ M'CLINTOCKA DO BIEGUNA PÓŁNOCNEGO.

W naszych czasach odbyło ku obu biegunom kilka podróży, które znacznie się przyczyniły do poznania tych miejsc niegościnnych. Co do bieguna południowego, zdaje się, że niemasz już tam żadnéj zagadki do rozwiązania. Odkrycia dokonane przez Cooka, Bellinghausena, Bristola i Wedella, uzupełnione zostały przez James Clarke Rossa, Dumont d'Urville'a i Wilkesa. Z nich przekonywamy się, że cała okolica bieguna południowego, przedstawia ląd stały, pod względem rozległości dorównywający Australii. Ogromne ściany lodu czynią brzegi tego południowego kontynentu zupełnie niedostępnemi; w głębi tego kraju, po którym nigdy niestąpała noga ludzka, gdzie nigdy żaden kwiat nie wystawiał swego kielicha na słońce, wznoszą się góry znacznéj wysokości; tak Erebus, odkryty przez Rossa, jest na 12,400 stóp angielskich wysoki, i wyrzuca z siebie słup dymu na 1200 stóp w górę. Nikomu dotąd nieudało się przezimować na południowym stałym lądzie i zbadać tę miejscowość, ponieważ, jak rzekliśmy wyżéj, góry lodowe niedozwalają dotrzéć do brzegów.

W okolicach bieguna północnego, które dotąd są znane, istnieją zupełnie inne stosunki. W miejscu stałego lądu widzimy tu mnóstwo wysp i półwyspów, z daleko wchodzącemi w ląd zatokami, tudzież znaczną ilość kanałów, któremi możnaby dostać się ze wschodniego do zachodniego morza, z Baffinskiéj zatoki do Drogi Behringa, gdyby niestawił temu nieprzebytéj zawady lód, daleko tu straszniejszy aniżeli pod biegunem północnym. Jeżeli i pod biegunem północnym ląd się znajduje, to należy go szukać pod najodleglejszemi jeograficznemi szerokościami, poza kanałami Kennedy i Wellingtona. Ale samo istnienie tego stałego lądu jest wątpliwe; długi czas przypuszczano nawet, że pod biegunem północnym znajduje się otwarte morze, wolne od lodów, dzięki ciepłemu prądowi powietrza od równika i prądowi ciepłéj wody, zwanemu Gulfstream, tak że okręty mogą tam pływać bez przeszkody.

Ponieważ w okolicach bieguna północnego można odbywać na sankach wyprawy w głąb lądu, i po lodzie od wyspy do wyspy, wszystkie więc okolice, gdzie tylko człowiek dotarł, są mniéj więcéj zbadane. Podczas jednéj takiéj podróży James Clarke Ross odkrył 1 czerwca 1831 roku biegun magnetyczny. Leży on na wschodnim brzegu półwyspu, noszącego nazwę Szczęśliwéj Beocyi, jakby

Tom X. 245

Figure 2 Illustration on the *Wędrowiec* cover page to the excerpt from the account of McClintock's voyage entitled 'McClintock's voyage to the North Pole'. Caption: 'The *Fox* ship ice-bound'.

Thus visiting all those places described on the pages of *Wędrowiec* (Mauritius, Africa, Australia, the Malay Archipelago) Conrad could have *experienced occasional feelings of déjà vu.* Later as a seaman naturally he combined travelling with writing and duly acknowledged 'Imagination, not invention, is the supreme master of art as of life' (Conrad 1994: 35); hence, to a certain extent, he did not invent those places, even as a child, telling stories to his friends, but creatively retold what he saw and read about in *Wędrowiec*. He admitted in his memoirs: 'Books may be written in all sorts of places', especially those places he read earlier about.

Sailing the seven seas

Conrad's memoirs begin in Rouen, the venue which he perceives through the lens of Flaubert's writing. The places he describes were first textualized for him by the French artist in his novel *Madame Bovary.*

> We had been shifted down there from another berth in the neighbourhood of the Opera House, where that same port-hole gave me a view of quite another sort of *café* – the best in town I believe, and the very one where the worthy Bovary and his wife, the romantic daughter of old Père Renault had some refreshment after the memorable performance of an opera which was the tragic story of Lucia di Lammermoor in a setting of light music. (Conrad 1994: 20–1)

The mistake in the surname of Mrs Bovary's father may testify to Conrad's indeed processing those recollections from memory of the texts read long ago. He perceived and associated those places in northern France, first by means of their textual images and only later physically and palpably.[32] Likewise, he could have experienced Borneo, Singapore, Congo and Mauritius through the texts he had read in *Wędrowiec*. Obviously, I do not wish to claim that Conrad remembered exactly what he read about but still he retained some images created while reading the travelogues which materialized when he visited those regions himself. For one thing, this process of excavating old memories is revealed in the case of the Africa-pointing scene when Conrad confesses:

> And of course I thought no more about it till after a quarter of a century or so an opportunity offered to go there – as if *the sin of childish audacity was to be visited on my mature head*. Yes. I did go there: *there* being the region of Stanley Falls which in '68 was the blankest of blank spaces on the earth's figured surface. A great melancholy descended on me. Yes, this was the very spot. But there was no shadowy friend to stand by my side [...]. What an end to the idealized realities of a boy's day-dreams. (Conrad 1994: 26, emphasis added)[33]

Paddling the Congo river Captain Korzeniowski recalls some scenes from his childish fascination with maps. It testifies to the fact that he remembered his readings and that they came back when he travelled and was exposed to the exotic surroundings. A similar process is described in the late essay *Geography* ... in which Conrad mentions his favourite pastime as a child – map-gazing and map-drawing and the echo of this activity when he became a sailor:

> I should have in the later sixties done my first bit of map-drawing [...]. It consisted in entering laboriously in pencil the outline of Tanganyika on my beloved old atlas [...]. And it was not all wasted time. As a bit of prophetic practice it was not bad for me. Many years afterwards as second officer in the Merchant Service it has been my duty to correct and bring up to date charts of more than one ship, according to Admiralty notices. I did this work conscientiously [...]; but it was not in the nature of things that *I should ever recapture the excitement of that entry of Tanganyika on the blank of my old Atlas.* (Conrad 2010: 12, emphasis added)[34]

This passage confirms that his later journeys and the landscapes he saw evoked the memories from his childhood and adolescence when he was left to himself and passed his time reading or copying maps. In the example above, it is his passion for studying maps and learning to draw them from memory which turned out to be useful when he was preparing maps for the government. Conrad also adds that he never felt alone at sea since he cherished 'the company of great navigators, the first grown-up friends of my early boyhood' (Conrad 2010: 14), which implies that he recalled his early readings while travelling as a seaman. He professes that he visited almost all places he read about except the North Pole. Hence, we can justifiably assume that he remembered a good deal from his readings of travel books and the travel journal *Wędrowiec* and recalled various aspects of it depending on the place he sailed to.

The outline of the narrative of the *Record* is drawn at the beginning of the discourse:

> It was always thus with this book, begun in '89 and finished in '94 – with that shortest of all the novels which it was my lot to write. Between its opening exclamation calling Almayer to his dinner in his wife's voice and Abdullah's (his enemy) mental reference to the God of Islam – 'The Merciful, the Compassionate' – which closes the book, there were to come several long sea passages, a visit (to use the elevated phraseology suitable to the occasion) to the scenes (some of them) of my childhood and the realization of childhood's vain words, expressing a light-hearted and romantic whim. (Conrad 1994: 26)

Indeed, during the composition of *Almayer's Folly* there were several journeys: two voyages to Australia, two visits to his uncle in the Ukraine, a journey to Africa, a convalescence travel to Champel and a voyage to Rouen (Watt 1994: xvii–xxx). Unsurprisingly for Conrad's life pattern then, his first book was written in transit, too. It is significant that his first novel was created in the course of his wanderings and it is not a mere literary technique to make Almayer follow Conrad in his travels (or to depict the novel's manuscript being dragged to every nook and cranny) in the *Record*, but it is a symbolic representation of the reiterative process that happened in the artist's life: (unwilled) translocation and reading (in childhood) – reading and (imaginary) journeying (in adolescence) – sailing and writing (maturity).

During one of those journeys back home to the Ukraine, the writer observes: 'I saw again the sun setting on the plains as I saw it in the travels of my childhood' (Conrad 1994: 33). He refers to the countless travels of his childhood to Nowochfastów, Kiev, Chernikhiv, Odessa, Lwów, Przemyśl and Kraków. At the same time, it is an echo of the fictive image of the sun setting for Nina or maybe, the other way round, the sun-setting scene in *Almayer's Folly* is the echo of the sun he saw as a child.[35] During the visit to the Ukraine after sixteen years, we get a rare chance to observe Conrad through the eyes of his friends there. Similarly to Kraków (through the recollections of 'Kocio'), we can take once again a glimpse of Conrad the raconteur – this time, however, spinning yarns about *real* journeys, the places he had explored himself:

> Those were unforgettable days – gathered round a blazing fire we spent long hours listening to Conrad who was talking about his voyages and impressions; he talked in Polish but occasionally lacking a word he would replace it with an English or French expression.[36]

As a Master Mariner Conrad returned to the Ukraine, the place he was born and where his migrant life began, to tell stories of his voyages around the world, which for the listeners were enviable tales of exotic adventure, while for him composed a sombre record of his displacement.

Conrad's volume of reminiscences exemplifies the type of writing which White dubs mental and existential geography, a narrative which employs 'shreds of memory', 'freewheeling association' (White 2015: viii, x). By sketching a mental map of his migratory life Conrad portrays his biography as a constant movement and creates 'a type of literature with uncertain borders' (Hazard in White 2015: viii). As has been pointed out above, Conrad's *Record* testifies that he was a transnational writer who was involved in cultural spaces which go across national borders (White 2010a: 24) and which enabled him to fully appreciate and cultivate the transnational spirit to 'uphold the notion of common space above […] particularisms' (25). *A Personal Record* is indeed a *record* of its author's *spacial* experiences which constitute an auto-bio-atlas showing his geographical, emotional and intellectual routes. Conrad's wanderings started very early in his childhood, then in adolescence moving from place to place between the Russian and Austrian partitions, he also travelled in his imagination thanks to the lively travelogues in *Wędrowiec*, later in his mature life as a seaman he explored on his own most of the places he read about and dreamt of as a youth, and in the end in Bessborough Gardens (but also in Postling [Pent Farm] and Bishopsbourne [Oswalds]) he textualized the turbulent life in transit. Finally, his nomadic life has come full circle.

Notes

1 I have discussed elsewhere *A Personal Record* as a form of 'autobiofiction' (the term was introduced by Alberca 2007: 195, Adamowicz-Pośpiech 2011).

2 Geopoetics, as an operative category, 'enables us to comprehend and to analyze the territorial, geographical and geo-ecological dimension of a literary text' (Italiano 2008).

3 White defines a *waybook* as a kind of narrative writing which 'employs an open structure, with loosely connected episodes' (White 2015: x).

4 I find particularly convincing Ambrosini's argument: 'It may be hard to believe in the age of Twitter and Facebook, but what we choose not to share with others plays an important part in our forging our own identity. […] How could the [English] public ever be expected to be interested, let alone understand [Conrad's Polish] past? […] Why not for once assume that Conrad was *compos mentis* and knew what he was doing?' (Ambrosini 2018: 38–40). Ambrosini proposes to replace the life-and-works paradigm with a memory-and-writing paradigm and pay close attention to what Conrad wanted to show.

5 All geographical names within the territory of the pre-partition Polish Commonwealth are given in their standard Polish form. I have followed in this Najder's edition of *Joseph Conrad. A Life*.

6 It was the kernel of the future National Government that was established during the 1863 January Uprising (Najder 2007: 18).

7 The relatives of the imprisoned men were not allowed to see them. They could only pass the parcels (with food and clothes) through the wire fence to the guards.

E. Korzeniowska described the heart-rendering scenes in a letter to her friends: 'Every morning I find a crowd of women by the Citadel gate; they are there for the same reason as myself. Sometimes we stand there a whole day, in rain and cold, waiting for a short note, for some news, and sometimes we wait in vain' (Najder 1983: 59). They were never sure if the prisoners got the packets. (See E. Korzeniowska's letters in Najder 1983: 58–62). On the basis of Conrad's letter to Lutosławski (and also on the dedication on the photo he sent from Vologda to his grandma) we can infer that Conrad may have accompanied his mother on some of those visits (Zabierowski 2016).

8 The fortress was built in 1832–6 by the orders of Tsar Nicholas I after the debacle of the 1830 November Uprising. It housed a prison in which thousands of Polish national activists were detained and/or executed (including A. Korzeniowski, R. Traugutt, leader of the 1863 January Uprising; J. Dąbrowski, later military chief of the 1871 Paris Commune; and the creator of independent Poland, Marshal J. Piłsudski). For the discussion of some other Polish *lieux de mémoire*, see Brodsky (2016b: 29–30).

9 A. Korzeniowski describes their lives just before the death of Ewa to his friend K. Kaszewski: 'My poor wife, who these two years has been destroyed by despair [...] has barely the strength to look at me [...]. For several months I have been everything in the house – master and servant. [...] *Konradek is of course neglected*' (26 February 1865, Najder 1983: 91–3; emphasis added). After the death of his wife Apollo broke down, yet he was increasingly concerned about his son. Again he wrote to Kaszewski: 'Poor child: *he does not know what a contemporary playmate is*; he looks at the decrepitude of my sadness, and who knows if that sight does not make his young heart wrinkled or his awakening soul grizzled. These are important reasons forcing me to tear this poor child away from my dejected heart' (18 September 1865, Najder 1983: 94–8; emphasis added). And Konradek got moved to Nowochwastów (May 1866).

10 GoGwilt cogently demonstrates that the novel *Almayer's Folly* (along with its eponymous hero) becomes the protagonist of the *Record* (GoGwilt 1995: 112).

11 On the biography and role of A.M. Pulman in Conrad's life, see Omelan 2004.

12 A. Korzeniowski commented on Konradek's activities: he 'burrows too deeply in books' (letter to K. Kaszewski of 1 February 1866 (Najder 1983: 103–4). He never read books for children, though (Conrad 1978: 77).

13 She was probably a daughter of Dr Tokarski (Najder 1983: 138). She met Konradek for the first time in 1867 when her family moved to Lwów and then in 1873 when he was placed at A. Syroczyński's pension (Omelan 2018: 111).

14 T. Bobrowski's letter of 28 June 1881.

15 Captain J. Craig, master of the *Vidar*, recalled that whenever he went down to his first mate's cabin to talk he 'usually found him writing' (Jean-Aubry 1927: 98).

16 *Wędrowiec* published also texts on literature, medicine, technology, science and industry (Kamisińska 2011: 73–83).

17 *Wędrowiec* (1867–74), no 1:1.

18 As delimiting dates for the discussion of the articles published in *Wędrowiec,* I chose the year 1866 since Konradek came to Nowochwastów in May that year and could have access to some issues of the journal at his uncle's library and the other date is the year of his departure from Poland – 1874.

19 I discuss extensively the texts published in *Wędrowiec* in the years 1867–74 in 'Conrad as a Reader of *Wędrowiec*', *The Conradian*, 46 (1), 2021.

20 A. Castelbolognesi (1836–75) – an Italian trader and explorer.

21 P. Belloni Du Chaillu (1831–1903) – a French-American traveller, zoologist and anthropologist.

22 J. H. Speke (1827–64) – an English explorer and officer in the British Indian Army.

23 E. A. Mage (1837–69) – a French naval officer and explorer of Africa.

24 P. Trémaux (1818–95) – a French architect, ethnographer and Orientalist photographer.

25 A. P. F. Tinné (1835–69) – a Dutch explorer in Africa who as the first European woman attempted to cross the Sahara.

26 C. Piagga (1827–82) – an Italian explorer of the region of the Southern Sudan and the Southern Nile.

27 'Lud Monbuttu w Afryce środkowej' [Monbuttu Tribe in Central Africa], *Wędrowiec* 1873 (161): 67, emphasis added. All translations, unless otherwise stated, are by the author of the chapter.

28 F. L. McClintock (1819–1907) – an Irish explorer in the British Royal Navy, known for his discoveries in the Canadian Arctic Archipelago. He published a on the fate of J. Franklin's lost polar expedition.

29 I. I. Hayes (1832–81) – an American Arctic explorer, physician and politician.

30 M. J. G. A. Lambert (1824–71) – a French hydrographer, he went on a voyage into Arctic seas and advocated the idea of an expedition to the North Pole; A. H. Petermann (1822–78) a German cartographer, he wrote a number of articles promoting exploratory missions, especially of the polar regions.

31 He mentions maps several times in his essay *Geography…* as he developed 'the taste for poring over maps', he showed 'proficiency in map-drawing' and he was able to draw the map of Western Sudan which he remembered till the end of his life (Conrad 2010: 10, 11, 13, Hampson 2003). Indeed this propensity for map drawing stayed with him till the end of his life which was substantiated by Warodell's essay on Conrad's hand-drawn maps on the margins of his manuscripts and on separate sheets of papers (Warodell 2017). *Wędrowiec* published many texts on the exploration of Eastern and Western Sudan, illustrated with maps, portraits of the natives and flora and fauna (e.g. in 1868–9

'Podróż po zachodnim Sudanie (odbytą przez p. Mage)' [Mage journey in Western Sudan].

32 White also emphasizes in his books the relation between a given author and the geography of the place, revealing in this way the work done in the context of the physical world (2010a: 21).

33 For a similar record of the process of bringing back to memory the scenes from childhood by current events, see a passage in *Geography …*: 'Yet it is a fact that about eighteen years afterwards a wretched little stern wheel steamboat I commanded lay moored to the bank of an African river […] The subdued thundering mutter of Stanley Falls hung in the heavy night air of the last navigable reach of the Upper Congo […]. I said to myself with awe "*this is the very spot of my boyish boast*"' (Conrad 2010: 14, emphasis added).

34 This fascination with atlases ran in the family. Conrad's aunt Regina Korzeniowska, who generously gave him one thousand roubles 'to buy shoes, galoshes, and a fur coat' (Najder 2007: 27), was a knowledgeable editor who produced historical atlases. Conrad could have read them, too.

35 For the manifold intertextual references of this line see J. Szczypień 2017: 31–50.

36 K. de Montrésor, letter to Jean-Aubry, 18 November 1927, qtd. in Najder 2007: 140.

Works Cited

Adamowicz-Pośpiech, A. (2009), 'Conrad's Play with Time in His Memoirs', in K. Bazarnik, B. Kucała (eds), *James Joyce and After: Writers and Time*, 143–54, Cambridge: Cambridge Scholars Publishing.

Adamowicz-Pośpiech, A. (2011), 'To Follow the Dream and again to Follow the Dream': Don Quixote, Almayer and Conrad as Multiple Reflections of the Dreamer, in P. Jędrzejko et al. (eds), *Secret Sharers: Melville, Conrad and Narratives of the Real*, 159–72, Zabrze: M-Studio.

Alberca, M. (2007), '*El pacto ambiguo*, Madrid: Biblioteca Nueva. Qtd', in M. Wagner-Egelhaaf (ed.), *Handbook of Autobiography /Autofiction*, section 2.3, Berlin-New York: De Gruyter.

Ambrosini, R. (2018), 'A Memoir "in the Shape of a Novel": Making the "Still Voice" of Conrad's Polish Past Resonate in *A Personal Record*', in W. Krajka (ed.), *Joseph Conrad's Authorial Self Polish and Other*, 37–56, Lublin and New York: Maria Curie-Skłodowska University Press, Columbia University Press.

Berthoud, J. (1978), '*A Personal Record*', in J. Berthoud, *J. Conrad. The Major Phase*, 1–23, Cambridge: Cambridge University Press.

Brodsky, S. (2005), 'Prester John's Workbook: Joseph Conrad, Edmund Candler, John Towson and Some Imperial Others', *Conradiana* 37 (1–2): 23–55.

Brodsky, S. (2016a), 'Dispossession Encoded: Conrad as Exile', in *Joseph Conrad's Polish Soul*, 79–124, Lublin, New York: M. Curie-Skłodowska Press, Columbia University Press.

Brodsky, S. (2016b), 'A Familiar Preface to *J. Conrad's Polish Soul*', in *Joseph Conrad's Polish Soul*, 11–42, Lublin, New York: M. Curie-Skłodowska Press, Columbia University Press.

Conrad, J. (1978), 'The Books of My Childhood', in Z. Najder (ed.), *J. Conrad, Congo Diary and Other Uncollected Pieces*, 77, Garden City, New York.

Conrad, J. (1983–2008), *The Collected Letters of Joseph Conrad*, gen. ed. L. Davies, Cambridge: Cambridge University Press.

Conrad, J. (1994), *A Personal Record*, ed. Z. Najder and J. H. Stape, Cambridge: Cambridge University Press.

Conrad, J. (2004), 'Poland Revisited', in J. H. Stape (ed.), *J. Conrad, Notes on Life and Letters*, 114–37, Cambridge: Cambridge University Press.

Conrad, J. (2010), 'Geography and Some Explorers', in H. R. Stevens and J. H. Stape (eds), with the assistance of M. Burgoyne, A. Fachard, *Last Essays*, 3–17, Cambridge: Cambridge University Press.

Gasyna, G. (2011), *Polish, Hybrid, and Otherwise. Exilic Discourse in J. Conrad and W. Gombrowicz*, London: Bloomsbury.

GoGwilt, C. (1995), *The Invention of the West. J. Conrad and the Double-Mapping of Europe and Empire*, Stanford: Stanford University Press.

Hampson, R. (2003), '"A Passion for Maps": Conrad, Africa, Australia, and South-East', *The Conradian* 28 (1): 34–56.

Hampson, R. (2005), '*Spatial Stories*', in P. Brooker and A. Thacker (eds), *Geographies of Modernism*, 54–64, London: Routledge.

Italiano, F. (2008), 'Defining Geopoetics', *Trans* (6). Available online: https://doi.org/10.4000/trans.299 (accessed 1 January 2020).

Jean-Aubry, G. (1927), *Joseph Conrad: Life and Letters*, vol. 1, London: Heinemann.

Kamisińska, D. (2011), 'Warszawski tygodnik "Wędrowiec" w latach 1863–1883. Part II', *Toruńskie Studia Bibliologiczne* 2011 (1): 65–86.

Karl, F. (1979), *J. Conrad: The Three Lives*, London: Faber and Faber.

Kertzer, J. M. (1974–5), 'Conrad's *Personal Record*', *University of Toronto Quarterly*, 44: 290–303. Reprinted in K. Carabine ed. (1992), *Joseph Conrad: Critical Assessments*, vol. III, 252–64, Mountfield: Helm Information.

Kmiecik, Z. (1965), 'Wydawnictwa periodyczne w Królestwie Polskim', *Rocznik Historii Czasopiśmiennictwa Polskiego* 4 (1): 142–60.

Knowles, O. (2010), 'Explanatory Notes', in Owen Knowles (ed.), *J. Conrad, Youth, Heart of Darkness, The End of the Tether*, 431–65, Cambridge: Cambridge University Press.

Lejeune, Ph. (2001), *Wariacje na temat pewnego paktu. O autobiografii*, ed. R. Lubas-Bartoszyńska, trans. W. Grajewski et al., Kraków: Universitas.

Meyer, B. (1967), '*A Personal Record*', in B. Meyer, *J. Conrad: A Psychoanalytic Biography*, Princeton: Princeton University Press.

Morf, G. (1930), *The Polish Heritage of J. Conrad*, London: Sampson Low.

Najder, Z., ed. (1964), *Conrad's Polish Background. Letters to and from Polish Friends*, trans. H. Carroll, Oxford: Oxford University Press.

Najder, Z., ed. (1983), *Conrad under Familial Eyes*, trans. H. Carroll-Najder, Cambridge: Cambridge University Press.

Najder, Z. (1988), 'Introduction', in Z. Najder (ed.), *J. Conrad, The Mirror of the Sea & A Personal Record*, xiv–xxi, Oxford: Oxford University Press.

Najder, Z. (2007), *Joseph Conrad. A Life*, trans. H. Njder, Rochester, New York: Camden House.

Nora, P. (1989), 'Between Memory and History', *Representations* 26 (1). Special Issues: Memory and Counter-Memory, trans. M. Roudebush, Oakland: University of California Press, 7–24.

Omelan, L. (2004), '"How Short His Years and How Clear His Vision!" Adam Pulman, Conrad's Unforgettable Tutor', *Conradiana* 36 (1–2): 131–42.

Omelan, L. (2018), '"A Man of Great Heart and Devotion": Antoni Syroczyński and His Role in Young Konrad's Education', in W. Krajka (ed.), *Joseph Conrad's Authorial Self Polish and Other*, 105–16, Lublin and New York: Maria Curie-Skłodowska University Press, Columbia University Press.

Pacukiewicz, M. (2012), 'Cultural Aspects of Joseph Conrad's Autobiography. On the Digressive Structure of *Some Reminiscences*', *Yearbook of Conrad Studies*, 7: 69–83.

Putnam, G. P. (1990), 'Conrad in Cracow', in M. Ray (ed.), *Joseph Conrad: Interviews and Recollections*, 205–7, Palgrave Macmillan.

Said, E. (1966) *J. Conrad and the Fiction of Autobiography*, Cambridge, MA: Harvard University Press.

Szczypien, J. (2017), *'Sailing towards Poland' with Joseph Conrad*, New York et al.: Peter Lang.

Tarnawski, W. (1984), '*A Personal Record*', in W. Tarnawski, *Conrad the Man, the Writer, the Pole*, 104–10, London: Polish Cultural Foundation.

Warodell, J. (2017), 'The Writer at Work: Hand-Drawn Maps in Conrad's Manuscripts', *Conradiana* 48 (1): 25–45.

Watt, I. (1994), 'Introduction', in F. E. Eddleman, D. L. Higdon (ed.), *J. Conrad, Almayer's Folly*, xxi–lxiv, Cambridge: Cambridge University Press.

Wędrowiec (1867–74). Available online: Digital Library of the University of Łódź, https://bcul.lib.uni.lodz.pl/dlibra/publication/387/edition/238/content?ref=desc (accessed 6 December 2019); https://bcul.lib.uni.lodz.pl/dlibra/publication/388/edition/239/content?ref=desc (accessed 6 December 2019).

White, K. (1992), 'Elements of Geopoetics', *Edinburgh Review*, 1992 (88): 163–78.

White, K. (2004a), 'An Outline of Geopoetics', in K. White, *The Wanderer and His Charts. Exploring the Fields of Vagrant thought and Vagabond Beauty*, 231–48, Edinburgh: Polygon.

White, K. (2004b), 'The Nomadic Intellect', in K. White, *The Wanderer and His Charts. Exploring the Fields of Vagrant thought and Vagabond Beauty*, 3–14, Edinburgh: Polygon.

White, K. (2010a), 'Wywiad z Pierre Boncenne [An interview with Pierre Boncenne]', in K. White, *Poeta Kosmograf*, trans. Kazimierz Brakoniecki, Olsztyn, 2010, 24–6. Originally published as: 'La danse de l'intellect. Entretien avec P. Boncenne', in K. White (1987), *Le poète cosmographe vers un nouvel espace culturel. Entreiens 1976–1986*, Pessac, Presses Universitaire de Bordeaux.

White, K. (2010b), 'Wywiad z Michel Phillippo [An interview with Michel Phillippo]', in K. White, *Poeta Kosmograf*, trans. Kazimierz Brakoniecki, 6–17, Olsztyn: Centrum Polsko-Francuskie. Originally published as: 'Portrait d'un nomade intellectuel. Entretien avec M. Phillippo', in K. White (1987), *Le poète cosmographe vers un nouvel espace culturel. Entretiens 1976–1986*, Pessac, Presses Universitaire de Bordeaux.

White, K. (2015), *Guido's Map: A European Pilgrimage*, Aberdeen: Aberdeen University Press.

Zabierowski, S. (2016), '"Conrad i Warszawa" [Conrad and Warsaw]', *Konteksty Kultury*, 13 (2): 125–37.

4

'The vision of a cosmopolitan': The transnational aesthetic of *A Personal Record*

Riccardo Capoferro
University of Rome, La Sapienza

This chapter will address the way in which Conrad fashions his identity in *A Personal Record*. As we will see, his self-presentation is intertwined with a definition of the novelistic imagination and its ethical function: *A Personal Record* articulates an aesthetic agenda that questions national boundaries and is meant to nourish a far-reaching sense of communal identity.[1] This agenda seems, however, at odds with the manifest purpose of Conrad's memoir. Permeated by far-fetched protestations of Englishness, *A Personal Record* was very probably written – like many other autobiographies – as a self-defence, sparked by Robert Lynd's disparaging criticism of Conrad's style in *The Daily News*:[2]

> Mr Conrad, as everybody knows, is a Pole, who writes in English by choice, as it were, rather than by nature. According to most people this choice is a good thing, especially for English literature. To some of us, on the other hand, it seems a very regrettable thing, even from the point of view of English literature. A writer who ceases to see the world coloured by his own language – for language gives colour to thoughts and things in a way that few people understand – is apt to lose the concentration and intensity of vision without which the greatest literature cannot be made. It was a sort of nationalism of language and outlook that kept wanderers like Turgenieff and Browning from ever becoming cosmopolitan and second rate … Mr Conrad, without either country or language, may be thought to have found a new patriotism for himself in the sea. His vision of men, however, is the vision of a cosmopolitan, of a homeless person. (Lynd [1908] 1973: 10–11)[3]

According to Lynd, Conrad's identity as a non-native speaker enfeebled his writing, undermining, in particular, his descriptive style. Excluded from a vivifying communal belonging, Conrad could not partake in that 'nationalism of language' which was, for Lynd, the source of all good literature.[4] This criticism seems to have shaped *A Personal Record*, which – sounding like a response to Lynd – is also a vindication of Conrad's identity as an English writer, an attempt to show how tight, how natural his relation to the English language and worldview was. Apparently, *A Personal Record* traces the story of a 'mysterious vocation' that is similar to a providential call: it presents Conrad's transformation into a British subject – implicitly, an English gentleman – and an English writer not only as a necessity, but also as an astonishing exception in a world where identities, both racial and national, are far more stable. As we will see, however, this view is by no means exclusive. To a minor extent, *A Personal Record* is also a *vocational* story: it suggests that Conrad's naturalization was the outcome of a path of professionalization that demanded hard work and staunchless dedication to the practical – secular – values of the British marine.

Nonetheless, the emphasis on Conrad's Englishness constitutes only one facet of this strange, two-pronged memoir, whose digressive structure – reminiscent of the Polish *gawęda* and of Sterne's oeuvre[5] – seems lacking in cohesion and has often puzzled readers. *A Personal Record* invites a search for an oblique, non-literal meaning, with an approach to narrative that Conrad himself compares to that of his fiction. This approach is ultimately instrumental to Conrad's self-definition as a novelist.[6] Superficially, the other manifest purpose of *A Personal Record* is to go back to his Polish past to show how 'formative' it had been. But this does not constitute an end in itself: it contributes to Conrad's self-representation as a writer who brings transnational concerns to an English audience. In accord with the Preface to *The Nigger of the 'Narcissus'* and with the author's note to *Almayer's Folly*, in *A Personal Record* Conrad characterizes his fiction as a tool to establish an emotional and intellectual bond between worlds. *A Personal Record* conveys a definition of Conrad the novelist and his art by means of an autobiographical narrative that is also a reassuring performance of identity. This aesthetic meditation, both covert and overt, unifies Conrad's memoir, knitting together the vindication of his Englishness and the remembrance of his Polish past. Needless to say, the realm of the aesthetic cannot be severed from the ethical and political realms: the artistic agenda of *A Personal Record* intimates how vital it is for the English public to focus on the complicated tales of a 'homo duplex'[7] who could 'make them see'.

At this point, a terminological remark is in order. While Lynd accused Conrad of an aesthetically unfruitful 'cosmopolitanism' – a category which prompts us to place *A Personal Record* both in current academic debates and in strains of the late nineteenth-century cultural debate – the idea of the 'transnational' may turn out to be more productive. The nineteenth-century discourse of 'cosmopolitanism', as expressed in reviews such as *The Cosmopolitan Review* and *Cosmopolis*, was attached, on the one hand, to post-Enlightenment ideas of urban refinement that valued the disinterestedness guaranteed by a detached, extra-national view of one's own nation; on the other, it encouraged a familiarity with other nations that was instrumental in strengthening one's own.[8] Ford's *English Review*, in which *A Personal Record* was published, reimagined cosmopolitanism for the literary world, updating the idea of the Republic of Letters and conceiving of (good) 'literature' as the result of an international cross-fertilization.[9] Conrad's view is certainly consistent with a post-Enlightenment, supranational disinterestedness, beautifully expressed by his utopian view of Europe as a political entity in 'Autocracy and War' (Conrad [1905] 1924). Moreover, it is consonant with Ford's agenda – Conrad being, in fact, the international writer par excellence. And it is perhaps significant that it was Conrad who had the idea of calling Ford's review *The English Review*: by specifying a national identity, he meant not so much to reinforce a sense of national affiliation as to suggest that the English identity was only one among many others, in accord with peaceful lines of nationalist thinking that envisioned a mutually beneficial coexistence of European peoples.

Nevertheless, as Richard Ambrosini (2013) has suggested, the retrospective concept of 'transnationalism' – long current in the social sciences – is more apt to theorize Conrad's own communal and aesthetic vision.[10] What Conrad does is, in fact, not so much elaborating on current ideas of cosmopolitanism as responding, imaginatively, to an expression of jingoism in the domain of the aesthetic. In *A Personal Record* he refashions his identity with a view to making his non-English experience relevant for an English audience. He places a premium on his own cultural assimilation while at the same time suggesting how that assimilation enabled him to act as a mediator between England and other, alien worlds, whose template is represented by Poland, itself a middle ground between the familiar and the foreign.[11] Conrad's attempt 'to make Polish life enter English literature'[12] through *A Personal Record* is meant to be exemplary of what Conrad sought to achieve in his fiction, which focuses on a range of reimagined cultures. The manifest end of the memoir – that of disclosing its author's 'personality' – does not stand in contradiction with this, 'the man behind the books' being, in fact, a novelist. The purpose of depicting 'a coherent, justifiable personality both in its origin and in its action' (Conrad 1919: 22) can be taken at face value, the action in question being, as a matter of fact, fiction-writing.

Superficially, however, *A Personal Record* is the narrative of a successful naturalization. While Conrad's transformation into a British subject was to a large extent dictated by circumstances, his memoir is a complicated, highly diversified rhetorical effort to *deny* those circumstances. Significantly, a main concern of Conrad is to explain how easily he acquired his command of the English language. In his Author's Note, added in 1919, he argues that his proficiency in English was not a matter of 'deliberate volition' (vi). Along the same lines, he adds:

> my faculty to write in English is as natural as any other aptitude with which I might have been born. I have a strange and overpowering feeling that it had always been an inherent part of myself. English was for me neither a matter of choice nor adoption. The merest idea of choice had never entered my head. And as to adoption – well, yes, there was adoption; but it was I who was adopted by the genius of the language, which directly I came out of the stammering stage made me its own so completely that its very idioms I truly believe had a direct action on my temperament and fashioned my still plastic character. (Conrad 1919: x)

By describing his inborn drive towards the English language, Conrad depicts his assimilation as an inevitable process, one on which he barely had any control. It was 'a very intimate action … too mysterious to explain', comparable to 'love at first sight' (x). To justify his naturalization, Conrad uses, among other things, the emergent language of the subconscious. He dissevers his English identity from his Polish roots, with an anti-deterministic – and anti-naturalistic – slant; his approach to the English language having been a 'matter of discovery and not of inheritance' (14). The fiction of a necessary assimilation – complemented, nonetheless, by a 'devoted practice' of the language – hints at the exceptionality of Conrad's parable, with a gesture that is recurrent in *A Personal Record*. Conrad echoes the Christian idea that identity is shaped by vocation, with a move that verges on self-contradiction: while in his fiction – for example in *Lord Jim*, *Typhoon*, and in *The Shadow Line* – he usually debunks providential plots,[13] his anxiety for assimilation prompts him to use rhetorical patterns that recall a Christian conception of the self, probably inherited via the Romantic imaginary.

At the same time, however, Conrad also seeks to downplay the differences between England and Poland. He highlights how the latter was foreign to 'Sclavonism' and had 'an exaggerated respect for individual rights', an attitude that translated into a 'special regard for the rights of the unprivileged of this earth' (xii–xiii). Conrad is probably evoking the universalist spirit of Polish Romanticism, which placed the Polish nation in a larger space in which even other nations could experience by right Poland's own desire for self-fulfilment. This spirit entailed a sense of co-responsibility for the fate of others that led Polish patriots to taking part in the 'Spring of nations' in 1848.[14] But the analogy between Poland and England – whose traditional defence of political and religious rights, emphasized by the Whig interpretation of history, remained fundamentally insular – is not only far-fetched, it is also marginal in the overall economy of *A Personal Record.* Conrad rather stresses the force of his mysterious vocation and, as we will see, builds up a universalist vision predicated on the power of fiction – of *his* fiction – rather than on overarching political or moral principles. Integral to this vision is a sympathetic representation of Poland, consonant with that of the remote places described by Conrad in his novels.

The episode that first stages the force of Conrad's vocation is prepared by the story of Uncle Nicholas B., a Polish patriot and a soldier in the Napoleonic army: a story of utter personal and national defeat, epitomized by a fact which left a deep mark in Conrad's memory.[15] On the run in a Lithuanian forest and desperate for survival, Nicholas and his companions were compelled to have an unconventional meal: 'Mr. Nicholas B. remains for me the unfortunate and miserable (but heroic) being who once upon a time had eaten a dog' (73). The misadventures of Nicholas B. set a backdrop for a key moment in the narrative of Conrad's own transformation into an Englishman. In the same chapter, he goes back to when, on a journey across the Swiss Alps with his tutor, he saw a group of 'English engineers' – examples of 'British Mankind' – involved in the works of the St. Gothard Tunnel. 'A bald-headed man … with a strong Scotch accent' (86) – significantly – failed to leave a strong impression on the boy. However, during an argument with his tutor over his plans to become a seaman, young Korzeniowski saw an 'unforgettable Englishman' who had 'the mien of an ardent and fearless traveller' (88). Characterized by an 'unextinguishable and comic ardour' (89) the Englishman sparked an epiphanic feeling in the boy, as the narrator of *A Personal Record*, with metaphors that prefigure the beginning of *The Shadow Line*, ironically highlights: 'Was he in the mystic ordering of common events the ambassador of my future … '? (89). The sight of the Englishman resonated with young Korzeniowski's dream of going to sea, that not long afterwards caused his tutor to blame him for being 'an incorrigible, hopeless Don Quixote' (94).

Two rhetorical strategies are interwoven in this chapter. On one level, it implies a stereotypically English practicality, which characterizes – although only to a minor extent – Conrad's presentation of his agency and motives. Retrospectively, his decision to leave appears only too understandable: 'fantastic meals of salt junk and hard tack upon the wide seas' (35) could certainly be preferable to Lithuanian dogs. The defeat experienced by Poland and, more specifically, by Nicholas B., invites, in other words, a comparison between the dead-end of Czarist domination and the cultural and political hegemony of a nation of engineers and seamen. But vocation seems to matter even more than reason. Conrad is led towards England by a powerful inner drive, objectified by his epiphanic view of the mystical ambassador in a knickerbocker suit that walks energetically across the mountains. Once again, his transition to England is presented in quasi-providential terms, although his view of the engineer has comic overtones that resonate with the underlying appeal that the episode makes to common sense.

Inevitably, Conrad's performance of Englishness is also inseparable from the narrative of his life as a seaman. The development of his identity is presented as the outcome of a path of professionalization – crucial to his development as a writer – in which there is no room for Quixotic temptations.[16] The illustration of how Conrad coped with the examiner's questions – feats that culminated with the exam for the degree of Master – is a key episode in his narrative of self-fashioning. Even Conrad's professional training seems, however, to have been shaped by a powerful inner drive. The crux of the episode is the conversation between Conrad and his 'loquacious' examiner, which contains more than one hint at Conrad's unusual status as a Pole who turned into an English sailor and places emphasis on his ability to make 'a homeward passage' (217) – 'home' being, in fact, England. The examiner – by whom Conrad feels 'adopted' (222) – remarks that he had never heard of another Pole in the British navy, asking whether Poles are 'inland people' and thus encouraging Conrad to explain that they are 'remote from the sea not only by situation, but also from a complete absence of remote association' (223). Conrad complements the anecdote with a new reference to his 'mysterious vocation', so strong that his 'wild oats had to be sown at sea'; 'the extraordinary psychology' of his 'sea going' being almost incomprehensible to the old man (223–4).

In this case too, Conrad remarks how exceptional his assimilation has been, taking silent pride in being the only one who was driven enough to have become a British master mariner, 'taking … a standing jump out of his racial surroundings' (227). His transformation into an Englishman appears to have been fuelled by a force so powerful as to overcome the inevitable constraints of biological determinism. Conrad's rhetorical effort becomes all the more apparent once we consider that in his author's note he does exactly the reverse: he *undermines* biological determinism. Nonetheless, it is worthy of note that his vocation did not exclude a degree of stubborn volition: 'if a seaman, then an English seaman' (229). Although in *A Personal Record* the British Marine is also characterized as, and to a certain extent was, a cosmopolitan community, Conrad clarifies that identities existed even on the sea, and that he both *chose* a specific identity and *was chosen* by it. Significantly, his decision to serve in the French marine appears to have been no more than the result of favourable circumstances, because in Europe 'it is with France that Poland has most connection' (228).

In this sequence, Conrad's devotion to professional seamanship and its secular values – which include a MacWhirr-like practical spirit – take centre stage. Conrad seems to have hardly won his identity as an English sailor. The defining turning points in the story of his assimilation, however, escape individual volition. Significantly, the ending of *A Personal Record* is devoted to another epiphanic moment: the first time Conrad *touched* an English ship. Similarly to chapter II – which revolves around the contrast between Uncle Nicholas B. and the Englishman walking on the Swiss Alps – chapter VII begins with Conrad's fond memories of his life in France and ends by foregrounding, once again, his lifelong fascination with England. Going back to his years in Marseilles, Conrad affectionately recalls how an old pilot of the Third Company – 'one grandfather, with a shaved, bony face' (242) – shared with him his Napoleonic memories, and 'honoured' him 'by a special and somewhat embarrassing predilection' so that he felt to be 'its temporarily adopted baby' (247). As J. H. Stape (2008) has noted, *A Personal Record* teems with adoptions and paternal figures, easing the weight of Conrad's Polish heritage and hinting at a more fluid sense of identity. The volatility of Conrad's self-fashioning is, however, balanced by fateful moments of being. Nothing in the chapter has the same emotional force of young Korzeniowski's first physical contact with an English ship, the *James Westoll* (in fact the *James Mason*). The space devoted to the approach of this 'big, high class cargo-steamer' (251) is itself meaningful. But the description also focuses on how young Korzeniowski volunteered 'to pull bow in the dinghy which shoved off … to put the pilot on board' (252) of the English ship. On the one hand, Conrad acknowledges that the event has been aggrandized by memory – 'small events grow memorable by the passage of time' (253) – but it is out of the question that the description of the moment he touched the ship amounted to a new, life-defining epiphany: 'when I bore against the smooth flank of the first English ship I ever touched in my life, I felt it already throbbing under my open palm' (252). The encounter with the *James Westoll* is a moment of self-recognition that carries the seeds of a necessary future. The flank of the ship is *already* throbbing, with young Korzeniowski experiencing, in a moment of revelation, a vital, organicist link with English ships which – in light of his irresistible, inborn, 'natural' drive – seems pre-given. Significantly, *A Personal Record* ends with this epiphanic, post-romantic but at the same time proto-modernist moment. In accord with

Conrad's general use of narrative discourse – which he disingenuously defines as 'informal' (21) – the memory of this realization appears to be so powerful as to disrupt chronological linearity. While Stephen Daedalus saw a girl on the beach, 'one whom magic had changed in the likeness of a strange and beautiful bird', young Korzeniowski felt an English craft throbbing under the palm of his hand.

But this is only a thread in the rich texture of *A Personal Record*, whose main purpose is in part concealed by Conrad's use of fragmented timelines and displaced emphases. If, as seems to be the case, Conrad wrote his memoir in response to Lynd's critique, *A Personal Record* should be read primarily as an artistic self-defence. And it is worthy of note that the memoir begins by focusing on Conrad's transformation into a writer. *A Personal Record* begins 'under the shade of old Flaubert' with a description of Conrad working on the tenth chapter of *Almayer's Folly* aboard the *Adowa*, 'gripped by the inclement weather alongside a quay in Rouen' (23). This overture sets the tone of the narrative, threading together a variety of crucial themes. Beginning in medias res like ancient epic, Conrad represents himself in an act of creation and self-creation through language, places himself in a genealogy that destabilizes national affiliations – with Flaubert acting as his muse – and describes his saint-like artistic dedication – once again, after the example of Flaubert. In doing so, he stresses how his identity is one with his work as a writer, while also suggesting, by implication, that his work has a broader communal significance, one that can be inferred in the light of Flaubert's quest for truth.[17] The same chapter focuses on other desultory attempts at fiction-writing: 'in the front sitting-room of furnished apartments in a Pimlico square' (33), and in the course of numerous sea-passages, over a time span that goes from 1889 to 1894. Conrad's vocation as a novelist appears to have been driven by forces not unlike those that energized his vocation as an English sailor:

> I had been treating myself to a long stay on shore, and in the necessity of occupying my mornings Almayer (that old acquaintance) came nobly to the rescue. Before long, as was only proper, his wife and daughter joined him round my table, and then the rest of that Pantai band came full of words and gestures. Unknown to my respectable landlady, it was my practice directly after my breakfast to hold animated receptions of Malays, Arabs, and half-castes. They did not clamour aloud for my attention. They came with a silent and irresistible appeal – and the appeal, I affirm here, was not to my self-love or my vanity. It seems now to have had a moral character, for why should the memory of these beings, seen in their obscure, sun-bathed existence, demand to express itself in

> the shape of a novel, except on the ground of that mysterious fellowship which unites in a community of hopes and fears all the dwellers on this earth?
>
> I did not receive my visitors with boisterous rapture as the bearers of any gifts of profit or fame. There was no vision of a printed book before me as I sat writing at that table, situated in a decayed part of Belgravia. After all these years, each leaving its evidence of slowly blackened pages, I can honestly say that it is a sentiment akin to pity which prompted me to render in words assembled with conscientious care the memory of things far distant and of men who had lived. (34)

Although fragmented by narrative discourse, the two thematic lines of *A Personal Record* turn out to be connected. If we place this episode in the overarching trajectory designed by the memoir, Conrad's irresistible urge to write appears to seamlessly follow from his drive towards England and the English language. And it appears to have been all the more irresistible because Conrad also emphasizes how his surrounding environment was not conducive to artistic concentration. At the beginning, he is interrupted by Young Cole, whose banjo-playing constitutes a prosaic – and perhaps, as Christopher GoGwilt (1995: 112) has suggested, Kiplingesque – counterpart to his creative effort. Nevertheless, Conrad's artistic drive has its own distinctive nature. The creative process he describes bears a strong resemblance to the unconscious, powerful, ecstatic inspiration typical of the Romantic creative experience, the call of his characters being 'silent and irresistible' (34). Later on, he remarks that he has been unable to trace his first book 'to any mental or psychological cause' (173), and that 'to survey with wonder the changes of one's own self is a fascinating pursuit', since they are 'the work of unseen forces' (176). Romantically, Conrad's artistic vision stems from the unfathomable wells of the inner self, but it has implications for the community as a whole (much like poetry for Adam Mickiewicz). His vision is permeated by keen moral awareness, appealing to 'a sentiment akin to piety' (34); the 'appeal' of Almayer and the 'Pantai band' to Conrad was, in fact, of a moral nature. Moral and aesthetic sensibility are, in other words, coextensive, the 'obscure' existence of the Pantai band demanding to be expressed in the 'shape of a novel'. Novelistic form is valuable insofar as it is able to weave emotional bonds and nourish the 'mysterious fellowship' that unites distant peoples – far beyond the national class-systems explored by the nineteenth-century novel.[18]

In this passage, not only does Conrad bolster and specify his identity as an English novelist, he also envisions an ideal audience: by extending the moral and emotional sensibility of their readers, his novels can cultivate a transnational community of feeling. Superficially, this idea sounds like a development of Mickiewicz's idea of a Christian brotherhood and of the view of art expressed by French novelists such as Anatole France (whose review of Maupassant's *Notre Coeur* has much in common with Conrad's Preface to *The Nigger of the 'Narcissus'*).[19] However, against the backdrop of the late nineteenth-century and early twentieth-century British public sphere – which revolved around the empire and its enlightening mission – Conrad's view of art cannot simply be seen as a conflation of received visions. Like other novelists before him, Conrad gestures towards a counter-public sphere that emerges within the realm of the aesthetic, but he does so to establish the priority of feeling as a communal bond over the self-proclaimed rational agency of British missionary imperialism. This idea, in accord with the Author's Note to *Almayer's Folly* and the Preface to *The Nigger of the 'Narcissus'*, finds further expression at the end of the chapter: 'An imaginative and exact rendering of authentic memories may serve worthily that spirit of piety towards all things human which sanctions the conceptions of a writer of tales, and the emotions of the man reviewing his own experience' (60). Conrad elaborates on the idea, recurrent in his oeuvre, that personal memories are sifted and reworked by the novelistic imagination and thus universalized.

In light of this, not only Conrad's memories of his first encounter with Almayer, but also his memories of Poland, turn out to have contributed to his novelistic imagination. The retrospective glance of *A Personal Record* is instrumental in defining a globally minded aesthetic ideal. Key to this ideal is the power of art to bring together worlds that are temporally, culturally and geographically distant. The sequences of *A Personal Record* devoted to the remote worlds experienced by Conrad in his Polish years and in his years as a seaman function both as examples and as formative templates of the social landscapes described in his fiction. Conrad's selection of the Polish materials was dictated not only by the affection he felt for specific characters or places, but also by the need to exemplify a historical experience made of three interconnected spheres: the personal, the familial and the national. The underlying meaning of Conrad's Polish memories also depends on their implicit value as a model for the narrative representation of historical experience, both personal and communal. In fact, as Richard Niland (2010) has shown, Conrad's early exposure to the ideals of Polish nationalism informed his view of international and global geopolitics as an ongoing process driven by the idea and the practice of national community. Steeped in the philosophy and rhetoric of nationalism since his early childhood, Conrad focuses on how national allegiances (in *Under Western*

Eyes), nation-formation (in *Nostromo*) and international geopolitics (in *The Secret Agent*) are dialectically related to individual lives. The story of Nicholas B. exemplifies, in particular, how personal destinies were shaped by a dream of national independence that turned out to be Quixotic – far more than the dream of becoming a sailor – and took a toll on Conrad's family. Nicholas B.'s quasi-cannibalistic meal is caused by a deadly interplay of imperial oppression and the 'false hope of national independence' (97) raised by Napoleon I. Chapter 3 of *A Personal Record* focuses more extensively on Polish matters, facing their painful intertwining of individual and collective life. It dwells on the fate of Nicholas B., on Conrad's mother's visit to her brother's house and on her obligation to return to exile despite her illness (a heart-wrenching passage that has been appropriated by W. G. Sebald in *The Rings of Saturn*).

A Personal Record suggests that Poland, the Malay Archipelago and their inhabitants have crucial features in common. Almayer is, apparently, radically different from Nicholas B. Nevertheless, they are both Quixotic. His self-image is impervious to the harsh pressures of colonial reality: he was 'ambitious, aiming at the grandiose'; 'the importation of that Bali pony might have been part of some deep scheme, of some diplomatic plan, of some hopeful intrigue' (149). Almayer's peculiar blend of visionary grandeur and damning impracticality is epitomized by his quirky demeanour – very rapidly, he grows uninterested in the pony. The crucial part he played in the unfolding of Conrad's vocation as a novelist suggests, however, that, likewise, he influenced the development of Conrad's novelistic imagination – 'The possessor of the only flock of geese on the East Coast is responsible for the existence of some fourteen volumes so far' (168). The memory of Almayer appealed to, and at the same time kindled, Conrad's fascination with peoples and contexts threatened by oblivion. 'Since you were always complaining of being lost to the world,' says Conrad to the imaginary ghost of Almayer, 'you should remember that if I had not believed enough in your existence to let you haunt my room in Bessborough gardens you would have been much more lost' (88). And in light of *Almayer's Folly* – a companion piece to *A Personal Record* – Almayer appears relevant not only individually, but in relation to the broader context that gives form and meaning to his actions. Much like Poland, the shores besides which Almayer lives and dreams are a tangle of political forces and group interests. As Cedric Watts reminds us,

> In his very first novel, he [Conrad] had dared to imply that what the imperial nations do on a big scale, with their gunboat diplomacy their international rivalry for 'spheres of influence' is essentially no different from what the

'uncivilised' people do on a small scale in their jungle settlements … whatever the race, nationality, colour or creed all men seem alike in their egoistic questing for material profit. (Watts 1993: 60)

Conrad's memories of his early experiences in *A Personal Record* are, therefore, instrumental in defining a transnational idea of the novel, the novelist and, prospectively, their public. In what relation do they stand, however, with Conrad's rhetorically strained performance of Englishness? As a matter of fact, the aesthetic subtext of *A Personal Record* is only half articulated. Much is left to conscious interpretation, as in Conrad's major fiction. In commenting on the narrative strategy of *Under Western Eyes*, Frank Kermode (1980) rightly argued that Conrad 'took a high view of art and a low view of his public' (89). Conrad's works are often characterized by a surface level of meaning and a covert level that demands decoding;[20] one writer makes sure that the audience is not too worried, while the other one encodes the narrative with secrets, whose shimmering traces invite a segment of the audience to piece the clues together and venture into precarious ground. This is, at least, what 'A Familiar Preface' itself seems to suggest:

these memories put down without any regard for established conventions have not been thrown off without system and purpose. They have their hope and their aim. The hope that from the reading of these pages there may emerge at last … a coherent, justifiable personality both in its origin and in its action. This is the hope. The immediate aim, closely associated with the hope, is to give the record of personal memories by presenting faithfully the feelings and sensations connected with the writing of my first book and with my first contact with the sea. In the purposely mingled resonance of this double strain a friend here and there will perhaps detect a subtle accord. (21–2)

'A friend here and there' able to 'detect a subtle accord' prefigure, within the much wider middle-class audience that Conrad addressed, the elite audience of *Ulysses* and the *Waste Land*. A strain of psychoanalytic or biographic criticism has highlighted Conrad's strategies of elusion and self-concealment in *A Personal Record*, focusing on the uneasy burden of his Polish past. However, while *A Personal Record* may contain hints at Conrad's sense of guilt, the context in which he lived and worked was probably more pressing.[21] The most unconventional of late-nineteenth- and early-twentieth-century English writers began his career on a Tory (not to say jingoist) periodical such as *Blackwood's Magazine* and – having to pay his bills – he desired to attain commercial success throughout his career.[22] His entire oeuvre has overt and covert meanings, and the fact that he published *A Personal Record* in *The English Review* does not mean that he addressed a restricted audience: in *A Personal Record* he sardonically mentions a conversation with a friend from his childhood that also touched on 'the last poem published in a very modernist review, edited by the very young and patronized by the highest society' (51). Arguably, the strategies of elusions and double-coding of *A Personal Record* have to do with the politics of the aesthetic. The half-expressed meanings of Conrad's memoir ran counter to widely shared moral and political tenets, identity being a rigid formation at the peak of European nationalism.

As we have seen, in fact, on one level Conrad over-performs his Englishness, structuring the parable of his assimilation around epiphanic moments and giving it providential overtones. His self-descriptions seem reminiscent of what M. H. Abrams has called 'the theodicy of the private life', a providential and redemptive design of individual life: an 'immanent teleology' which owes much to St. Augustine's *Confessions* and informed the development of the self in the imaginary of Romantic poetry.[23] This pattern, also akin to Hegel's philosophy of history, includes a circuitous journey from alienation to integration, which culminates in a final self-development that coincides with a conscious fusion with the whole. While Abrams finds these features especially in British romanticism, epiphanic moments (such as Novalis's *Augenblick*) and redemptive patterns that combine mystical inspiration and epic nostalgia – such as the parable of Jacek Soplica in Mickiewicz's *Pan Tadeusz* – are recurrent in European Romanticism. In a Romantic fashion, Conrad's transformation into an Englishman appears to be the expression of a super-individual, quasi-teleological necessity, although individual volition also plays a part. To emphasize the exceptionality of his life-trajectory, Conrad goes so far as to essentialize national identities. Nevertheless, he also describes his mind as a Lockean *tabula rasa* that was filled by English words and notions. This rhetorically overloaded performance of Englishness, which is meant to assuage the fear of the alien, expresses Conrad's anxiety over assimilation and personal identity.

On another level, however, Conrad's memoir does something very different: it portrays a hybrid identity which unfolds in the process of artistic creation, ultimately encompassing the English one. This second level appears less visible because, characteristically, Conrad makes use of a fragmented timeline. In strictly chronological terms, his transformation into a novelist should follow his transformation into an Englishman, with the English seaman finally becoming the cosmopolitan author. However, like in a movie or a TV series that interlaces two narrative sequences, one of which is a prequel to the other – for example

The Godfather: Part II or, more recently, *True Detective* – the two trajectories of individual development are not presented sequentially. Conversely, they appear to be only marginally connected and the overall meaning of *A Personal Record* does not seem to emanate from their overall unity. In fact, the memoir ends with Conrad's epiphanic contact with an English ship, his mysterious vocation appearing to be that of an English *sailor*.

Nevertheless, this displaced emphasis – probably a fruitful result of the writing process of *A Personal Record*, itself fragmented – does not completely obscure the other main purpose of Conrad's unconventional memoir: his self-definition as an artist. That he used a narrative to express his artistic ideals should not come as a surprise, because his critical and his fictional discourses are often imbricated.[24] It is significant that *A Personal Record* is tightly interconnected to the entire corpus of Conrad's fiction. Explicitly, this connection is provided by *Almayer's Folly*, which laid the groundwork for Conrad's subsequent production. But the narrative of how *Almayer's Folly* was born sheds light on the seeds out of which other works grew. The story of how Konrad Korzeniowski decided to go to Africa echoes the beginning of *Heart of Darkness*, both Marlow and Conrad recalling their early fascination with maps and making the fateful decision of exploring the blank spaces of the earth: 'When I grow up I will go there' (Conrad 1946: 52), says young Marlow, which sounds much like young Korzeniowski's resolve: 'When I grow up I shall go there'! (141). A few lines later, Conrad recalls how his earliest reader, 'the young Cambridge man', laconically appreciated his work and urged him to continue to write: a story of life-changing trust – or an expression of Conrad's ironic desire for trust – introduced by the same line by Novalis that opens *Lord Jim*: 'It is certain my conviction gains infinitely the moment another soul will believe in it' (43). Moreover, *A Personal Record* is also a theoretical playground in which Conrad tests ideas he was to use in subsequent works. He devotes some reflections to the differences between fiction and autobiography, disparaging Rousseau's *Confessions* to justify his own autobiographical practice. He argues that, unlike the autobiographist, the novelist makes use of his imagination, probing its utmost limits, but even his work is confessional: 'A writer of imaginative prose (even more than any other sort of artist) stands confessed in his works' (182). The awareness of the semi-autobiographical nature of fiction-writing – a cornerstone of Conrad's theory of the novel – would fructify in *The Shadow Line*, which presents itself as a 'confession'. (Needless to say, Conrad always showed a pervasive awareness of the relation between his fiction and his personal experience.) And it is perhaps worthy of note that *A Personal Record* also highlights the emergence of the genre label that appears in most Conrad subtitles, reminiscent of the Polish *gawęda* but also expressive of a proto-modernist dislike for genre constraints. The young Cambridge man asks Conrad what kind of work he is giving him to read. Conrad's answer – 'It is a sort of tale' (45) – does far more than voice his insecurity as a would-be novelist; it resonates with his impatience with received aesthetic categories, conveyed precisely by his recurrent use of 'tale' in his subtitles (and by his scepticism of the notions of 'realism' and 'romanticism').

However, in *A Personal Record* the aesthetic is not divorced from the ethical and political domains. Conrad's self-representation stresses the public role of the artist. It entails an idea of the audience as, potentially, a transnational community. The ability of the novel to establish sympathetic links independently of social boundaries assumes a global reach. According to *A Personal Record*, the moral and political sensibility that Conrad's novels seek to nourish overcomes the boundaries of the British nation, and, concomitantly, the sense of moral superiority that attended the missionary nationalism of the empire, reaching out towards foreign worlds as diverse as Poland and the Malay Archipelago. The transnational community imagined by Conrad is, loosely speaking, an expression of early-twentieth-century 'cosmopolitanism'. However, we should keep in mind its distinctive features. It is predicated on an aesthetic universalism: it is art that, more than anything else, envisions and enables an ever-increasing human community, one that is capable of accommodating the alien – and of making the familiar strange.

Notes

1 The multifaceted problem of identity is a crucial one in *A Personal Record* and in Conrad's oeuvre as a whole. For a relevant analysis of the themes and turning points of *A Personal Record* that also provides a useful overview of previous criticism, see Stape (2008). On Conrad's performed Englishness in his early works, see Simmons (2004). On Conrad's authorial identity in *A Personal Record*, see Purssel (2016).

2 See Najder (1997).

3 Lynd was not the only one who regarded Conrad as, essentially, an alien. For this aspect of the reception of *A Personal Record*, see Purssel (2016: 174–6).

4 Lynd's view is part of the surge of 'Anglo-Saxonism' that marked the late Imperial period. See Kumar (2003: 187–225).

5 See Tarnawski (1969). On the *gawęda*, see Busza (1966). The relation between *A Personal Record* and *A Sentimental Journey* is suggested by Najder (1997: 105).

6 As Richard Ambrosini has suggested, *A Personal Record* should be read against the backdrop of Conrad's work as a transnational author – similar, in this respect, to Luigi Pirandello, James Joyce and Franz Kafka, Conrad being 'an English writer and a transnational novelist' (2013: 12). Ambrosini, from whose work mine take its cue, highlights how *A Personal Record* is tightly connected to Conrad's 'more theoretical essays' (2018: 47).
7 Conrad (1991: 89); 5 December 1903, to Kazimierz Waliszewski.
8 See Agathocleous (2011: 56).
9 See Attridge (2008).
10 For a broad-ranging introduction to the concept and its implications at the level of cultural production, see Vertovec (2009).
11 On the 'Polonism' of *A Personal Record*, see Szczpien (1989). Christopher GoGwilt (1995) has found, conversely, a pervasive destabilization of identity, time and place in *A Personal Record*, which responds to contemporary geopolitical developments: 'in its attempt to extricate Conrad's life and work from the increasingly charged stereotype of the "Slav", *A Personal Record* stands as a historical record of the emerging cultural and political division between eastern and western Europe' (3). For a thorough reading of Conrad's work, see Chapter 5.
12 Conrad (1988: 138); 7 October 1908, to J. B. Pinker.
13 On this aspect, especially in *The Shadow Line*, see Capoferro (2015).
14 See Skórkzewski (2018).
15 According to Najder, the 'sense of an inherited catastrophe, both personal and communal, was also part of [Conrad's] mental background' (Najder 2000: 321).
16 'Sobriety' as a literary value appears to be the side effect of a professional requirement, certified during Conrad's exams at the Marine Department of the Board of Trade.
17 On these aspects, see Stape (2008).
18 Undeniably, Conrad's theory bears a strong resemblance to William Wordsworth's theory of poetry, which exerted a powerful influence on the tradition of British realism, in particular on George Eliot. However, Conrad was more directly influenced by French theories of art as well as by Polish Romanticism. Ian Watt's thesis that Conrad's theory of art is indebted to the preface to *The Lyrical Ballads* is an Anglicization of Conrad that downplays his lifelong connection to other European cultures. See Watt (1979: 79–80).
19 See Hervouet (1990: 139).
20 Ian Watt's 'delayed decoding' and Cedric Watts's 'covert plots' constitute, it goes without saying, different facets of this expressive strategy. See Watt (1979) and Watts (1984).
21 On the elusiveness of *A Personal Record* and its causes – especially Conrad's sense of guilt in relation to his Polish past and his anxiety about

reputation – see Prescott (2004). For a recent reading of *A Personal Record* as 'a thinly veiled apology for Conrad's desertion of his native land and language', see De Vinne (2014, quotation p. 82).

22 On Conrad and *Blackwood's Magazine* – from a point of view that is both ideological and material – see Simmons (2004).

23 See Abrams (1971: 95–6).

24 On this, see Ambrosini (1991).

Works Cited

Abrams, M. H. (1971), *Natural Supernaturalism. Tradition and Revolution in Romantic Literature*, New York & London: Norton.

Agathocleous, T. (2011), *Urban Realism and the Cosmopolitan Imagination in the Nineteenth Century: Visible City, Invisible World*, Cambridge: Cambridge University Press.

Ambrosini, R. (1991), *Conrad's Fiction as Critical Discourse*, Cambridge: Cambridge University Press.

Ambrosini, R. (2013), 'Reconceptualizing Conrad as a Transnational Novelist: A Research Programme', *Studia Neophilologica*, 85 (1–4): 5–16.

Ambrosini, R. (2018), 'A Memoir "in the shape of a novel": Making the "still voice" of Conrad's Polish Past Resonate in *A Personal Record*', in W. Krajka (ed.), *Joseph Conrad's Authorial Self: Polish and Other*, 37–55, Lublin: Maria Curie-Skłodowska University Press, New York: Columbia University Press.

Attridge, J. (2008), '"We Will Listen to None but Specialists": Ford, the Rise of Specialization, and the English Review', in A. Gasiorek and D. Moore (eds), *Ford Madox Ford: Literary Networks and Cultural Transformations*, 29–42, Amsterdam: Rodopi.

Busza, A. (1966), 'Conrad Polish Literary Background and Some Illustrations of the Influence of Polish Literature on His Work', *Antemurale*, 10: 109–255.

Capoferro, R. (2015), 'Providence, Anti-Providence and the Experience of Time in *The Shadow Line*', *Conradiana*, 47 (1) (Spring): 17–42.

Conrad, J. (1919), *A Personal Record*, London and Toronto: Dent.

Conrad, J. (1924), 'Autocracy and War', in *Notes on Life and Letters*, 111–52, New York: Dent.

Conrad, J. (1946), *Heart of Darkness*, in *Youth, Heart of Darkness, The End of the Tether*, London: Dent.

Conrad, J. (1988), *The Collected Letters of Joseph Conrad, Volume 4*, ed. F. R. Karl and L. Davies, Cambridge: Cambridge University Press.

Conrad, J. (1991), *The Collected Letters of Joseph Conrad, Volume 3*, ed. F. R. Karl and L. Davies, Cambridge: Cambridge University Press.

De Vinne, C. (2014), 'Begging the Question of Confession: Joseph Conrad's *A Personal Record*', *Prose Studies: History, Theory, Criticism*, 25 (3): 82–99.

GoGwilt, C. (1995), *The Invention of the West. Joseph Conrad and the Double-Mapping of Europe and Empire*, Stanford: Stanford University Press.

Hervouet, Y. (1990), *The French Face of Joseph Conrad*, Cambridge: Cambridge University Press.

Kermode, F. (1980), 'Secrets and Narrative Sequence', *Critical Inquiry*, 7 (1) (Autumn), *On Narrative*: 83–101.

Kumar, K. (2003), *The Making of English National Identity*, Cambridge: Cambridge University Press.

Lynd C. (1973), 'Review', *The Daily News*, 10 August 1908, reprinted in N. Sherry (ed.), *Conrad: The Critical Heritage*, 10–11, London: Routledge.

Najder, Z. (1997), 'A Personal Record', in Z. Najder, *Conrad in Perspective: Essays on Art and Fidelity*, 102–9, Cambridge: Cambridge University Press.

Najder, Z. (2000), 'Polish Inheritance', in O. Knowles and G. M. Moore (eds), *Oxford Reader's Companion to Conrad*, 321, Oxford: Oxford University Press.

Niland, R. (2010), *Conrad and History*, Oxford: Oxford University Press.

Prescott. L. (2004), 'Autobiography as Evasion: Joseph Conrad's *A Personal Record*', *Journal of Modern Literature*, 28 (1), *Autobiography and Memoir* (Autumn): 177–88.

Purssel, A. (2016), '"The Speech of my Secret Choice": Language and Authorial Identity in *A Personal Record*', in K. I. Baxter, R. Hampson (eds), *Conrad and Language*, 168–85, Edinburgh: Edinburgh University Press.

Sherry, N., ed. (1973), *Conrad, The Critical Heritage*, London: Routledge Kegan Paul.

Simmons, A. H. (2004), 'The Art of Englishness: Identity and Representation in Conrad's Early Career', *The Conradian*, 29 (1) (Spring): 1–26.

Skórkzewski, D. (2018), '(Polish) Romanticism, from Canon to Agon', in T. Trojanowska, J. Niżyńska and P. Czapliński (eds), *Being Poland: A New History of Polish Literature and Culture*, 68–104, Toronto: University of Toronto Press.

Stape, J. H. (2008), 'Narrating Identity in a Personal Record', in J. Lothe, J. Hawthorn, J. Phelan (eds), *Joseph Conrad: Voice, Sequence, History, Genre*, 217–35, Columbus: The Ohio State University Press.

Szczpien, Jean M. (1989), 'Joseph Conrad's *A Personal Record*: Composition, Intention, Design: Polonism', *Journal of Modern Literature*, XVI (1) (Summer): 3–30.

Tarnawski, W. (1969), 'Conrad's *A Personal Record*', *Conradiana*, 12: 55–8.

Vertovec, S. (2009), *Transnationalism*, London: Routledge.

Watt, I. (1979), *Conrad in the Nineteenth Century*, Cambridge: Cambridge University Press.

Watts, C. (1984), *The Deceptive Text: An Introduction to Covert Plots*, Brighton: Harvester.

Watts, C. (1993), *A Preface to Conrad*, London: Longman.

Part Two

Empire, movement and migration

5

'New shades of expression': Death and Empire in Conrad's unrestful tales

Richard Niland
Imperial College, London

Conrad's first collection of short stories, *Tales of Unrest* (1898), was crucial in his evolution as an author, confirming his transformation from professional sailor to professional writer. Commenced during his honeymoon in Brittany in 1896, the five tales reveal an expanded thematic and geographical range that allowed Conrad to dramatize liminal spaces and to negotiate the boundaries that shaped his own process of redefinition and realignment, not least the protocols and codes of Empire. As early reviewers noted, these stories were 'in harmony with the spirit of our times' (*Boston Evening Transcript* 1898: 18). That 'spirit' was a spirit of 'unrest', individual and global – and it is inscribed in the struggles for personal identity within patriarchal space in 'The Idiots' and 'The Return' and the necessity of (and resistance to) cultural assimilation in 'Karain', 'An Outpost of Progress' and 'The Lagoon'. In particular, unrest comes through the pervasive spectre of death as the ultimate migration, in the face of which Conrad explores the sources of our inexorable strivings; what *The Nigger of the 'Narcissus'* expressively terms 'desired unrest' (Conrad 1926: 90). The range of 'crossings' that articulate Conrad's 'duplex' nature is also evident in the diverse perspectives and the sources of inspiration: France, the country of his second language, and England, his adopted homeland; and, drawing upon his memories of the colonial world, Africa and Malay Archipelago, forging a rich transnational nexus of literary and cultural traditions. True to its title, this is a volume founded upon and reflective of the 'unrest' in Conrad's own experiences and vision. Such transnational concerns have led historians such as Maya Jasanoff to label Conrad the key writer of late nineteenth- and early twentieth-century globalization for his probing scrutiny of receding and emerging political, economic and cultural forces (Jasanoff 2017). Similarly, Marianne DeKoven has observed that Conrad's 'unrest is another name for the discontents of modern, particularly colonialist civilization' (DeKoven 1997: 241). In addition, the composition of *Tales of Unrest* is intimately linked with Conrad's time in Brittany in 1896, and this chapter will examine his encounter with Breton culture before turning to the global engagements of empire.

Death and Breton culture in 'The Idiots'

If the ultimate crossing of death stalks the stories linked to Conrad's honeymoon, it is fitting that the author's marriage proposal to Jessie George took place in the shadow of Hans Holbein's celebrated *The Ambassadors* (1533) in the National Gallery in London. Holbein's painting treats the promise of transnational encounters, exploration and empire, but is importantly qualified by its anamorphic representation of a human skull; one of European art's most celebrated *momento mori*. The Conrad's crossing to Brittany only extended such connections. According to Baedeker's guide to Northern France of 1894, 'curious old superstitions and legends are met at every turn' in Brittany (Baedeker 1894: 204). Coincidentally, one of the newspaper sensations of June 1896, when Conrad worked on 'The Idiots' and 'An Outpost of Progress', was the sinking of the *Drummond Castle*, with the loss of 242 lives, off the Breton coast. In a letter to T. F. Unwin, Conrad felt that 'Inevitableness is the only certitude' (Conrad 1983: 303), and writing to Edward Garnett from Brittany, Conrad discussed the fishermen of the region as captives in a zone between life and death; 'a few old fellows forgotten by the capricious death that dwells upon the sea [who] shuffle about amongst the stones of this sterile land and seem to wonder peevishly at having been left so long alive' (Conrad 1983: 272). In the eighteenth century, Brittany experienced epidemics of dysentery and enteric fever, suffering disastrous mortality rates. The population declined, but consequently Brittany became a prolific centre of publishing for books about death, and this cultural association persisted at the close of the nineteenth century (McManners 1985: 89).

Notably, the village of Kermaria-an-Isquit lies twenty miles from where Conrad spent his honeymoon in 1896, and its church, whose late-fifteenth-century frescoes were uncovered in 1856, houses some of the best-preserved examples of the medieval *danse macabre* in Europe. In European print culture the most widely known images of the dance of death, Hans Holbein's *Les Simulachres et Historiées Faces de la Mort*, were published in Lyon in 1538, and

Conrad often drew on this tradition for political critique. 'Heart of Darkness' undertakes a journey to 'places with farcical names, where the merry dance of death and trade goes on in a still and earthy atmosphere as of an overheated catacomb' (Conrad 1903: 70–1). *Nostromo's* Guzman Bento 'reached his apotheosis in the popular legend of a sanguinary land-haunting spectre whose body had been carried off by the devil in person' (Conrad 1984: 47), while, later, in Montpellier in 1907, Conrad wrote (proleptically in light of both Thomas Mann's *The Magic Mountain* (1924) and the modern World Economic Forum) of 'Davos-Platz' where the 'modern Dance of Death goes on in expensive hotels' (Conrad 1988: 420). Amongst Conrad's literary influences, Dickens frequently recalled the dance of death. In *Little Dorrit*, Henry Gowan 'was like the dressed-up Death in the Dutch series; whatever figure he took upon his arm, whether it was youth or age, beauty or ugliness, whether he danced with it, played with it, or prayed with it, he made it ghastly' (Dickens 1857: 506). In *The Mystery of Edwin Drood*, 'two skeleton journeymen out of the Dance of Death appear' (Dickens 1870: 89), and according to Michael Hollington, 'Dickens remained haunted by the blighting impact of the skeleton of the Dance of Death upon youth and beauty throughout his career as an artist' (Hollington 1978: 74). In France, one of Conrad's favourite writers, Anatole France, wrote 'La danse des Morts' (1869), continuing a European engagement with Holbein found in the writers who shaped Conrad's work. As Sarah Webster Goodwin has observed, the Holbein images contain 'the medieval motif that we find still in murals and incunabula. But the nineteenth century has a dance of death all its own; Goethe, Baudelaire, Flaubert, Gautier, Dickens, Hardy, Mann, and Joyce … allude to the dance of death and use it, with varied ironies, as an image, a metaphor, or a structuring device' (Webster Goodwin 1988: 3–4). The engagement with the *danse macabre* feeds into the iconography of *fin-de-siècle* culture, from Camille Saint-Saens' *Danse Macabre* (1874) and Oscar Wilde's *The Picture of Dorian Gray* (1890) to the imperialist verses of Henry Newbolt's 'Admiral Death' (1898), capturing a sense of anxiety and unrest at the heart of the outwardly aesthetic and imperial. As Allan H. Simmons and J. H. Stape have stressed, the stories in *Tales of Unrest* speak to 'prevailing *fin-de-siècle* fears associated with "decadence" and "degeneration"' (Conrad 2012: xxxv), and Conrad's early work is haunted by death and disturbance, as the stories span, like Holbein's engravings, the social spectrum of death's victims, from peasants to chiefs. The unrest in *Tales of Unrest* comes from an awareness of both death as an external event or visitation, but also, as his 'Author's Note' asserts, from Conrad's pressing awareness that 'We cannot escape from ourselves' (Conrad 2012: 6).

Landscape and death figure prominently in Conrad's first published short story, 'The Idiots', and it is the initial fruit of his encounter with Brittany and the culturally residual on the fringes of European modernity. Later dismissed by Conrad for being derivative of Maupassant and strands of nineteenth-century French naturalism, the story nevertheless acquires much of its interest from its engagement with Breton culture. The first glimpse of the 'idiots' at the roadside introduces 'creatures [who] are forgotten by time, and live untouched by years till death gathers them up into its compassionate bosom: the faithful death that never forgets in the press of work the most insignificant of its children' (Conrad 2012: 53). In Breton legend, Ankou is the embodiment of death and often drives an ancient chariot (Le Braz 1893), and the narrator learns much of the story from 'an emaciated and sceptical old fellow with a tremendous whip' (Conrad 2012: 55). The wedding ceremony of Jean-Pierre Bacadou that initiates the series of familial disasters is presented as a dance of death akin to that of Bergman's *The Seventh Seal*: 'In front the violin sang a strident tune, and the *biniou* snored and hummed while the player capered solemnly, lifting his heavy clogs. The sombre procession drifted in and out of the narrow lanes, through sunshine and through shade, between fields and hedgerows' (Conrad 2012: 56). When Jean-Pierre asserts his authority on the farm 'the old folks felt a shadow – precursor of the grave – fall upon them finally' (Conrad 2012: 56). Ultimately, Susan stabs Jean-Pierre in the throat with scissors. When she encounters the old soldier Millot, before her own suicide, she mistakes him for the ghost of her dead husband. Millot condemns that superstition of the Breton community: 'As if there were such things as ghosts! Bah! It took an old African soldier to show those clodhoppers' (Conrad 2012: 72). Anticipating the subsequent tales in the collection, this evocation of the wider experience of Africa and empire acts as a corrective to European traditions, shifting understandings of death from the domain of the supernatural to that of the material and human.

Where do such recurring concerns and images derive from in addition to their general place in the local culture? On 3 July 1896 Conrad told Unwin that he had met 'the local poet … who bestowed upon me three volumes of his immortal works'. This was Charles le Goffic, who was 'going to impart to me some Breton documents – I don't know of what nature. Still there may be something in them' (Conrad 1983: 290). Le Goffic was one of the most famous nineteenth-century Breton writers, a keen promoter of local heritage, and he later edited an anthology of *Poets of the Sea* in 1928. Richard M. Berrong has examined the parallels between Le Goffic's *Le Crucifié de Keraliès* (1891) and 'Les Sept Innocents de Pleumeur' and 'The Idiots', examining also how some of these elements make their way into stories such as 'An Outpost of Progress' (Berrong 2010). In his later collection *L'Ame Bretonne* (1902), Le Goffic wrote in detail of the celebrated *Grands Calvaires de Bretagne*, stone sculptures of the Crucifixion dotted throughout the landscape, while *Le Crucifié de Keraliès* specifically mentions 'idiots' moving in pilgrimage past these Breton structures. One of the most prolific writers on Breton themes in the late nineteenth century was the poet and folklorist Anatole Le Braz. Amongst many other works, his *La Légende de la mort en Basse-Bretagne, croyance, traditions, et usages des Bretons Armoricains* (1893) discusses the prevalence of the skeletal image of death in Brittany and other local legends. In 1898 an English translation of Le Braz's work appeared, entitled *Dealings with the Dead*. The preface by A. N. Whitehead noted, 'The tenderness felt by Bretons for the dead, – above all, for the drowned, whether of their own or any other land or nation, – was not long since signally and most touchingly exhibited, when the steamship *Drummond Castle* foundered on their coast' (Le Braz 1898: 19). According to Le Braz, one of the *intersignes* or harbingers that announces impending death in Breton culture is 'when dogs howl in the night, meaning that death is approaching' (Le Braz 1893: 7). In 'The Idiots', prior to the mortal afflictions that unfold, Jean-Pierre challenges the Gods by the graveyard at the gate of the church. As they drive home through the night, the 'country rang clamorous in the night with the irritated barking of farm dogs, that followed the rattle of the wheels all along the road' (Conrad 2012: 63). Le Braz also collected tales of 'Violent Deaths: Drowning and Hanging' (Le Braz 1893), offering a Breton precursor to the cards of Madame Sosostris in *The Waste Land*, evoking the literal and figurative hangings and drownings that mark the fate of Conrad's characters in *Tales of Unrest*.

Conrad's engagement with Breton culture merges with his portrait of the East elsewhere in *Tales of Unrest* to offer an idiosyncratically transnational collection, and the stories as a whole 'share a concern with what the nineteenth-century termed "the primitive", a world-view and psychology (relatively) untouched by modernity and anchored partly in animism and in a heightened emotional awareness and receptivity' (Conrad 2012: xli). In a British and Irish literary context, W. B. Yeats is the best-known purveyor of the other-worldly energies coursing through Celtic folk culture, with characteristic views found in articles such as 'The Broken Gates of Death', which appeared in *The Fortnightly Review* in 1898. The depiction of death and folklore in 'The Idiots' can be read against contested notions in English literary criticism, shaped by Matthew Arnold, that a Celtic Element in writing and thought would spiritualize the body of English literature. As William Atkinson has noted, 'The Idiots' was first published in *The*

Savoy, a publication with decadent associations, and the story can be situated within that magazine's interest in the Celtic fringe, as the 'theme of Celtic decline threads its way through the entire run of *The Savoy*' (Atkinson 2015: 121). In the face of such concerns, Yeats's 'The Celtic Element in Literature' (1898), first published in *Cosmopolis*, which would also see the appearance of 'An Outpost of Progress', forwarded an attachment to a traditional Celtic world 'where anything might flow and change, and become any other thing' (Yeats 1993: 193). Such writing is drawn to 'unbounded and immortal things' (Yeats 1993: 194), and in 'The Idiots' 'the landscape takes on some of the sinister magic' found elsewhere in *The Savoy* (Atkinson 2015: 127), but only as a prelude to disenchantment. Conrad's regionalism suggests death will be victorious in its finality, but unlike the fascination of Yeats with a Celticism that would infuse a problematic modernity with nurturing elements of tradition, Conrad finds a traditionalism that compels only due to its precarity and imminent demise. In this sense, despite Conrad's sense of its derivative and anomalous nature, 'The Idiots' is consistent with the writer's recurring themes in a wider imperial context, depicting 'the anxiety of a pre-modern or not quite-modern society in the face of modernity' (Atkinson 2015: 126).

Death and empire in 'Karain: A Memory'

The transnational connections between both European fringes and imperial margins were not lost on Conrad and other contemporary writers. An introduction to Anatole le Braz's work on death observed that one could find 'very close affinities between the beliefs … documented in Brittany and the animistic ideas of certain remote peoples', establishing an anthropological field of enquiry extending to Celebes and Borneo (Le Braz 1893: xli). In *Tales of Unrest*, the Celtic atmosphere of death derived from Brittany spreads to the Malay world of Conrad's experience and memory, making the collection a transnational hybrid of European and Asian currents, an Orientalism channelled through the filter of a marginalized European modernity, that of the Celtic Fringe.

Despite its brevity, V. S. Naipaul noted that 'The Lagoon' has 'a lot of Conrad in it – passion and the abyss, solitude and futility and the world of illusions' (Naipaul 1981: 200). Later parodied by Max Beerbohm in *A Christmas Garland* (1912), and a tale that Conrad himself felt contained 'lots of secondhand Conradese' (Conrad 1983: 301), 'The Lagoon' relies for its unrestful effects on a contrast between an 'immobility perfect and final' (Conrad 2012: 155) in the setting and the disturbance recounted in the narration which deals with betrayal and death. It is a story characterized by both double-crossing and the crossing of mortality, with the narration occurring beside a dying woman who expires at the end of the tale. Preoccupied with 'the wonder of death – of death near, unavoidable, and unseen' (Conrad 2012: 159), Arsat concludes that 'There is no light and no peace in the world ... but there is death ... death for many' (Conrad 2012: 167).

'An Outpost of Progress', the best-known story in *Tales of Unrest*, charts an alienating European encounter with Africa, occurring in sight of the 'dwelling place' of death (Conrad 2012: 204), whose 'grim humour' (Conrad 2012: 78) oversees the cross marking the resting place of the previous imperial administrator. The lethargy of Kayerts and Carlier is contrasted with the 'vibrating brilliance' (Conrad 2012: 82) of the wilderness, and their descent towards violence, breakdown and death is conveyed through a frantic quickening of the story, the 'surprising flash of violent emotion' (Conrad 2012: 94) that takes over events and actions. Exploiting Kayerts and Carlier's growing confusion and ineptitude, Makola arranges a midnight bonfire dance for the workers of the station so that they can be sold off, producing a ritualistic dance of death that echoes the wider atrocities taking place in the name of empire: 'I think you had better give some palm wine to our men to make a dance this evening' (Conrad 2012: 88); and a *danse macabre* occurs as the men are traded for ivory. Later, the *calvaires* of Brittany are impressionistically reconfigured as 'a dark smudge, a cross-shaped stain, upon the shifting purity of the mist' (Conrad 2012: 98), and Kayerts is discovered 'hanging by a leather strap from the cross' (Conrad 2012: 99). Composed amidst the death-filled traditions of Brittany, and constituting an exercise in sustained Flaubertian irony, the story dredges up Conrad's dark encounter with the dance of empire in his journey to Africa in 1890. Writing to T. Fisher Unwin about 'An Outpost of Progress', Conrad said, 'All the bitterness of those days, all my puzzled wonder as to the meaning of all I saw – all my indignation at masquerading philanthropy – have been with me again while I wrote' (Conrad 1983: 294).

While often regarded as Conrad's most unrepresentative story, Alvin Hervey's deliberations in 'The Return' occur in the death-like and Dantesque city of London, reflecting the monstrous, brooding gloom of 'Heart of Darkness', with the narrator imagining 'a silent flood, as though the great night of the world had broken through' (Conrad 2012: 148). In particular, women become an originating source of anxiety, and Henry Staten has discussed how in the story 'the darkness of the heart and the horror of the existential abyss are probed strictly in relation to an anxiety and a need that the protagonist feels in relation to a woman' (Staten 1995: 141), with 'The Return' presenting a 'domestic and eroticized version' of 'Heart of Darkness' (Staten 1995: 140). Death is evoked from the beginning, as the passengers walk 'with the hurried air of men fleeing from something compromising; from something suspected and concealed … like truth or pestilence' (Conrad 2012: 103). Hervey is later consumed by 'thoughts he had never had before; thoughts disintegrating, tormenting, sapping to the very core of life – like mortal disease; thoughts that bred the fear of air, of sunshine, of men – like the whispered news of pestilence' (Conrad 2012: 142). Conrad's pestilential imagery, of course, famously extends to 'Heart of Darkness' to describe the 'moribund shapes' of the dying Congolese in the 'Grove of Death' as 'some picture of a massacre or a pestilence' (Conrad 1903: 75, 76), where, as Andrew Purssell has observed, 'if colonialism is to be compared with Nature, it is as a kind of disease' (2020: 359).

Alongside 'An Outpost of Progress', 'Karain: A Memory' is the most accomplished tale in the collection and reveals Conrad's stylistic development in retrospection and frame narration, techniques that presage the appearance of Marlow in 'Youth', 'Heart of Darkness' and *Lord Jim*. At the same time, the story is acutely concerned with transnational exchanges and (mis)understandings. As a Malay story that draws on various traditions of empire writing, 'Karain' 'turns popular material against the assumptions of the genre' (GoGwilt 1995: 44), and the premise of 'Karain' initially echoes aspects of Rudyard Kipling's *Barrack-Room Ballads* (1892) in presenting a striking figure from the East, such as Gunga Din, as an object of scrutiny and contested meanings. As with 'The Lagoon', it is a story of death and memory, intricately linking a British culture of mourning embodied in Queen Victoria to the world of Karain and his troubled past (Adams 2001). Karain speaks 'nonchalantly of life and death' (Conrad 2012: 14), and in his pomp he sees himself as the owner of his splendid land, evoking Holbein's privileged figures shadowed by mortality. Conrad introduces the image of the constant companion, presented in an enigmatic and macabre register throughout: 'There was indeed always one near him, though our informants had no conception of that watcher's strength and weapons, which were both shadowy and terrible' (Conrad 2012: 18). Karain's world, like a woodcut or painting, mirrors 'the suspicious immobility of a painted scene' (Conrad 2012: 16). The presence of the sword-bearer who keeps Karain's past at bay weds the iconography of the dance of death to cultural recollections of a Faustian bargain with summoned forces: 'The old fellow, impenetrable and weary, was always there. He shared his food, his repose, and his thoughts; he knew his plans, guarded his secrets' (Conrad 2012: 19).

Death and the diabolic abound in the story as a means of conventionally setting an exotic East against the seemingly rational scrutiny of the West; although, in a foreshadowing of the tale's coda on the Strand in London, these elements become conflated and confused as the story unfolds, illustrating the complexity of transnational encounters and imperial hermeneutics. The phantasmagorical landscape of the story features 'strange stone idols – carved images of devils with many arms and legs, with snakes twined around their bodies, with twenty heads a holding a hundred swords' (Conrad 2012: 32). Likewise, Karain's obsession with the past manifests itself in language that recalls the dance of death. After the unexplained death of the sword-bearer, Karain appears 'looking over his shoulder, like a man pursued' (Conrad 2012: 25). Later, the otherwise protected space of ship's cabin, where 'the firm, pulsating beat of the two ships chronometers ticking off steadily the seconds of Greenwich Mean Time' are 'a protection and a relief' (Conrad 2012: 38), harbours a macabre tableau: 'Hollis, stripped to the waist, lay stretched out on the lockers, with closed eyes and motionless like a despoiled corpse' (Conrad 2012: 25), and, indeed, Hollis ultimately emerges as an ambiguous preserver and destroyer of sustaining illusions to both Karain and his shipmates. Karain is a 'fugitive' (Conrad 2012: 27), one who comes to resemble a skeleton:

> His cheeks were hollow, his eyes sunk, the muscles of his chest and arms twitched slightly as if after an exhausting contest ... but his face showed another kind of fatigue, the tormented weariness, the anger and the fear of a struggle against a thought, an idea – against something that cannot be grappled, that never rests – a shadow, a nothing, unconquerable and immortal, that preys upon life. (Conrad 2012: 27)

Not surprisingly, the narrator feels that he, Jackson and Hollis have 'been called to the very gate of infernal regions' (Conrad 2012: 41). Indeed, for David Adams, Karain' is about 'the problem of forgetfulness, of silencing the voices of the unrestful, unplacated dead', with Karain embodying 'an impoverished Odysseus: he lacks the means to exploit—or simply to control and contain—the dead' (Adams 2001: 728, 729).

'Karain' captures elements of Conrad's liminal style, as he explores two worlds, 'one open and without belief, one closed and ruled by old magic', with Conrad's remote locations places that 'continuously made and unmade themselves' (Naipaul 1981: 201, 208). In its intricate use of the language, symbols, and tropes of empire, 'Karain' contains the seeds of what has been termed a 'geopolitic of knowledge' emerging 'from the wounds of colonial histories, memories and experiences' (Mignolo 2012: 37). The story is a product of 'the sense of the marvellous' (Greenblatt 1991: 73) that characterized early European colonial encounters and the disenchantment central to the later production of the idea of the West (GoGwilt 1995). Key to this is the meeting between the imagined wonders of the East, in both cultural and monetary terms, and the contents of the individual archives of the West, which when opened momentarily summon 'all the homeless ghosts of an unbelieving world' (Conrad 2012: 44). Once these ghosts have vanished, Hollis's box acts as a demystified archive of modernity, with its various cheap but emotionally resonant contents shaping the fluctuating sense of value found in the story. If 'classification is indispensable to the ideology' (Spurr 1993: 69) of empire and colonization, then Hollis's collection, and the ideological project of which it is a personal manifestation, is a bric-a-brac of disparate objects rather than the unified body of knowledge sought by imperial taxonomies:

> There were there a couple of reels of cotton, a packet of needles, a bit of silk ribbon, dark blue; a cabinet photograph, at which Hollis stole a glance before laying it on the table face downwards. A girl's portrait, I could see. There were, amongst a lot of various small objects, a bunch of flowers, a narrow white glove with many buttons, a slim packet of letters carefully tied up. Amulets of white men! Charms and talismans! Charms that keep them straight, that drive them crooked, that have the power to make a young man sigh, an old man smile. Potent things that procure dreams of joy, thoughts of regret; that soften hard hearts, and can temper a soft one to the hardness of steel. Gifts of heaven – things of earth. (Conrad 2012: 43)

Selected from this repository is, of course, one potent symbol: a Victorian Golden Jubilee Sixpence minted in 1887, bequeathed to Karain to ward off the ghosts of his past, but inviting associations of fraud, deception and inflated value (Adams 2001). The likely mutations of the 'gilt' sixpence infuse the story with an awareness of the protean nature of currency and exchange, both monetary and cultural. As Andrew Purssell has noted, 'the course traced by the sixpence offers an ironic reversal of the conventional trajectory of a European modernism which searches through the symbolic systems of other cultures to find alternative meaning and value' (Purssell 2020: 366). Karain's acquisition of the coin marks his 'moment of entry into the symbolic world of Empire' (GoGwilt 1995: 61), and its effect is to render Karain 'the incarnation of the very essence of still excitement' (Conrad 2012: 45); passively engaged, but latent with other responses, something borne out in renewed political activity by Karain's people at the end of the story. Indeed, the meeting of the exotic and the imperial, and the enacted shifting meanings of objects and symbols observed at the climax of the story, demonstrates, as Michael Levenson has argued, that the culture reflected and produced in modernism 'was not a collision between novelty and tradition, but a *contest of novelties*, a struggle to define the trajectory of the new' (Levenson 2011: 5).

Despite the atmosphere of obscure imperial intrigue integral to the othering processes of colonial fiction, 'Karain' also possesses a transparent fascination with power and celebrity found elsewhere in late-nineteenth-century literature. Karain is 'insatiable of details' (Conrad 2012: 19) of Queen Victoria, and, in some respects, he is an unlikely brother to a figure in American writer Sarah Orne Jewett's 'The Queen's Twin' (1899), in which an elderly New England widow believes herself to be Queen Victoria's sister, thereby engaging in a trans-Atlantic obsession with the correspondences between her own life and that of Karain's 'Great Queen' (Conrad 2012: 44). As in 'Karain', time and its sonic register effect a curious montage of modernity, where in the presence of 'a loud-ticking clock' the narrator observes 'an early newspaper portrait of Her Majesty the Queen of Great Britain and Ireland. On a shelf below were some flowers in a little glass dish, as if they were put before a shrine' (Orne Jewett 1899: 30). Juxtaposing the two tales establishes Karain as already 'one of us', readily experiencing global culture and its conventional politico-cultural distractions by way of various circulating media. Of course, despite the exotic meeting of cultures that forms the centrepiece of Conrad's story, the assuaging of Karain's anxiety through the object of the coin is no more fantastic than the unrestful quests of capital that take place around him and which drive the endeavours of the narrator and his fellow seamen. 'Karain' reveals that the links between primitive fetishism and capitalist fetishism are strikingly close. As Michael T. Taussig has observed, 'the mystery of capitalist economic growth and accumulation of capital' is achieved in the way in which 'An inert medium of exchange becomes a self-breeding quantity, and in this sense becomes a fetish – a thing with lifelike powers' (Taussig 1980: 128). Indeed, in 'An Outpost of Progress' the 'storehouse was in every station called the fetish, perhaps because of the spirit of civilization it contained' (Conrad 2012: 82). In 'Karain', Victoria 'commands a spirit, too—the spirit of her nation; a masterful, conscientious, unscrupulous, unconquerable devil' (Conrad 2012: 44); an unrestful spirit that will dazzle the 'startled, never-resting eyes' (Conrad 2012: 81) of those who fail to submit to its workings, but equally those who conspire in its operations.

With the chronometers that accompany the narrative, one important encounter in 'Karain' is between what Claude Lévi-Strauss has labelled the 'domesticated' history of the West and the fluid temporal categories of Karain's 'primitive' imagination. The narrator seeks to 'enlighten' the chief, but 'attempts to make clear the irresistible nature of the forces which he desired to arrest failed to discourage his eagerness to strike a blow for his own primitive ideas' (Conrad 2012: 23). As Simmons and Stape note, 'Karain' imaginatively yet accurately captures the persistence of 'a deeply held belief in the supernatural – ghosts, spells, charms, sorcery – and a strongly animistic world-view [which] survived the Islamization of Malay culture and co-existed with it more or less compatibly' (Conrad 2012: xxxvii). In *The Savage Mind*, Lévi-Strauss observed that to the chronological determinations and understandings of modernity the 'characteristic feature of the savage mind is its timelessness; its object is to grasp the world as both a synchronic and a diachronic totality'. If the historical mind of Western culture in 'Karain' is 'concerned with closing gaps and dissolving differences' (Lévi-Strauss 1989: 263) as a homogenizing agent of burgeoning globalization, that of the East and the primitive both preserves and constructs a space for heterogeneous otherness across transnational and transcultural divides. This is captured in the closing coda set in London, where the memory of Karain heightens the sense of alienation at the imperial centre amidst the 'gaudy', 'shabby' and 'dirty' (Conrad 2012: 48) novelties and conventions of the modern urban scene, thereby positing a rejection of the outward manifestation of the same stabilizing signs, figures and culture against which Marlow rails in 'Heart of Darkness'. This element also has its roots in popular imperial writing, such as Kipling's 'Mandalay' (1890), which engenders a provincializing of Eurocentric metropolitanism. Elsewhere, in 'Our Overseas Men' (1892), Kipling wrote that 'There is no provincialism like the provincialism of London .... Look back on her from ten thousand miles, when the mail is just in at the Overseas Club, and she is wondrous tiny. Nine-tenths of her news – so vital, so epoch-making over there – loses its significance, and the rest is as the scuffling of ghosts in a back attic' (Kipling 1920: 49). In effect, the hauntings and unrest of 'Karain' lie in the suggestion that, as Walter Mignolo has observed, 'Western epistemic hegemony has created more problems than solutions' (Mignolo 2012: xxi).

Karain's physical appearance and theatrical demeanour promise 'to awaken an absurd expectation of something heroic going to take place – a burst of action or song' (Conrad 2012: 15), and the same can be said for the project of Empire and its place in contemporary English literature. Heroics, real and imaginary, informed much Victorian empire writing, and the 1890s saw the 'irreverent West' (Conrad 2012: 15) as reverent as ever on the subject of expansion and dominion. If, as discussed, a medieval and renaissance strand from the *danse macabre* colours

Tales of Unrest in the context of death, a retrospective Elizabethan strand makes its presence felt through a subtle consciousness of Victorian imperial nostalgia. This appears from the outset in the epigraph from *II Henry 4th*: 'Be it thy course to busy giddy minds/With foreign quarrels', in which overseas adventures are promoted as a means of distraction from domestic political scrutiny. *Tales of Unrest* also registers topical political developments relating to Spanish imperial control in the Philippines, something captured in the story's reference to 'moribund Spanish gun-boats' and the fact that the distant news of an uprising in Karain's lands will 'make it hot for the *caballeros*' (Conrad 2012: 15, 47). If the semantically charged Jubilee Sixpence and its enabling power on Karain serve as a qualified reminder of the zenith of one imperial power, Britain, it also later participates in the death throes of another, Spain. In Victorian writing there is an awareness of the long decline and impending end of Spanish imperialism (something effected by the Spanish-American War of 1898), a triumphalism that is registered through a turn to British, and especially Elizabethan history. 'Karain' is contemporary with Henry Newbolt's *Admirals All* (1897), which explored the exploits of the Elizabethan age, and, in particular, his popular 'Drake's Drum', which cultivated the legend of a drum belonging to the famous privateer that would sound in Cornwall in times of national need. Writing of 'Drake's Drum', Newbolt later proudly asserted that 'I did give my Country a Legend of real value' (Newbolt 1942: 224), providing British imperialism with a literary charm akin to the sustaining value of Karain's coin. Such late-Victorian texts continued the Elizabethan nostalgia of J. A. Froude's 'England's Forgotten Worthies' (1852), Charles Kingsley's *Westward Ho!* (1855) and John Everett Millais's *The Boyhood of Raleigh* (1870). Conrad ironically draws on this rhetoric in 'Heart of Darkness', linking the Elizabethan world of Drake to the nineteenth century of Franklin, ambiguously conjuring the spell of history by invoking men and ships 'whose names are like jewels flashing in the night of time' (Conrad 1903: 53), but whose romantic aura masks both piratic plunder and exploratory extinction. Such texts reveal anxieties about the course of empire through a fascination with figures that initiated its rise and furthered its reach, harbouring an unspoken unrest about the destiny of imperial power, one later vocalized in Kipling's 'Recessional' (1897).

Conrad's early work gestures towards reassuring imperial dreams while revealing the strife and unrest of imperial nightmares. 'Karain' concludes in the company of death's 'perfect and severe' agents outside Bland's firearms store on the Strand, 'amongst the dark and polished tubes that can cure so many illusions' (Conrad 2012: 47); the rifles that will fire into the bush in 'Heart of Darkness', thereby echoing Sir Walter Raleigh's words on the power of the executioner's axe: 'This is a sharp and fair medicine to cure all my diseases' (Waldman 1950: 236). *Tales of Unrest* explores the tensions of life lived in the shadow of empire and death from Brittany to Borneo, with unrest the animating force behind the people and politics of Conrad's transnational fiction. At the opening of the *Confessions*, St. Augustine states that hearts find no 'peace until they rest' in God (Augustine 1961: 21). In turn, Conrad's preface to *The Nigger of the 'Narcissus'*, a tale of the death of James Wait composed in the wake of the stories that comprise *Tales of Unrest*, asserts that, if successfully accomplished, an artist's work might contain 'all the truth of life', including 'the return to an eternal rest' (Conrad 1926: xvi). The artist purportedly embraces the subject of death in the context of rest and repose, but throughout Conrad's fiction death is stripped of comfort and other-worldliness. Instead, through its constant shadow and intrusions into individual lives and imperial polities, it is intertwined with the transnational cultural, political and economic forces shaping the modern world.

Works Cited

Adams, D. (2001), '"Remorse and Power": Conrad's Karain and the Queen', *Modern Fiction Studies*, 47 (4): 723–52.

Atkinson, W. (2015), '"The Idiots" in *The Savoy*: Decadence and the Celtic Fringe', *Conradiana*, 47 (2): 113–31.

Augustine (1961), *Confessions*, trans. R. S. Pine-Coffin, London: Penguin.

Baedeker, K. (1894), *Northern France from Belgium and the English Channel to the Loire, Excluding Paris and Its Environs, etc*, Leipsic: Karl Baedeker.

Berrong, R. M. (2010), 'The Revenge of the Raped Woman: "The Idiots" and Charles Le Goffic's *Le Crucifié de Keraliès*', *The Conradian*, 35 (2): 117–20.

Boston Evening Transcript (1898), 30 April: 18.

Conrad, J. (1903), *Youth and Two Other Stories*, New York: Grosset and Dunlap.

Conrad, J. (1926), *The Nigger of the 'Narcissus: 'A Tale of the Sea*, New York: Doubleday, Page & Company.

Conrad, J. (1983), *The Collected Letters of Joseph Conrad, Volume 1, 1861–1897*, ed. F. R. Karl and L. Davies, Cambridge: Cambridge University Press.

Conrad, J. (1984), *Nostromo: A Tale of the Seaboard*, ed. K. Carabine, Oxford: Oxford University Press.

Conrad, J. (1988), *The Collected Letters of Joseph Conrad, Volume 3, 1903–1907*, ed. F. R. Karl and L. Davies, Cambridge: Cambridge University Press.

Conrad, J. (2012), *Tales of Unrest*, ed. A. H. Simmons and J. H. Stape, Cambridge: Cambridge University Press.

DeKoven, M. (1997), 'Conrad's Unrest', *Journal of Modern Literature*, 21 (2): 241–9.

Dickens, C. (1857), *Little Dorrit*, London: Bradbury & Evans.

Dickens, C. (1870), *The Mystery of Edwin Drood*, London: Chapman and Hall.

GoGwilt, C. (1995), *The Invention of the West: Joseph Conrad and the Double-Mapping of Europe and Empire*, Stanford: Stanford University Press.

Greenblatt, S. (1991), *Marvellous Possessions: The Wonder of the New World*, Chicago: University of Chicago Press.

Hollington, M. (1978), 'Dickens and the Dance of Death', *The Dickensian*, 74 (2): 67–75.

Jasanoff, M. (2017), *The Dawn Watch: Joseph Conrad in a Global World*, London: William Collins.

Kipling, R. (1920), *Letters of Travel (1892–1913)*, London: Macmillan.

Le Braz, A. (1893), *La Légende de la mort en Basse-Bretagne, croyance, traditions, et usages des Bretons Armoricains*, Paris: Honoré Champion.

Le Braz, A. (1898), *Dealings with the Dead: Narratives from 'La Légende de la Mort en Basse Bretage'*, trans. A. E. Whitehead, London: George Redway.

Levenson, M. (2011), *Modernism*, New Haven, CT: Yale University Press.

Lévi-Strauss, C. (1989), *The Savage Mind*, London: Weidenfeld and Nicholson.

McManners, J. (1985), *Death and the Enlightenment: Changing Attitudes to Death in Eighteenth-Century France*, Oxford: Oxford University Press.

Mignolo, W. D. (2012), *Local Histories/Global Designs: Coloniality, Subaltern Knowledges, and Border Thinking*, Princeton: Princeton University Press.

Naipaul, V. S. (1981), *The Return of Eva Peron*, London: Penguin.

Newbolt, H. (1942), *The Later Life and Letters of Sir Henry Newbolt*, ed. M. Newbolt, London: Faber & Faber.

Orne Jewett, S. (1899), *The Queen's Twin and Other Stories*, New York: Houghton, Mifflin and Company.

Purssell, A. (2020), 'Empire and Modernism in Joseph Conrad's "Karain: A Memory"', *The Review of English Studies*, New Series, 71 (299): 355–69.

Spurr, D. (1993), *The Rhetoric of Empire: Colonial Discourse in Journalism, Travel Writing, and Imperial Administration*, Durham, NC: Duke University Press.

Staten, H. (1995), *Eros in Mourning: Homer to Lacan*, London: Johns Hopkins University Press.

Taussig, M. T. (1980), *The Devil and Commodity Fetishism in South America*, Chapel Hill: University of North Carolina Press.

Waldman, M. (1950), *Sir Walter Raleigh*, London: Collins.

Webster Goodwin, S. (1988), *Kitsch and Culture: The Dance of Death in Nineteenth-Century Literature and Graphic Arts*, London: Garland.

Yeats, W. B. (1993), *Writings on Irish Folklore, Legend and Myth*, ed. R. Welch, London: Penguin.

6

'Queer foreign fish': Food and migration in *Almayer's Folly* and *The Secret Agent*

Kim Salmons
St Mary's University, London

Joseph Conrad's migratory experiences – first as the child of political exiles in Russian occupied Ukraine, then as a sailor in the Merchant Navy, and finally as an author of English fiction – can be charted by the food and manners of eating that he has encountered on his travels. As he writes in *A Personal Record*: 'I know the taste of shark, of trepang, of snake, of nondescript dishes containing things without a name' (2008: 234). For Conrad food represents not only a barrier to belonging – Almayer in Conrad's first novel, *Almayer's Folly* (1895) can never adjust to the 'preponderance of rice diet on the family table'[1] – but also as a cross-cultural rite of entry to a new community. In the 'Preface' to his wife Jessie's *A Handbook of Cookery for a Small House* (1923), Conrad emphasizes the role of food in transnational relations, citing good cooking as the common ground between different cultures:

> The intimate influence of conscientious cooking by rendering easy the processes of digestion promotes the serenity of mind, the graciousness of thought, and the indulgent view of our neighbours' failings which is the only genuine form of optimism. (vi)

Conrad was the living embodiment of transnationalism as seen through his food preferences: despite his Polish heritage, his favourite food was the British version of macaroni cheese as cooked by his wife, a dish that originated in Italy in the thirteenth century. Notably, Jessie's recipes cross and intermix cultural boundaries with her version of 'Risotto' made from Indian 'Patna rice' (48, 49). These Conradian culinary crossings inform both our understanding of the author and the place of food in the gustatory experience of his migrant characters through the assimilation and adaptation of ingredients and recipes.

For Conrad food also represents home. His first piece of recorded writing was on the verso of his photograph as a six-year-old: 'To my dear Granny who helped me send pastries to my poor Daddy in prison – grandson, Pole-Catholic and szlachcic' (Najder 2007: 22). This culinary offering to his father Apollo, a political prisoner in Warsaw during the early 1860s and at a time when Poland was partitioned between Russia, Germany and Austria, establishes the connection between food, home, nationality, religion and class. Conrad's pastries – small pieces of portable food – bring to a space of alienation a taste of the familiar, at the same time reinforcing the aristocratic status of the family name. Despite the nationalist loyalties of his parents, Conrad left his Polish homeland at the age of seventeen and opted for a life at sea in the French and then British Merchant Navy, abandoning his agricultural roots (Conrad's father Apollo, was an estate manager and the Szlachta were landowning aristocrats), but taking with him the reputation of the Szlachcic: 'honourably known in the wide countryside for the delicacy of their tastes in the matter of eating and drinking' (Conrad 2008: 232). This delicacy of taste was borne out in Conrad's later life. In a memoir of her husband, *Joseph Conrad as I Knew Him*, Jessie writes of his culinary sensitivities:

> Once a new maid, unaware of his dislike of having the joint on the dining-table, proudly placed before him half a calf's head. It was quite elegantly prepared, but unfortunately it looked what it was. He gave one disgusted glance at it, promptly reversed his chair, and sat with his back to the dish. (1926: 19)

This aversion is, perhaps, explained in *A Personal Record*, in which Conrad recounts the tale of his Grand Uncle Nicholas B. a Knight of the Legion of Honour in Napoleon's army fighting against the Russians. Separated from his main column, Nicholas Bobrowski, starving and lost, 'chanced upon a "Lithuanian village dog" which, along with two of his fellow officers', he 'decapitated, skinned, cooked and devoured' (Salmons 2017: 2). Conrad, writing in *A Personal Record*, recalls the moment after his grandmother told him this story:

> A silence in which a small boy shudders and says firmly:
> 'I could not have eaten that dog.'
> And his grandmother remarks with a smile:
> 'Perhaps you don't know what it is to be hungry.' (Conrad 2008: 234)

I have previously claimed that the story combines the 'human survival instinct' with 'patriotic fervour' (Salmons 2017: 3), but Conrad's reaction communicates the fascination and disgust of a small boy who listens to a tale about a Polish nationalist eating not only an animal that is not commonly considered food for

Europeans, but an unhealthy-looking specimen of a Russian occupied nation. This inability to accept – both physically and psychologically – a food that is representative of the other, is a theme that I want to investigate in this chapter, from both the point of view of the colonizer in the East, and the immigrant food that is introduced to Britain – primarily London – at the end of the nineteenth century. My argument is that food acts predominantly as a barrier to belonging between nations and as a point of fascination and appropriation for the dominant culture.

The word 'miscegenation', coined in 1863 by the American journalist David Goodman Croly,[2] originally described interracial marriage, but has latterly been used to depict the metaphorical act of 'eating the other', a metaphor more recently employed by modernist and postcolonial writers such as bell hooks (*sic*), who in her 1992 essay, 'Eating the Other', describes the commodification and resulting consumption of the other as a 'spice that can liven up the dull dish that is mainstream white culture' (366). hook's use of the word 'spice' not only points to obvious sexual phraseology, but references the West's desire for the condiments of the East and the resulting lucrative trade.[3] More importantly, however, it embodies the argument of this chapter that when immigrant and native food is mixed, a more culturally acceptable hybrid is born. That 'miscegenation' took on negative overtones was partly down to the underlying political intentions of Croly in which he advocated for a new world based on interracial marriage, a political ploy that intentionally incited the alarm of the white working class in America to turn them against the Republican Party.[4] Before Croly's intentionally problematic terminology was adopted, interracial marriage was previously referred to as an 'amalgamation', a process of combining or uniting. The latter has more positive overtones, whereas 'miscegenation' suggests a contamination and an element of disgust. This is important when considering native food and the experience of the colonial migrant in Conrad's Malay novel, *Almayer's Folly* and when considering immigrant food in *The Secret Agent* (1907). The first demonstrates the cultural inability of the European – albeit in Almayer's case a second-generation European – to adapt to the local diet as a means of sustenance or wealth, fearing contamination and a dilution of identity; while in *The Secret Agent* migrant food goes through a process of adaptation to make it more palatable to European tastes, but in so doing becomes an inauthentic commodity. In both instances, food and foodways create barriers to belonging.

This argument could be extended to include Conrad's African fiction in which he recreates with irony the inability of the European colonizer to either provide for themselves, or physically withstand the local diet. In 'An Outpost of Progress' (1898), the two hapless white colonials, Kayerts and Carlier, left in charge of a Central African trading station, rely on the 'goodwill' of the local chief Gobila, whose villagers bring every morning, 'fowls, and sweet potatoes, and palm wine, and sometimes a goat' because 'the Company never provisions the stations fully' (Conrad 1945b: 96). But after losing that 'goodwill' through a wilful inability to understand the culture they inhabit, Kayerts and Carlier find themselves existing merely on 'rice boiled without salt … One must have lived on such diet to discover what ghastly trouble the necessity of swallowing one's food may become' (109). Alienated from the natives and unable to provide for themselves they engage in a fight to the death over 'the last fifteen lumps' of sugar (109). Interestingly, the 'ten station men' from a distant tribe who are employed by the Company also sicken under the rice rations, 'a food unknown to their land, and to which they could not get used'. These Africans become 'unhealthy and miserable', but 'belonging as they did, to a warlike tribe with filed teeth, they had more grit, and went on stupidly living through disease and sorrow. They did very little work, and had lost their splendid physique' (100). Similarly, in *Heart of Darkness* (1899) the Western constitution is no match for the native diet. As the station manager asserts, 'Men who come out here should have no entrails' (Conrad 1967: 74). The incompatibility of cross-cultural diets is further explored when in the same novel the native workers are 'fed on unfamiliar food', sicken and die (66).

Food in Conrad's colonial novels does not simply equate with nourishment or act as a rite of entry into a host culture, but instead can create a barrier to belonging. However, in his political novels, food is not so much a material obstruction to assimilation, but a metaphorical and psychological one. In *The Secret Agent*, food establishes a migrant narrative that speaks to emerging globalization, heterogeneity and the commodification of food – not least the 'foreign preserved milk firm' where Stevie works as an office boy – that represents the ideological tensions created by an immigrant population to London while anticipating the urban dietary melting pot. Where the cultural divide in *Almayer's Folly* is embedded in food, creating barriers to assimilation, in *The Secret Agent*, food as a rite of entry can only be – at least at first glance – on the terms of the host culture with the migrant going through a process of adaptation. However, this adaptation creates a paradox in that migrant food loses its authenticity, creating a tension between fraudulence and hybridity. Any attempt to retain authenticity is met with resistance through the English inability to overcome inherently negative responses to the unfamiliar. The aim of this chapter is to explore the colonial migrant experience in a non-European and European context through the commodification of food and ways of eating. This will be done by focusing on two foodstuffs, Trepang and birds' nests – as portrayed in *Almayer's Folly* – to argue that both Almayer and Lingard fail because they do not value the culture in which they reside. I will then link these foods to their cultural significance and economic value in the London of *The Secret Agent*. This will provide the backdrop for a wider discussion about the representation of immigrants in the capital through their national food, and the tensions that exist around hybridity, adaptation and assimilation embodied in the figure of Conrad's Assistant Commissioner.

The European in the east

Conrad's first novel *Almayer's Folly* recounts the story of a white man fated to exist in a state of cultural limbo. Born of Dutch parentage in Batavia, Kaspar Almayer belongs neither to his European heritage nor to his birthplace of Java or to the place where he has resided for the last twenty years, Sambir. As Andrew Francis in Chapter 8 of this volume affirms, '[i]t is a function of Almayer's failure to exist transnationally that he is denied a true place in the community he has supposedly adopted' (146). Rather than accept his transnational status, Almayer asserts his identity as a 'white man', refusing to adjust to the rhythms and traditions of his Malay surroundings – a multicultural domain that finds common ground in the cultivation of wet rice, a crop introduced to Malaysia by Sumatran immigrants during the 1600s and which in its production and harvest demands communal cooperation rather than individualistic labour. Food cultivation for Malays was very much a transnational cooperative endeavour and personal gain was not encouraged (Jackson 1972: 79). The Sambir of Conrad's novel is an exemplar of transnationalism – albeit not always a harmonious one[5] – through its mix of Arab, Chinese, Sulu, Bugis, Siamese and Balinese occupants or traders, but with rice as the common denominator. This foodstuff formed a cross-cultural bridge of communication, acting not only as a metronome for the rhythm of daily life but also as a form of currency as demonstrated by the benevolent Morrison in *Victory* (1915) who supplies the hungry upriver communities of Timor with rice. However, to focus on rice as the only food of cross-cultural and transnational importance in the novel is as short-sighted as Almayer's inability to understand or appreciate the culture of the archipelago into which he was born. The foodstuffs that overwhelmingly represent the economy, physical and cultural rites of entry, and barriers to belonging and which play a small but significant role in this novel, are that of Trepang (sea cucumbers or otherwise known as sea slugs) and birds' nests.

Trepang are echinoderms that feed on aquatic animals and come in various shapes, sizes and colours, growing up to three feet long. When attacked they can change their shape and, depending on the environment in which they are cultured, they can change their colour too. The Chinese call them 'seamen' because they are shaped like a penis and have 'invigorating qualities'. During the Qing Dynasty (1644–1911), Trepang was much sought after and a substantial trade took place between Xiyang and Macassar, the town in which Hudig has his warehouse and where Almayer works as a young man (Dai Yifeng 2002: 31). Birds' nests are made from the saliva of the Swift and when placed in hot water dissolve and can be eaten as soup. Neither trepang nor birds' nests have much taste, but both are highly valuable food commodities which the Chinese believe have medical, aphrodisiacal and rejuvenating properties. Since the Tang Dynasty of 618–907 AD, there has been a prosperous trade in birds' nests between China and the Idahan tribe of Eastern Borneo (Ismael 2002: 45). The villages of the Idahan include Madai, Baturung, Segarong and Tepadung, all locations around the Berau River, which, as critics of Conrad have confirmed, is the 'real life source' for Conrad's Pantai River and the settlement near and around Sambir (Berthoud 1992: xi). The Idahan – like most Malays – had no interest in consuming birds' nests themselves but understood the cultural value to the Chinese: 'According to the Idahan, upon realising that the Chinese had a keen interest in the nests, their ancestors were cautious not to disclose the exact locations of the nesting caves, but rather assured them of a continuous supply if the Chinese agreed to wait on the coast' (Dai Yifeng 2002: 45). The location of these caves, plus the right to trade in birds' nests, was inherited, passed down through families and, as James F. Warren has shown in his extensive study of Sino-Sulu trade, birds' nests realized a gain of 90 to 100 per cent when sold and became comparatively more valuable than gold (Warren 1977: 55).

Birds' nests are first mentioned in Chapter One of *Almayer's Folly* when the reader is introduced to Lingard's secret river: 'Many tried to follow him and find that land of plenty for gutta-percha and rattans, pearl shells and birds' nests, wax and gum-dammar' (Conrad 1945a: 8). These are the waters from which 'Lingard came and went on his secret or open expeditions, becoming a hero in Almayer's eyes by the boldness and enormous profits of his ventures' (8). In addition, Lingard's encounter with the Sulu pirate ship from which he kidnaps the Sulu child – later to become Mrs Almayer – suggests he is trading in waters controlled by the Sulu Sultanate that used slaves to collect birds' nests that were duly traded with China (Jun 2010: 151). It is likely that the young Mrs Almayer might also have known the location of the caves in which birds' nests were harvested. Almayer too could have known about these locations having been on 'long cruises' with Lingard 'when he was wont to visit almost every island in the archipelago' (Conrad 1945a: 9). Although 'trepang' is not mentioned in this first reference to the 'secret river' this area, known as the Spermode Archipelago, near Macassar was home to the shallow coastal waters where the most expensive of the trepang species, the 'Trepang Pasir' could be harvested (Jun 2010). However, Lingard's successful enterprise in local food is soon replaced by 'new combinations that were in the future to bring profits bigger still' (Conrad 1945a: 9). When he leaves to pursue his 'mysterious work which was only spoken of in hints, but was understood to relate to gold and diamonds in the interior of the island', no mention is made of birds' nests or trepang, instead he goes to seek the 'Gunong Mas – the mountain of gold' (82).

The question therefore becomes why Lingard and Almayer do not continue the trade in these valuable foodstuffs. Possibly 'escaped dangers' (Conrad 1945a: 9) (a reference perhaps to encounters with Sulu Pirates) were too much for the ageing Rajah Laut, although the harvesting of trepang would have been far more in keeping with his title of 'King of the Sea' (24). As Berthoud has noted, there was a 'speculative boom' in gold in Borneo at the end of the nineteenth century driven by Europeans, but for the local people these were 'always more important in legend than in fact' (1992: 219, n. 24). This is supported in the novel: 'The coast population of Borneo believes implicitly in diamonds of fabulous value, in gold mines of enormous richness in the interior' (Conrad 1945a: 39) with 'implicitly' being the operative word, suggesting the mythological rather than the factual. But Lingard's pursuit of 'gold and diamonds' fit comfortably and culturally with Almayer's dreams of a 'future' which 'gleamed like a fairy palace' (10), in a way in which the unappetizing trepang and birds' nests do not. This is demonstrated when Dain arrives at Almayer's kampong and afterwards when questioned by his wife, Almayer claims the Bali Prince was wanting to 'collect Trepang and birds' nests on the islands'. But Almayer tells Dain, 'You have come to the wrong house, Tuan Maroola, if you want to trade as you say. I was a trader once, not now, whatever you may have heard about me in Macassar' (52). Having lost his monopoly in the trade, Almayer tells Dain to try the Rajah or the Arabs: 'Abdulla is the man you want. There is nothing he would not buy, and there is nothing he would not sell; believe me, I know him well' (52). Dain could be selling Sulu slaves, much needed in the area for the collection of birds' nests and Trepang – although it later becomes clear that Dain's purpose is to acquire gunpowder –

however, the narration corresponds with Dain's claim: 'He said he was a trader and sold rice. He did not want to buy gutta-percha or beeswax, because he intended to employ his numerous crew in collecting trepang on the coral reefs outside the river, and also in seeking for birds' nests on the mainland. Those two articles he professed himself ready to buy if there were any to be obtained in that way' (Conrad 1945: 57). The point here is that Almayer's psychological investment in Western artefacts – the fairy palace, the gold and diamonds – has replaced the cross-cultural trade in local foodstuffs.

The other explanation for Almayer's lack of interest in Dain's proposal, not ignoring the fact that he has little to trade anyway, is a familial one. His Sulu wife is associated with the trade of trepang and birds' nests and, as we know, Almayer suffers a cultural and sexual aversion to her. On their wedding night he is 'uneasy, a little disgusted and inclined to run away' (Conrad 1945a: 23). Similarly, he assumes that the 'disgust' he feels for the 'preponderance of rice diet on the family table' is also experienced by his mixed-race daughter Nina (31). The association between the sexual disgust Almayer has for Mrs Almayer, and the disgust he has for the local food which taints the 'family table', synchronizes the act of eating with the mixing of blood and therefore his ingestion of the local food brings him racially closer to the natives of Sambir.[6] This is further implied by the aphrodisiac qualities of both birds' nests and trepang. The negativity associated with this 'miscegenation' is emphasized by Conrad's claim in *A Personal Record* that he ate 'foods without a name', combining the exotic with the incomprehensible and rendering Mrs Almayer – who also has no name – as a cultural taboo.

Robert Hampson has shown that readers of *Almayer's Folly* are drawn into a complicity with Almayer, interpreting the novel from a Western perspective. As Hampson suggests, 'the novel's initial emphasis on the savage/civilized binary might perhaps be seen as a strategy directed against the European reader' (2000: 114). Almayer's use of the word 'disgust' reinforces the unfamiliar and undervalued nature of Malay culture such as the 'betel-nut chewing mother', the 'communal cooking pot' and the dilapidation of Almayer's existence signalled by the 'cracked glass tumbler' and significantly the 'tin spoon', a step down from the more valuable Malay spoons fashioned from Mother of Pearl (Conrad 1945a: 16). However, as Hampson has also shown, the perspective shifts and it becomes clear that Conrad is playing a trick on his readers tapping into an inherent Western prejudice. I would argue that the same is true when it comes to the trading of birds' nests and trepang. Conrad's 'nondescript dishes containing things without a name' (Conrad 2008: 234) suggests that the unspeakable is synonymous with the uneatable. For Europeans in the 1800s, Chinese food was considered with some disgust as it included foodstuffs which the West regarded as 'offensive to ingest or which flout ethical … principles' (Bell and Valentine 1997: 220). Even Alfred Russel Wallace described 'tripang' [*sic*] as 'looking like sausages which have been rolled in mud and then thrown up the chimney', claiming the sea creatures held 'no charms for me!' (1869: 79). As such, Almayer's inability to assimilate into the culture of the East through his feelings of disgust, not just for his wife, but for the food that he must eat, is simultaneously experienced by the Western readers of Conrad's fiction, who become vicarious migrants to South East Asia and complicit in the aversion that Almayer has for the society in which he lives.

Food, sex, belonging and economic prosperity sit at the same table in this novel, thus Almayer's decision to resist the rites of entry offered to him by his wife through trade and communal eating relegate him to perpetual exile, from both his European heritage and his host culture. On a broader scale, both Lingard and Almayer fail to capitalize on a transnational monetary system based on foodstuffs. Almayer's insularity, prejudice and determination to protect an abstract European identity – as mythical as the mountain of gold upon which he rests all his hopes – stifle his ability to learn the 'rhetoric and practice of global trade [and] cultural pluralism' (Warren 2010: 3).

Immigrant food in *The Secret Agent*

While Almayer resists and ignores the significant monetary benefits of South East Asian food commodities in the Eastern Borneo of the early 1880s, in London at the 1884 International Health Exhibition, the Victorian food writer Vincent M. Holt was extolling the physical benefits of eating insects and exotic Eastern foods. In his pamphlet entitled *Why Not Eat Insects* (1885) he opens with the lines, 'In entering upon this work I am fully conscious of the difficulty of battling against a long-existed and deep-rooted public prejudice', that of eating sea animals and insects that are not considered 'food' by the West. Despite this, he goes on to write excitedly about witnessing European visitors to the Health Exhibition sampling the culinary delights of South East Asia:

> watching, with wonder, the most refined ladies and gentlemen, in correct evening costume, sitting down to partake of a dinner, whose most attractive items, as shown in the menu, were such objects as bird's [*sic*] nests soup, cuttlefish, sea slugs, and shark's fins for no other reason than that it was the fashion to do so.

> I will venture to say that if it had been previously suggested to those people to have such items included in the menu at a country house they would have expressed disgust at the idea. (*International Health Exhibition Literature*, 1884)

Holt's enthusiasm for foreign and exotic food was not solely based on reasons of health. In his pamphlet he continues: 'the annual value of these nests imported into China and Japan exceeds £200,000. Surely considering the general approbation expressed of this soup at the Health Exhibition, it would pay some enterprising London merchant to import nests into England.' The menu offered at the Health Exhibition is copied out in Holt's pamphlet and describes the sea slugs as 'Biche de Mer a la Matelote Chinoise'.[7] The purpose of adopting the French appeals to discerning diners of this fashionable cuisine,[8] while also creating a transnational space for a sea creature found in the seas of Borneo but prized by the Chinese as a delicacy, now described in a European language. Moreover, the French disguises negative associations with the common slimy, terrestrial mollusc of British gardens.

Unsurprisingly, Holt's argument for the eating of insects failed to catch on in nineteenth-century London, while sea slugs and birds' nests only fleetingly adorned the menus of the city's restaurants. By 1914, it was still possible to enjoy birds' nests or sharks' fins at *The Cathay*, but only on half a day's notice (Panayi 2008: 91). The first Chinese restaurant, named *The Chinese Restaurant*, opened in 1908 in Glasshouse Street, Piccadilly, and the same year Chung Koon opened *Maxims* in Soho. Soon after this came *The Cathay*, also in Glasshouse Street.[9] However, in the 1880s, Chinese immigrants set up small eating houses around the docks catering to sailors, while well-to-do Londoners would have been exposed to Chinese cuisine through temporary eating places such as The Health Exhibition. By 1914, Panayi claims there were nine Chinese restaurants in London. However, *the Times* of 1913 writes of thirty Chinese restaurants operating in London's East End (Assael 2013). Once established, Chinese restaurants did not attempt to cater to the growing immigrant population from the homelands, but instead for the British natives who had a taste for the 'exotic'. Chinese restaurants such as *The Cathay* became westernized, offering dishes that were more suited to local tastes such as chicken and pineapple and bamboo shoots (91), and taking agency in developing hybrid dishes to make a profit. The same was also true of Italian restaurants, including the most famous of its time, *Pagani's* in Great Portland Street, just north of Soho, which opened in 1871 and was described as 'A La Carte Italian'. Despite this, the famous restaurant reviewer Nathanial Newnham-Davies highlights a menu offering typically English and

French food as well as 'Bortsch soup [*sic*] ... the customary Sunday soup at Pagani's' (1899: 299). By the 1880s there were 440 different types of national and international eating establishments in London listed in Kelly's London Trade Directory (Assael 2013: 17). However, the traditional 'Chop House' continued to uphold the characteristics of Englishness with its 'homely character' where 'huge joints of cold roast and boiled meat, bread and half a pint of porter or mid ale in a pewter tankard' could be taken (685). *The Cheshire Cheese* in Fleet Street[10] was one such establishment. This is the place Verloc, who describes himself as 'a natural born British subject', choses to go to 'think about' how to break the news of Stevie's death to Winnie. But despite the claim of 'Englishness', many of these chop houses served dishes such as turtle soup, a testament to the growing transnationalism of the food market diversified by immigrants. Assael claims that these immigrants became more 'visible' due their distinctiveness not just in their appearance and language, but because of 'the smell of their food' (2013: 688). Thus, in *The Secret Agent*, the 'smell of fried fish'[11] that Stevie, Winnie and her mother smell on their way to the new residence in South London would probably have been from Jewish street food sellers. At the beginning of the 1890s, large numbers of Russian and Polish Jews arrived, making their homes in the slums of Soho. Equally, the journey from Soho to Peckham would have taken in the Old Kent Road,[12] 'populous precincts of the working poor' (Assael 2018: 50).

The first identified recipe for the preservation of fish through deep frying with batter was written by the Jewish cookery writer Hannah Glasse in 1781 (Panayi 2014: 20). Up until the 1850s most fish would have been smoked, salted or dried and available only to the wealthy. However, the advent of the railways made fish an affordable meal for the masses of London and, by the end of the nineteenth century, outlets combining fried fish with fried potatoes soon emerged, producing another hybrid, the fish and chip shop. Quickly losing its Jewish culinary provenance, this fast and cheap source of food was established as a great British Institution, which may be one reason why Conrad's Sir Ethelred is intent on getting his Bill through parliament to nationalize the fisheries.

Many of the foreign restaurants of London diversified their cuisine to cater to the myriad tastes of cosmopolitan London, not least those members of the middle classes who served in the colonies. Newnham-Davis, reviewing the Italian restaurant *Romano's* on the Strand, references a 'Malay curry cooked as it is in Malaya and served in a Malay fashion, with sambals and with shining Malayan shell spoons for the rice' (1914: 110). The Assistant Commissioner in *The Secret Agent* is one such colonial who, amidst the cold and wet of London, comfortingly recalls the 'colonial climate' and mentally returns to the world of Alfred Russel Wallace's *The Malay Archipelago* (Conrad 1947: 98, 118). In many respects he serves as an interesting comparator to Almayer: he too feels he does not belong in the place where he resides, but, as a man born in Europe, he longs to return to the East, where he has spent much of his professional life. The Assistant Commissioner straddles both East and West imbricating the orient and the occident. For example, the 'speaking tubes resembling snakes' which are tied to the back of his desk with their 'gaping mouths … ready to bite his elbows' (Conrad 1947: 97) sit comfortably in the headquarters of the Metropolitan Police, the description fusing an oriental king with the man in charge of 'Special Crimes' (117). Similarly, Heat, on entering the commissioner's office, finds his superior posed as if in front of an oriental altar: 'bent over a great table bestrewn with papers, as if worshipping an enormous double inkstand of bronze and crystal' (97). In these instances, the Assistant Commissioner relieves the tension between authenticity and fraudulence, by creating a hybrid space within the Italian restaurant he visits in the novel, an establishment which may be contrasted with the situation described in a column, entitled 'Looker On', featured in the London trade newspaper *Hotel*:

> The London foreign population has its own restaurants … it is a common remark that these restaurants of London are in the hands of foreigners, but strangely enough foreigners in London do not patronize to any great extent those restaurants which the average Londoner regards with the most favour. Instead they go to those 'unpretentious' restaurants where 'the cooking is just as good and everything is just as nice and clean, but the charges are only about a fourth of those the poor deluded native pays'. (16 October 1895 p. 17 in Assael 2013: 688)

Not only does the exclusivity of these restaurants attest to a resistance to the dominant host culture, but the geographical locations were 'known only to a very few Londoners' as if local knowledge and agency are held not with the native, but with the more gastronomically discerning foreigner.

Other Italian restaurants were referred to by magistrates as being run by 'low Italians and foreigners' who used the restaurant business as a 'cover for illegitimate and despicable activities'.[13] Hampson claims the three time periods that span *The Secret Agent* – 'just prior to 1886' at the end of the Fenian bombing campaign; 1894, the date of the Greenwich bombing; and December 1905 to May 1907 'when [Conrad] was writing the novel'[14] – are united in 'the theme of immigration' and the beginning of the 'anti-alienist' movement which started with the *London Evening News* campaign of 1886 against 'The Foreign Flood'

(Hampson 2012: 99). Judith Walkowitz, in her 2012 study of London from the late Victorian era to the First World War,[15] claims there is a relationship between the 'dangerous cosmopolitanism' of Soho's catering industry and the 'adulterated food' that some of these establishments sold. She articulates this as an 'alimentary threat to the body politic' creating a relationship between 'urban danger and hybrid food culture' (in Assael 2013: 704). Conrad sets the scene for such culinary criminality when he has the Assistant Commissioner leave his departmental office where he has observed London 'as if swept clear suddenly by a great flood' and 'as vast as a sea' (Conrad 1947: 100, 102) and descend into the 'slimy aquarium'[16] of the Strand; the watery metaphors enhancing the association between the submerged world of foreigners and undesirables. Entering this murky world, the 'genius of the locality assimilated him', and he becomes a 'queer foreign fish' (Conrad 1947: 147). Although the analogy at first glance appears to reinforce the negative overtones of an immigrant underworld made more dangerous by its ability to seduce the native population through its cooking, the scene in the Italian restaurant undermines these preconceptions. The Assistant Commissioner makes his way to 'one of those traps for the hungry … without air, but with an atmosphere … of fraudulent cookery' where he eats a 'short meal' (148). The restaurant becomes a site of cultural hybridity and foreignness which is simultaneously 'a peculiarly British institution' (149). In other words, Conrad is suggesting that the whole idea of Britishness is fraudulent. He drives this home by asserting that the 'patrons of the place … seemed created for the Italian restaurant, unless the Italian restaurant had been perchance created for them' (149). The result is a cosmopolitan-gastronomy that subverts any attempt at identification or nationalization: 'these people were as denationalized as the dishes set before them' (149). Dining at this inauthentic eating place, the Assistant Commissioner is at leisure to lose his identity: 'he himself had become unplaced' and donning a 'foreign appearance' he experiences a 'pleasurable feeling of independence' (150). The Italian restaurant offers the denationalized Assistant Commissioner freedom in its own denationalization. After eating the meal, the Assistant Commissioner's journey from the Italian restaurant to Brett Street becomes not just a walk through a 'wet London night', but a journey past 'dark mysterious houses, temples of petty commerce … He felt light-hearted, as though he had been ambushed all alone in a jungle many thousands of miles away from departmental desks and official inkstands' (150). Where the Assistant Commissioner had felt like an immigrant in his own country, he now transposes the familiarity of the East on to the London streets through eating a meal that in its inauthenticity strips him of an identity and allows him to perceive the world through a transnational lens. This moment reclaims the experience of the reader, who, like the Assistant Commissioner, is freed from the inherent prejudices of a national identity. The Assistant Commissioner can now live up to his conviction – the conviction of a man whose name we never know – that '[w]e can never cease to be ourselves' (118).

The Secret Agent is a story about 'a complex cultural interaction taking place in the everyday life of the city', a melting pot of nationalities and ethnicities in which the existence of 'Englishness' is questioned (Young 2006: 2). The 1906 'Alien's Act' attempted to prevent the influx to Britain of Italians, Germans, Jews and Chinese, but the popularity of their food with the native population created a paradox with the emergence of London's Chinatown established around Limehouse in the 1880s with its grocery stores and 'cheap and cheerful cafes' offering favourites such as 'sweet and sour pork' and chop suey. The immigrant enters the metropolitan world through adaptation, assimilation and the fusing and adjusting of food to carve out a hybrid space, while at the same time maintaining – albeit secretly – an authentic identity. As Assael has shown, foreign restaurants preserved their culture by withholding knowledge to the native population of their 'secret' establishments. However, they were also able to develop establishments that catered to the native population, removing – or disguising – those items of food that excited disgust. While the 'Alien's Act' attempted to prevent the entry of Jews, Italians and Chinese immigrants, their food culture thrived by creating 'British Institutions', not least the quintessentially English Lyons's tea house, set up by J. S. Lyons, a German Jewish immigrant (Assael 2013); and Tesco, founded in 1919 by Jack Cohen, a Jewish immigrant who ran a small grocery stall in East London. The assimilation of these establishments into the British national psyche has ensured all knowledge of their foreign history has conveniently been forgotten.

Conclusion

An exploration of migrant food in *Almayer's Folly* and *The Secret Agent* crosses the boundaries of cultural difference through trade and portable foodways. But if the visibility of the immigrant was submerged in the murky and dank places of the western psyche, their presence was asserted in the food that everyday Londoners ate and desired. However, the fishy smells that emanated from the street food that signalled the presence of the 'other' became a register for the complicated relationship that Britain had, not only with its colonies, but with the migrants who came to live in London. The simultaneous rejection of the 'other', combined with a desire for their food, created an alienating tension in the Western psyche. To survive, the immigrant adapted to their surroundings, but at the same time retained their sense of identity through the traditions of a secret, authentic food culture that became as mysterious and talked about by the natives of London as Lingard's 'secret river' in Borneo.

Almayer's Folly and *The Secret Agent* are counterpart novels, not only through their focus on political intrigue and the liminality of their characters, but in the way that the emblems and environs of the East are transposed on to the wet streets of London. But where Almayer represents the inflexibility of the colonial in the East, the Assistant Commissioner – a man to whom Conrad gives no name – straddles both East and West, and in so doing becomes a 'Queer Foreign Fish'. The reference not only encapsulates strangeness, difference and obliqueness, but endows the Assistant Commissioner with versatility and the ability to assimilate. By extension, this versatility affords him the exoticism, value and adaptability of the immigrant.

Notes

1 For a detailed analysis of the significance of rice in *Almayer's Folly*, see 'Food as Cultural Narrative in Almayer's Folly' in Salmons (2017).

2 From the Latin miscere, 'to mix'. The term originally appeared in 'Miscegenation: The Theory of the Blending of the Races, Applied to the American White Man and Negro' (www.etymonline.com/search?q=miscegenation).

3 In 1498, the Portuguese explorer Vasco da Gama made the first sea voyage from Europe to India, via the southernmost tip of Africa. The mission was driven by a desire to find a direct route to the places where spices were plentiful and cheap, cutting out the middlemen. His arrival on India's Malabar Coast, the heart of the spice trade, marked the start of direct trading between Europe and South East Asia (https://www.bbc.com/future/bespoke/made-on-earth/the-flavours-that-shaped-the-world)

4 For a more detailed explanation of Croly's intentions, see http://hoaxes.org/archive/permalink/the_miscegenation_hoax/and for the etymology of 'miscegenation' see https://www.etymonline.com/search?q=miscegenation

5 J. H. Stape claims the gramophone scene in AF 'plays up misunderstanding, cultural dominance and appropriation, and the clash of civilizations' (*Conrad in Context*, 2009: 141).

6 Robert Hampson has pointed out that 'the precise coding of Almayer's meal of "rice and a little fish" is made clear in "Falk". Schomberg scornfully contrasts Falk's meal of "rice and a little fish" with the "meat" he provides all year round for his patrons; he hammers home the point by adding, "I am not catering for a dam' lot of Coolies"' (2000: 213, note 11).

7 Biche de Mer refers to trepang and derives from the Spanish Bicho dei mar. 'Bicho' has sexual connotations and thus the term evolved into 'bêche de mer' which confirms that 'biche de mer' and trepang are the same type of sea cucumber.

8 In the 1820s, France established itself as the height of culinary fashion with its arcades and restaurants with Marie Antonin Carême publishing *L'Art de la Cuisine Française* which was seminal in its differentiation of home and restaurant cooking.

9 http://www.britishchineseheritagecentre.org.uk/timeline/british-chinese-food

10 Although there was more than one Cheshire Cheese in London, the Fleet Street branch is probably the most likely place for Verloc to go after travelling from Maze Hill back to Charing Cross after Stevie is blown up.

11 One reason why Conrad may have made mention of the smell of fried fish was the abundance of complaints about the smell. The Public Health Act of 1875 (amended in 1891) tried to put controls on emissions (Panayi 2014: 39).

12 For a more detailed geography of Winnie's mother's trip to the Licensed Victuallers' Asylum, see Hans Van Marle, 'Of Lodgings, Landladies and *The Secret Agent*', *The Conradian*, 12 (2) (November 1987): 138–49.

13 'Disreputable Restaurant Keepers', *Daily News*, 11 April 1900 p. 9.

14 This timing coincides with Hans Van Marle's argument that *The Secret Agent* is set in 1886, Winnie and Verloc having married – according to Winnie's wedding ring – in 1879 (1977: 6–8).

15 *Nights Out*, Yale: Yale University Press, 2012.

16 The reference could be to the Royal Aquarium (aka 'The Tank') which opened on 22 January 1876 in Westminster. It was intended as an exhibition centre and had thirteen tanks which were meant to house unusual sea creatures. However, the only marine life that was put on show was a dead whale and the hall was eventually closed down after gaining a reputation for soliciting. It was sold in 1903 to the Methodist Church (Munro 1971).

Works Cited

Assael, B. (2013), 'Gastro-cosmopolitanism & The Restaurant in Late Victorian and Edwardian London', *The Historical Journal*, 56 (3): 681–706.

Assael, B. (2018), *The London Restaurant 1840–1914*, Oxford: Oxford University Press.

Bell, D. and Valentine, G. (1997), *Consuming Geographies: We Are Where We Eat*, London: Routledge.

Berthoud, J. (1992), 'Introduction' to *Almayer's Folly*, London: Wordsworth.

Carabine, K. (2008), 'Introduction' to *A Personal Record*, Herts: Wordsworth.

Cheung, S. and Wu, D. Y. H., eds (2002), *The Globalisation of Chinese Food*, Florence: Taylor & Francis.

Conrad, J. (1923), *A Handbook of Cookery for a Small House*, London: William Heinemann.

Conrad, J. (1926), *Joseph Conrad as I Knew Him*, London: William Heinemann.

Conrad, J. (1945a), *Almayer's Folly & Tales of Unrest*, London: J. M. Dent.

Conrad, J. (1945b), 'An Outpost of Progress', in *Tales of Unrest*, London: J. M. Dent.

Conrad, J. (1947), *The Secret Agent: A Simple Tale* [1907], London: J. M. Dent.

Conrad J. (1967), *Youth, Heart of Darkness, the End of the Tether*, London: J. M. Dent.

Conrad, J. (2008), *The Mirror of the Sea & A Personal Record*, Hertfordshire: Wordsworth.

Francis, A. (2021), 'A "Settled Resident": Movements of Peoples and Cultures in Conrad's Malay Fiction', in K. Salmons and T. Zulli (eds), *Joseph Conrad: Migration, Modernity & Transnationalism*, London: Bloomsbury.

Glover, D. (2012), *Literature, Immigration, and diaspora in fin-de-siecle England: A Cultural History of the 1905 Aliens Act*, Cambridge: Cambridge University Press.

Hampson, R. (2000), *Cross-cultural Encounters in Joseph Conrad's Malay Fiction*, London: Palgrave.

Hampson, R. (2012), *Conrad's Secrets*, London: Palgrave Macmillan.

Holt, V. M. (1885), *Why Not Eat Insects?* London: Field & Tuer.

hooks, b. (1992), 'Eating the Other: Desire and Resistance', in *Black Looks: Race and Representation*, 21–40, Boston: South End Press.

International Health Exhibition Pamphlet. (1884), ed. Henry W Acland. London School of Hygiene and Tropical Medicine Printed and Published for the Executive Council of the International Health Exhibition and for the Council of the Society of Arts by William Clowes, b28045324. Available online: https://wellcomelibrary.org/item/b28045324

Ismael, M. Y. (2002), 'Sacred Food from the Ancestors: Edible Bird Nest Harvesting among the Idahan', in David Y. H. Wu and Sidney C. H. Cheung (eds), *Globalisation of Chinese Food*, Oxon: Routledge.

Jackson, J. C. (1972), 'Rice Cultivation in West Malaysia: Relationships between Culture History, Customary Practices and Recent Developments', *Journal of the Malaysian Branch of the Royal Asiatic Society* 45, 2 (222): 76–96.

Jun, A. (2010), 'The Role of Samas/Bajaus in Sea Cucumber Trades in the Sulu Sultanate Economy: Towards a Reconstruction in Perspectives on Bajau-Sama Diaspora', in Kathleen Schwerdtner Manez and Sebastian C. A. Ferse (eds), *The History of Makassan Trepang Fishing and Trade*; gen ed: Sharyn Jane Goldstien. PLoS One. 5, 6. Available online: https://journals.plos.org/plosone/article?id=10.1371/journal.pone.0011346 (accessed 30 April 2020).

Munro, J. M. (1971), *The Royal Aquarium: Failure of a Victorian Compromise*, Beirut: American University of Beirut.

Najder, Z. (2007), *Joseph Conrad. A Life*, Rochester; New York: Camden House.

Newnham-Davis, N. (1899), *Dinners and Diners: Where and How to Dine in London*, London: Grant Richards.

Newnham-Davis, N. (1914), *The Gourmet's Guide to London*, New York: Brentano's.

Panayi, P. (2008), *Spicing Up Britain: The Multicultural History of British Food*, London: Reaktion Books.

Panayi, P. (2014), *Fish and Chips: A History*, London: Reaktion Books.

Plotz, J. (2009), *Portable Property: Victorian Culture on the Move*, Princeton: Princeton University Press.

Salmons K. (2017), *Food in the Novels of Joseph Conrad: Eating as Narrative*, London: Palgrave Macmillan.

Stape, J. H. (2009), 'The Far East', in Allan Simmons (ed.), *Joseph Conrad in Context (2014)*, 139–62, Cambridge: Cambridge University Press.

Van Marle, H. (1997), 'Shades of Reality: A Little Conrad in *The Secret Agent*', *The Conradian*, 3 (1): 6–8.

Walkovitz, J. (2012), *Nights Out: Life in Cosmopolitan London*, London and New Haven: Yale University Press.

Wallace, A. R. (1869), *The Malay Archipelago, Volume II*, London: Macmillan.

Walton, J. (1989), 'Fish and Chips and the British Working Class, 1870–1930', *Journal of Social History*, 23 (2): 243–66.

Warren, J. F. (1977), 'Sino-Sulu Trade in the Late Eighteenth and Nineteenth Centuries', *Philippine Studies*, 25 (1): 50–79.

Warren, J. F. (2010), 'Saltwater Slavers and Captives in the Sulu Zone, 1768-1878', *Slavery and Abolition: A Journal of Slave and Post-Slave Studies*, 31 (3): 429–49.

Yifeng. D. (2002), 'Food Culture and Overseas Trade: The Trepang Trade between China and South East Asia during the Qing Dynasty', in David Y. H. Wu and Sidney C. H. Cheung (eds), *Globalisation of Chinese Food*, 21–42, Oxon: Routledge.

Young, R. J. C. (2006), *Colonial Desire: Hybridity in Theory, Culture and Race*, London & New York: Routledge.

7

'The east spoke to me, but it was in a western voice': Perlocutionary acts and the language of migration in Conrad's fiction

Tania Zulli
'G. d'Annunzio' University of Chieti-Pescara

1

Language carries ideological and cultural meaning and, in turn, culture, ideology, history and society find their expression through words and communication. These basic principles of language theory are true for both spoken and written communication, even if the use of speech acts in writing must consider a number of variables linked to the written nature of the texts themselves.[1] If every speech act represented in a narrative work is inseparable from its social and cultural context, equally, every utterance will be best understood if placed in the stratified dialogical background it belongs to, since 'each successful text produces for its readers a social fact. The social facts consist of meaningful social actions being accomplished through language, or speech acts' (Bazerman and Prior 2004: 311). Also, language creativity can be more suitably valued in the perspective of the meaning and values the author wants to express. These theorizations are at the core of Mikhail Bakhtin and V. N. Vološinov's book *Marxism and the Philosophy of Language*,[2] which focuses on the idea that every individual speech act – either real or narrative – is far from being individual and always susceptible to sociological analysis, with the consequence that '[t]he stylistic shaping of an utterance is shaping of a social kind, and the very verbal stream of utterances, which is what the reality of language actually amounts to, is a social stream. Each drop of that stream is social and the entire dynamics of its generation are social' (Vološinov 1973: 93–4). Thus, not only literary texts, but also the very words used to write them, especially those used by the writer to give life to his characters, are dependent on contextual dynamics able to enrich their connotation.

Much earlier than the above-mentioned language and speech-act theorists, Joseph Conrad had recognized the power of the word not only in artistic terms, but also as a carrier of social and ideological values. In *A Personal Record* he expresses this awareness thus:

> You perceive the force of a word. He who wants to persuade should put his trust not in the right argument, but in the right word. The power of sound has always been greater than the power of sense. I don't say this by way of disparagement. It is better for mankind to be impressionable than reflective. Nothing humanely great – great, I mean, as affecting a whole mass of lives – has come from reflection. On the other hand, you cannot fail to see the power of mere words; such words as Glory, for instance, or Pity. I won't mention any more. They are not far to seek. Shouted with perseverance, with ardour, with conviction, these two by their sound alone have set whole nations in motion and upheaved the dry, hard ground on which rests our whole social fabric. (Conrad 2008: 205)

The authority of words 'to set whole nations in motion' and 'upheave the ground of social fabric' finds its expression in the role played by language, communication and speech within the sociocultural context to which they belong. In this context, the power of 'sound' has a peculiar function, one Conrad had considered as the main aesthetic objective of his writing – as confirmed by the famous statement 'to make you hear' of his Preface to *The Nigger of the 'Narcissus'*. Conrad's interest in language and his literary representations of speech as a crucial carrier of personal and social relationships make his *oeuvre* apt for an analysis which takes into account linguistic studies, such as those of pragmatics and, more specifically, speech-act theories. This chapter will explore narrative speech acts in Conrad's works to determine how voices and utterances represent the cultural forces lying behind them, becoming a way to explore migration and its consequent experiences of exclusion and relocation. When presenting expatriate characters, Conrad delves into the thematic and moral description of marginalization and acceptance not only through a skilful use of characterization, but also by introducing dialogues which exemplify the construction and violation of cultural barriers. The way his characters speak unveils different attitudes to their condition as outcasts – regardless of their origins and landing places – shedding light on some crucial elements, such as the wish for intercultural contact through communication and, at the same time, the complications and hardships of integration. Eventually, the connection between language and migration opens up to wider areas of exploration in the author's aesthetic vision, leading to a reconsideration of his status as a transnational writer.

In this chapter, the axiological value of speech acts will be considered in *Almayer's Folly* (1895) and 'Amy Foster' (1901) by concentrating on the analysis of two specific utterances that will lead to reflect on his artistic philosophy and the making of his 'persona poetica' (Ambrosini 2019: 21). Dialogues and communication will be scrutinized in order to disclose a crucial characteristic of the author's *oeuvre*, that of making textual structures speak about wider artistic visions. This is an issue Richard Ambrosini has introduced in his recent book *Le storie di Conrad* where he affirms that the 'story' of a fine intellectual with a clear artistic project in mind emerges through the textual analysis of Conrad's work. According to Ambrosini, in fact, Conrad 'transformed his abstract ideal in fictional practice by creating different forms, techniques, and narrative structures in his *stories*, by modifying plots, characters' types, as well as geographical and historical settings' (Ambrosini 2019: 17).[3]

The investigation of Conrad's work in relation to the sociocultural background of migration finds its roots in his itinerant life which drove and shaped his own social attitude as well as his personal search for individual stability resulting, from a literary viewpoint, in the creation of 'a kind of novel which can neither fully accept, nor fully escape, the conventions and habits of its own culture' (Eagleton 1970: 32). Wavering between his status of naturalized British citizen and the various representations given by his contemporaries for whom he remained 'a literary homeless', a man 'without either country of language' (Lynd [1908] 1973: 211), and 'our guest' (Woolf 1948: 282), Conrad succeeded in bringing his immigrant perspective on English life (see Simmons 2007). Both his personal experience and his interest in contemporary migration policies (see Zulli 2019b: 302–3) were introduced in his fiction through a range of viewpoints. Grounded in three countries and in three languages (Davies 2016: 208), he brought a highly cosmopolitan, transnational and transcultural perspective to British literature. His frequent journeys at sea allowed him to face racial and cultural multiplicity, and to come into contact with a variety of speech types. Seen from a contemporary perspective, Conrad's world is a world 'in movement', inhabited by characters who communicate in different idioms in the attempt to compromise – despite frequent clashes – their diverse transitions. Not surprisingly, the communities represented in his Malay stories are multiracial, multicultural and multilingual, while foreign idioms are spoken in all his novels. An extensive picture of the variety of languages in Conrad's fiction is given by Michael Greaney, who claims that

> a … survey of [Conrad's] fiction would reveal that Dutch, Malay, Arabic, and Chinese are spoken in *Almayer's Folly* and *An Outcast of the Islands*; French and a number of unidentified African languages are spoken in *Heart of Darkness*; French and German are spoken in *Lord Jim*, Spanish and Italian are spoken in *Nostromo*; Russian, French, and German are spoken in *Under Western Eyes*. … At times in Conrad the language barrier is solid and visible … but elsewhere it seems rather conveniently to evaporate. (Greaney 2002: 19)

This plurilingualism complicates the question of speech acts, since it makes the message conveyed in communication dependent not only on sociocultural contextualization, but also on phonetic and semantic plurality.

2

The idea of spoken language as a channel to configure social relationships is presented from the very beginning of Conrad's writing career, in *Almayer's Folly*. As is well known, the famous opening words of his first novel, 'Kaspar! *Makan*!' are not in English. Mrs Almayer calls her husband to dinner by using his Dutch name ('Kaspar') and a Malay word ('makan') meaning 'to eat', both being foreign words to her (Ambrosini 2019: 70). Difficult to understand if not contextualized, these words have triggered numerous interpretations mainly focusing on the hermeneutical potential of the different languages in which they are spoken – indeed, they are pronounced by a Malay woman and addressed to a Dutchman. This has drawn attention on the linguistic and cultural variety which repeatedly emerges in Conrad's later novels through the setting of his works, his characters and their way of speaking.

An interesting aspect concerns the effect that this expression has on Almayer's consciousness, further clarified when read through the lens of narrative pragmatics, allowing light to be shed on the social implications of communicative phenomena in fictional texts. Specifically, by going beyond its literal meaning and paying attention to what has been defined the 'perlocutionary' power of speech acts, one can investigate the potential of Mrs Almayer's (the speaker's) words on Almayer's (the listener's) temperament and explore the value of one of the main dogmas of perlocutionary acts, 'to say something is to do something' (Austin 1962: 120). As for the perlocutionary power of speech acts, J. L. Austin[4] has singled out the several effects that may be produced by an utterance in the act of communication. In his book *How to do Things with Words* (1962), he deals with speech acts and their effect on the feelings, thoughts and actions of both speaker and listener. Austin distinguishes the locutionary act, which is characterized by 'meaning' – the meaning the speaker wants to convey – the illocutionary act, which 'has a certain force in saying something' – and produces conventional effects on the addressee – and the perlocutionary act 'which is the achieving of certain effects by saying something' – that is, it relates to the listener's reaction upon the declaration (Austin 1962: 120). Perlocutionary acts ultimately refer to 'what we bring about or achieve by saying something' (Austin 1962: 108), thus emphasizing the effect on the listener more than on the speaker and referring to an area which is, ultimately, external to the speech performance itself.

A suitable case of perlocutionary speech act in Conrad's fiction can be found in *Youth* (1898), when Marlow hears a voice on the steamer *Celestial* from Singapore after his boat has made it safely into the Muntok port. He recounts that

> before I could open my lips, the East spoke to me, but it was in a Western voice. A torrent of words was poured into the enigmatical, the fateful silence; outlandish, angry words, mixed with words and even whole sentences of good English … The man up there raged aloud in two languages, and with a sincerity in his fury that almost convinced me I had, in some way, sinned against the harmony of the universe. (Conrad 2010: 37)

The consequential effect of the man's speech and tone is that of making Marlow believe that he has 'sinned against the harmony of the universe'. Even if the speaker's words are not intended to affect his listener and we actually don't know which words are pronounced exactly, it is easy to detect their consequence on Marlow:[5] they make him feel guilty and responsible for some unspecified sin. Although they are unrelated to Marlow's behaviour – who has not actually provoked them – their harshness hints directly at his own sensibility, influencing his sense of responsibility towards the world. This leads back to the meaning of the short story itself which analyses the protagonist's youth, expressed in the conclusion where he describes his 'first vision of the East'. After listening to those 'angry words', facing the Eastern silence and hearing some of its languages, he '[sees] the men of the East … brown, bronze, yellow faces, the black eyes, the glitter, the colour of an Eastern crowd [staring] without a murmur, without a sigh, without a movement' (Conrad 2010: 37). In that precise moment the East unveils to young Marlow, such a vision containing the very idea of his youth. In general, the link to Marlow's consciousness and the reference to an existential, universal condition is a clear example of how the pronouncement of an utterance can go beyond linguistic frames of reference and connect to conceptual considerations. Moreover, the stereotyped East/West dichotomy is further problematized if we consider that Marlow has apparently been mistaken for a native by the skipper of the *Celestial* who addresses him with the vehemence he would reserve to an Eastern. This reveals a more complex conceptualization of the migrant condition, based on ambiguity in dialogic exchanges across different cultures. The same ambiguity in dialogues can be observed in a number of works written by Conrad.

By applying the principles of speech-act theory on Mrs Almayer's 'Kaspar! *Makan*!' it is not difficult to detect that the unintentional perlocutionary power of her words triggers a drastic change in Almayer's mood – he 'shuffle[s] uneasily' (Conrad 2011: 7) at the call. Moreover, the utterance is followed by a description of the protagonist's past life and future engagements. Both perspectives (past life and future actions) are shaped around Almayer's felt condition of exile in Sambir and his life of migration, while his changed disposition applies to both circumstances in equal terms. The perlocutionary 'sequel' (Austin 1962: 117) of the call works both intradiegetically and extradiegetically, by extending to the social sphere and to the author's ethical views and narrative strategies, too. From a linguistic point of view, the accent on Mrs Almayer's 'shrill' voice recalls Conrad's general interest for the phonetic aspect of words, expressed in his idea that 'The power of sound has always been greater than the power of sense' (Conrad 2008: 205) previously quoted in this chapter. In semantic terms, the crucial link between Mrs Almayer's shouted words and her husband's corrupted ideal of a glorious life substantiate Almayer's inability to assimilate to the native community, making him one of the first Conradian outcasts, a solitary, marginalized migrant. By calling her husband to dinner, not only does Mrs Almayer trigger vexing thoughts about his desolate situation in Sambir, but she also allows the narrator to introduce the protagonist's desire to emigrate to Europe. Not a migrant *strictu sensu*, Almayer behaves as if he was one. Moving among Macassar, Java and Amsterdam, 'Almayer's quickened fancy' (Conrad 2011: 8) retraces his past life in the days when he had met Lingard. At that time, Macassar was the crossroads of overseas trade, 'teeming with life and commerce. It was the point in the islands where tended all those bold spirits who, fitting out schooners on the Australian coast, invaded the Malay Archipelago in search of money and adventure' (Conrad 2011: 8). When he left his unhappy parents in Java – an irritable father and a moaning mother living with the nostalgic thought of her youth spent in Amsterdam – he was excited at the idea of a new, wealthy future. After twenty years, the hope of that future has not abandoned him, but his condition has turned into one of despair and exclusion. His alienation is further reinforced by how Mrs Almayer addresses him: the woman discordantly speaks with the authority of the master. As a matter of fact, she is the ruler of her family and manages to control her daughter's (and consequently her husband's) life. Almayer is an outcast in Sambir, and his wife does not lose the opportunity to shout at him reinforcing the sense of social exclusion he experiences. His estrangement is firstly dramatized by Mrs Almayer's communicative approach, apt to 'acknowledge by a scanting remark or an insulting exclamation the accidental presence of her husband' (Conrad 2011: 23). Before being elaborated as an individual and existential condition, Almayer's marginalization is expressed verbally through his wife's language – to which he nevertheless responds in a similarly aggressive way.[6]

This linguistically achieved exclusion has direct references to Conrad's artistic and ethical views. Among the several readings of the novel's *incipit*, Fausto Ciompi's interpretation detects three main connotations in Mrs Almayer's words: after considering that the two words used by the woman are spoken in as many different languages, he underlines the value of the 'shouted' *incipit* with which Conrad inaugurates his career, and finally draws attention to the fact that Almayer's unrealized dream of wealth lays the foundations of Conrad's typical representation of 'defeated idealism' or his deconstructions of an equally 'corrupted oneiric idealism' (Ciompi 2012: 22–3). That is, Mrs Almayer's cry becomes the carrier of a specific type of Conradian characterization, that of the defeated and corrupted idealist eventually yielding to the trials of experience – characters like Jim, Kurtz, Michaelis and Gould belong to this group. This type of idealism is partly linked to Conrad's Polish legacy and partly derives from the Romantic fascination for invisible and powerful enemies. Traces of it surface throughout his scepticism, nihilism and Hobbesian pessimism.[7] Therefore, apart from being the first Conradian character defeated in his ideals and dying in solitude far away from the place he considers as 'home' (Europe), Almayer is also the first representative of a central aspect of Conrad's aesthetic and ethical vision.

In fact, the perlocutionary power of Mrs Almayer's words reveals crucial aspects about the novel's complex narrative structure in terms of sequential plans and chronological shifts. In Chapter Five, another important reason for the woman's call is disclosed to the reader. The chapter goes back to the events described at the beginning of the story extending Almayer's limited perspective: that cry is actually a way to give 'the signal of unwilling separation' (Conrad 2011: 49)[8] to Nina and Dain Maroola, who are secretly meeting. The reason for Mrs Almayer's speech act, what she wants to 'achieve by saying something' (Austin 1962: 108), is related to her plan to support Nina's escape with Maroola and, in wider terms, to her will to contrast her husband's goal – one he has pursued throughout all his life – to make her a European. Not only are Mrs Almayer's words charged with meaning and intentions hidden to Almayer himself, but the question of transnational identity and cross-cultural exchanges emerges again as a crucial trope underlying speech acts.

3

Unlike Almayer, Yanko Goorall, the protagonist of 'Amy Foster', is a 'proper' emigrant, a Carpathian mountaineer shipwrecked on the coast of south-west England while trying to reach America. As in every story of migration, he finds himself among hostile people unable to understand his language and unwilling to accept his difference. The story's focus on language has elicited great critical attention. Yanko's disturbing, indecipherable voice, his 'senseless speech' (Conrad 1974: 120), besides serving 'as a vocal record of cultural difference' (Israel 1997: 371), is also meant to convey specificities on the individual condition of the migrant. Yanko's use of language reveals different attitudes to his condition as outcast, shedding light on his wish for interpersonal exchange through communication and, at the same time, showing the complications and hardships he encounters in his attempts to integrate in the village. As such, the emigrant's speech expresses both his sense of exclusion (his are 'words from an unearthly language', Conrad 1974: 117) and his struggle to be accepted in a new society (he approaches Smith imploring him 'in God's name to afford food and shelter', Conrad 1974: 120). After spending a night and day wandering around the village, he is locked in Mr Smith's woodshed. Early in the morning, Mr Smith's servant, Amy Foster, visits the lodge to give him a piece of bread. The episode represents one of the crucial scenes in the story:

> The girl had not been able to sleep for thinking of the poor man, and in the morning, before the Smiths were up, she slipped out across the back yard. Holding the door of the wood-lodge ajar, she looked in and extended to him half a loaf of white bread — 'such bread as the rich eat in my country', he used to say.
>
> At this he got up slowly from amongst all sorts of rubbish, stiff, hungry, trembling, miserable, and doubtful. '*Can you eat this?*' she asked in her soft and timid voice. He must have taken her for a 'gracious lady'. He devoured ferociously, and tears were falling on the crust. Suddenly he dropped the bread, seized her wrist, and imprinted a kiss on her hand. She was not frightened. (Conrad 1974: 124, my italics)

The description introduces a revealing division, semantically and structurally adjusted to the representation of the two characters. The figure of Amy as perceived by Yanko – a 'gracious lady', allegedly rich, with a mild, sweet disposition conveyed through her 'soft and timid voice' – is juxtaposed against the outcast described by the narrator as a 'stiff, hungry, trembling, miserable, and doubtful' man. The individual and cultural boundaries introduced here become less marked throughout the story, as Yanko tries to adapt to his new identity and Amy proves an outsider herself, isolated from the social life of the village. However, such blurring does not serve to fill the enduring gap between two national and cultural realities that are ostensibly detached. On the contrary, the story confirms Conrad's declared aim to explore 'the essential difference of the races' (Karl and Davies 1986: 402).

The key utterance pronounced by Amy, 'Can you eat this?' is anticipated by her bread offer, a meaningful gesture that distinctly contextualizes her words. The religious symbolism of the scene is evident; several biblical representations are recalled, mainly those contained in the New Testament, which associate bread with a gift from God, denoted as both physical (Matthew 26: 26) and spiritual (John 6: 5) nourishment.[9] The meaning Yanko gives to Amy's gesture is emphatically religious also because, as a fervent Catholic, he has an animated reaction testifying to his strong faith.[10] However, despite its intense connotation, the symbolism contained in the passage is there to strengthen the idea of the protagonist's Eastern cultural heritage more than to deliver any personal religious message on the author's part.[11] In the story, religion is an essentially 'material' act linked to objects, churches and customs while it hints at the inner perception of faith (Salmons 2018). Even Amy's determination to meet Yanko's needs through charity and generosity answers the social standards of reception and hospitality.

In terms of communication, the question pronounced by Amy is one of the few sentences heard from her own voice, her speech being mainly filtered through Kennedy's reports. The locutionary effect of her words (the intention to convey the message that Yanko must eat the bread) and the illocutionary power the sentence holds (the invitation, Amy's urging the man to accept it) conflate into Yanko's action of 'ferociously devouring' the bread (perlocutionary act). The perlocutionary power of Amy's expression is exemplified by Yanko's emotive response – he sheds tears on the crust and kisses her hand in sign of gratitude. His reaction is unsurprisingly linked to the sphere of his emigrant experience. If, on the one hand, the three levels of meaning of Amy's sentence converge in the axiological field of hospitality and charity, on the other hand, the perlocutionary power of such words represents the potential of integration contained in language only deceptively. As a matter of fact, Yanko's reaction conforms the behaviour of a migrant who has just experienced a first act of reception, but the final effect of the words accompanying the offer does not lead to the integration the sentence seems to announce. The question reveals that the bread offer carries within itself the suggestion of an acceptance which is impossible to achieve, and this will be clear once the sentence is read in the perspective of the subsequent events of the story. The words pronounced by Amy, 'Can you eat this?' acquire multiple meanings if considered both in the context of the narration itself and against the background of the migration experience. The bread he is offered provides for his immediate sustenance but is inadequate to support his physical health in more durable terms. As Kim Salmons affirms, Yanko's distance from the social life of the Kent village results also in the difficulty to accept its inhabitants' eating habits. Ironically, he should not be able to eat the bread he is offered, since 'digestion, like the furrows of the brain which have developed overtime by external conditions, is affected by habits, traditions and locally available food' (Salmons 2020: 19). And as a consequence, his ingestion of the bread has real and symbolic harmful consequences.[12]

Amy's gesture and words are meant to express compassion, but in the long term they are empty and ineffective. Equally, her charitable attitude described earlier in the narrative – 'She had never been heard to express a dislike for a single human being, and she was tender to every living creature' (Conrad 1974: 109) – seems to apply only to the restricted social area of the village community. In brief, while handing the bread, she is offering a product of her land and a symbol of her social world as a sign of acknowledgement of the migrant's condition, but when asked to detach from that world to meet her husband's individual and cultural needs her humanity fails. On the other hand, and even more importantly, she is not able to allow for the broadening of that setting to include the foreigner. In fact, she resents Yanko singing Polish songs to their child – 'such as the mothers sing to babies in his mountains' (Conrad 1974: 137) – and 'object[s] to him praying aloud in the evening [expecting] the boy to repeat the prayer aloud after him by-and-by' (Conrad 1974: 137). At the end of the story, she is unable to save him from death, and she proves unable to understand his cry for help, a single word pronounced in the spasms of fever, 'water', to which she responds by opening the door and running out with the child in her arms (see Conrad 1974: 140).

As in the case of Almayer, Yanko's alienation is principally conveyed in linguistic terms and even if the story displays Conrad's interest in some 'potentially integrative aspects of language' (Fraser 1988: 184), the emigrant's attempts at communication only reinforce his marginalization. If, according to pragmatics, context is fundamental to understand the meaning of a sentence, the context of the story confirms that the real significance of Amy's initial gesture and sentence is deprived of those values it seeks to convey. This happens because in their attempt at communication Yanko and Amy lack the kind of interaction taking place in every dialogue, based on a unique language which talks to both of them. Understanding Yanko's request means locating that request in a hermeneutical framework – that of a different culture with different values – which Amy is not able to grasp.

4

Giuseppe Sertoli has lately revitalized a crucial intuition on the theme of racial difference as linked to location in 'Amy Foster'. He has observed that the 'fear of the other' narrativized in the short story does not differ much from the 'fear of the other' the author was investigating, by using a different environmental context, in *Heart of Darkness*.[13] Both works reflect the tragic consequences ensuing from an atavistic impulse leading to rejection (Sertoli 2019: 7). Even if in 'Amy Foster' the racial confrontation takes place within European boundaries[14] the rules of exclusion work in exactly the same way, regardless of geographical settings. This consideration brings to the fore Conrad's personal feelings as an emigrant and hits back at the definition of his individual and artistic identity, which was a major concern in the years from 1897 to 1902. We could then say that *Almayer's Folly* (1895) and 'Amy Foster' (1901) mark the beginning and the end of a period in which Conrad worked on the reassessment of his artistic personality and the aesthetic nature of his works by shifting between two identities, that of the Polish citizen and that of the English writer.[15] He undoubtedly felt an outsider and at the same time developed the awareness – traces of which are to be found in his later novels – that his real authorial identity had to be structured in much wider terms, taking into account both European and extra-European contexts and accommodating his emigrant, cosmopolitan and transnational nature.

At the time when Conrad was establishing himself permanently in Britain (1984), the negotiation between his Polish origins and British adoption worked on both personal and artistic levels and the problem of language and communication played a central role. National belonging was a conscious choice, and Conrad's self-representation as a writer was also to be detected in his concern with the English language. The awareness of his personal limits at mastering spoken English[16] emphasized the importance he gave this language in his writing career. In fact, 'Conrad's experience is distinct from that of the "average" assimilated immigrant, who (gradually) acquires a language and increasingly identifies with the espoused national polity, while inhabiting two cultural contexts: original and adopted' (Simmons 2004: 4). Rather, his declared 'vocational' drive towards the English idiom (and culture) conceals a much deeper awareness for the need of a hybrid, diversified, transnational identity. This message is conveyed throughout his narrative in ethical, ideological and structural terms, as well as through the use of fictional communication intended as conveyor of cultural and social messages. This way, he is able to merge aesthetic and sociopolitical aims and fulfil the demand exerted on writers to establish a writer–reader communication in which they create 'the context, the purpose, and the relationship between them-selves and their readers within their texts, so that meaning can survive long after the original writers, readers, and contexts cease to exist' (Horner 1981: 10). In wider and symbolical terms, if we consider Conrad's writing as conveying a long-lasting meaning, we will find that the perlocutionary power contained in his message impacts today's readers, too, while Conradian strategies of dialogue and language express his transnational artistic project. Besides speaking to Almayer and Yanko Goorall, the two utterances analysed in this chapter ('Kaspar! *Makan*!' and 'Can you eat this?') speak to us today. They speak to contemporary readers about migration, exclusion and integration. They speak to us about the communicative power of literature itself and, most importantly, they articulate the artistic credo of the author, who tirelessly continued 'to invent stories and manipulate forms, pursuing the art of the word and performing a dialogue at times provocative and at times ironic with the English public' (Ambrosini 2019: 321).[17]

Notes

1 For example, writers and readers are usually detached from each other in time and space and a writer's discourse can be distant from its original context. However, such context is established in the text in a way that allows meaning to survive in acts of speaking and readers to catch that meaning despite temporal and spatial distance.

2 Some details are needed on the genesis and composition of this book. It was first published in Leningrad in 1929, signed by V. N. Vološinov. Even if Bakhtin never claimed its authorship, it has been demonstrated that he was the main author of the

book, while his friend Vološinov only played a marginal part in its composition. However, even today *Marxism and the Philosophy of Language* appears under the name of V. N. Vološinov in library catalogues.

3 Conrad 'trasformò il suo ideale astratto in pratica romanzesca, inventando nelle sue *storie* forme, tecniche, strutture narrative sempre diverse, modificando trame, tipologie di personaggi, ambientazioni geografiche e storiche'. *My translation.*

4 John Langshaw Austin was one of the most famous British philosophers of language in the twentieth century. He is known for his theory of speech acts (further developed by J. R. Searle) which considers the relationship between utterances and their potential to perform the above-mentioned definition of locutionary acts, illocutionary acts and/or perlocutionary acts (see Miller 2001, Petrey 2016, Searle 1979).

5 Even though Austin affirms that 'saying something will often, or even normally, produce certain consequential effects upon the feelings, thoughts, or actions of the audience, or of the speaker, or of other persons: and it *may* be done with the design, intention, or purpose of producing them' (Austin 1962: 101, my italics), the speaker's intention is not always a requisite of perlocutionary speech acts.

6 As a matter of fact, Almayer either addresses his wife rudely or becomes passively silent. To her, he is utterly 'impenetrable – impenetrable to persuasion, coaxing, abuse; to soft words and shrill revilings; to desperate beseechings or murderous threats' (Conrad 2011: 31).

7 An interesting analysis of Conrad's critical perspectives on abstract idealism (with a focus on *Heart of Darkness*) is in Ciompi (2012: 87–110).

8 'Mrs. Almayer had undertaken the easy task of watching her husband lest he should interrupt the smooth course of her daughter's love affair, in which she took a great and benignant interest.' Ibid.

9 Amy's act can also be read as a metaphor of the biblical event of Christ sharing the bread (Matthew 14:19-20) with its subsequent symbolic connotation of nourishing the crowds. 'And he directed the people to sit down on the grass. Taking the five loaves and the two fish and looking up to heaven, he gave thanks and broke the loaves. Then he gave them to the disciples, and the disciples gave them to the people. They all ate and were satisfied, and the disciples picked up twelve basketfuls of broken pieces that were left over' (Matthew 14:19-20).

10 It is just worth mentioning that the references to Yanko's Catholic faith are often given a 'verbal' connotation – '[he is] heard every evening reciting the Lord's Prayer, in incomprehensible words and in a slow, fervent tone' (Conrad 1974: 131). The Lord's Prayer includes the same double symbolism of bread providing for physical survival and the salvation of the soul.

11 In his approach to religion, Conrad seemed to follow the Polish trend of a very nationalistic kind of religion. Also, to make a very simplistic generalization, Conrad

acknowledged the presence of God while harshly attacking Christian doctrines. On the theme of religion in Conrad, see Lester (1988).

12 White bread leads back to the process of bread whitening through the use of particular substances, such as alum – a detrimental, if widely extended, practice in the nineteenth century (see Salmons 2018). This thesis is supported in the text by the physical evolution of Yanko himself. Initially described as strong, 'light' and healthy (Conrad 1974: 111), with the passing of time he loses all his energy, and becomes 'depleted, diluted and exhausted' (Salmons 2018).

13 See also Ruppel (1996).

14 To be precise, Yanko comes from the Tatra Mountains, the highest mountain chain of the Carpathians forming a natural barrier between Poland and Slovakia.

15 According to David Glover, ' "Amy Foster" was written during a phase which saw a marked rise in organised hostility towards "aliens" – that is, during the months between the official foundation of the British Brothers' League in Stepney on 9 May and the setting up of the Parliamentary Pauper Immigration Committee on 31 July 1901, two pressure groups arising from opposite ends of the sociopolitical scale. [...] If Jósef Teodor Konrad Korzeniowski ever ceased to think of himself as a foreigner, it would not have been in 1901' Glover (2012: 131).

16 On Conrad's concerns with spoken English see Davies (2007: 23–4) and Schwab (1965: 346).

17 'a inventare storie e a manipolare forme, inseguendo l'arte della parola e conducendo un dialogo a volte provocatorio a volte ironico con il pubblico inglese'. *My translation.*

Works Cited

Ambrosini, R. (2019), *Le storie di Conrad. Biografia intellettuale di un romanziere*, Roma: Carocci.

Austin, J. L. (1962), *How to Do Things with Words*, Cambridge, MA: Harvard University Press.

Bazerman, C. and Prior, P., eds (2004), *What Writing Does and How It Does It: An Introduction to Analyzing Texts and Textual Practices*, Mahwah, New Jersey and London: Lawrence Erlbaum Associates.

Ciompi, F. (2012), *Conrad. Nichilismo e alterità*, Pisa: Edizioni ETS.

Conrad, J. (1974), *The Nigger of the 'Narcissus', Typhoon, Falk and Other Stories*, ed. Norman Sherry, London: Everyman's.

Conrad, J. (2008), *The Mirror of the Sea and A Personal Record*, London: Wordsworth.

Conrad, J. (2010), *Youth, Heart of Darkness, The End of the Tether*, ed. Owen Knowles, The Cambridge Edition of the Works of Joseph Conrad, Cambridge: Cambridge University Press.

Conrad, J. (2011), *Almayer's Folly and The Rover*, Introduction and Notes by John Lester, London: Wordsworth.

Davies, L. (2007), 'Clenched Fists and Open Hands: Conrad's Unruliness', *The Conradian*, 32 (2): 23–35.

Davies, L. (2016), Afterword to *Conrad and Language*, ed. Katherine Isobel Baxter and Robert Hampson, Edinburgh: Edinburgh University Press.

Eagleton, T. (1970), *Exiles and Émigrés. Studies in Modern Literature*, New York: Schocken Books.

Fraser, G. (1988), 'Conrad's Revisions to "Amy Foster"', *Conradiana*, 20 (3): 181–94.

Frederick R. Karl and L. Davies, eds. (1983–2008), *The Collected Letters of Joseph Conrad*, Cambridge: Cambridge University Press.

Glover, D. (2012), *Literature, Immigration, and Diaspora in Fin-de-Siècle England. A Cultural History of the 1905 Aliens Act*, Cambridge: Cambridge University Press.

GoGwilt, C. (2016), 'Conrad and Romanised Print Form: From Tuan Almayer to "Prince Roman"', in Katherine Isobel Baxter and Robert Hampson (eds), *Conrad and Language*, Edinburgh: Edinburgh University Press: 117–31.

Greaney, M. (2002), *Conrad, Narrative, and Language*, Cambridge: Cambridge University Press.

Horner, W. B. (1981), 'Speech-act Theory and Writing', *FFORUM: A Newsletter of the English Composition Board*, University of Michigan, 3: 9–11.

Israel, N. (1997), 'Exile, Conrad, and "La Différence Essentielle des Races"', *NOVEL: A Forum on Fiction*, 30 (3) (Spring): 361–80.

Karl, F. R. and Laurence Davies, eds (1986), *The Collected Letters of Joseph Conrad*, Cambridge: Cambridge University Press.

Lester, J. (1988), *Conrad and Religion*, London: Macmillan.

Lynd, R. ([1908] 1973), 'A Set of Six', *Daily News*, 10th August 1908, in Norman Sherry (ed.), *Joseph Conrad. The Critical Heritage*, 210–12, London: Routledge.

Miller, J. H. (2001), *Speech Acts in Literature*, Stanford: Stanford University Press.

Petrey, S. (2016), *Speech Acts and Literary Theory*, London: Routledge.

Ruppel, R. (1996), 'Yanko Goorall in The Heart of Darkness: "Amy Foster" as Colonialist Text', *Conradiana*, 28 (2): 126–32.

Salmons, K. (2018), '"Without Phosphorus, No Thought": The Importance of a Healthy Diet in Joseph Conrad's "Amy Foster"', Unpublished conference paper presented at the 45th Annual International Conference of the Joseph Conrad Society (UK), 5–7 July, Writtle University College, Chelmsford, Essex.

Salmons, K. (2020), 'Jam Puffs and White Bread: Habits of Eating and Othering in George Eliot's *The Mill on the Floss* and Joseph Conrad's "Amy Foster"', *RSV. Rivista di Studi Vittoriani*, 49: 7–20.

Searle, J. R. (1979), *Expression and Meaning. Studies in the Theory of Speech Acts*, Cambridge: Cambridge University Press.

Sertoli, G. (2019), 'Conrad e la tragedia della paura dell'altro. Un montanaro dei Carpazi nella civilissima Inghilterra', *L'Indice*, 5 (May): 7.

Simmons, A. (2007), 'How Joseph Conrad Formed an Identity as an English Novelist', *Language&Literature*, 27 September. Available online: https://culture.pl/en/article/how-joseph-conrad-formed-an-identity-as-an-english-novelist#2 (accessed 22 May 2019).

Simmons, A. (2004), 'The Art of Englishness: Identity and Representation in Conrad's Early Career', *The Conradian*, 29 (1) (Spring): 1–26.

Schwab, A. T. (1965), 'Conrad's American Speeches and His Reading from "Victory"', *Modern Philology*, 62 (4) (May): 342–7.

Vološinov, V. N. (1973), *Marxism and the Philosophy of Language*, New York: Seminar Press.

Watt, I. (2000), *Conrad in the Nineteenth Century*, Berkley, Los Angeles: University of California Press.

Woolf, V. (1948), 'Joseph Conrad', in *The Common Reader*, 282–91, London: The Hogarth Press.

Zulli, T. (2019a), *Joseph Conrad. Language and Transnationalism*, Chieti: Solfanelli.

Zulli, T. (2019b), '"Undesirable Immigrants": The Language of Law and Literature in Joseph Conrad's "Amy Foster"', *POLEMOS*, 13 (2): 299–312.

8

A 'settled resident': Movements of peoples and cultures in Conrad's Malay fiction

Andrew Francis
Independent Scholar, Cambridge

'I believe I am the only white man on the east coast that is a settled resident', declares Almayer to the two Dutch naval officers who come to investigate his wrongdoing over gunpowder in *Almayer's Folly* (Conrad [1895] 1923: 122). Although at first sight a simple statement of fact, it is a declaration full of significance, both for Conrad's representation of Almayer and for the wider representation in this novel and his Malay fiction more generally of the troubled issues of belonging and residence. These are issues that are very much to the fore in this fiction, a significant part of which is set in settlements – Sambir and Patusan – where immigrants of various ethnic groups are present and which effectively act as test sites for considering Conrad's thinking about migration.[1] The issues underpin Conrad's portrayal of the changing social relations brought about by migration, informing our understanding of transnationalism, making readers engage with the extent to which these social relations move beyond any single national culture and towards the possibility of the transnational being achieved.

While this chapter will examine the implications and cultural impacts of colonial migration, it will also consider Arab, Chinese and Malay migration, and, for colonial migrants, the tombstones and graves that often marked their ends abroad. While it is usually the case in Conrad studies that migrations are viewed in terms of the migrants themselves, much can also be understood by considering what I shall term the 'transnationalism of things', those material objects that accompanied the migrants or that were acquired or built by them, things that deserve consideration as being the voiceless, but not expressionless, indicators of change and movement that contribute to Conrad's construction of character and context.

Belonging, residence and citizenship

The popular *Bos-Niermeyer schoolatlas der geheele aarde* (Bos-Niermeyer School Atlas of the Whole World), as it later became known, has been published under various titles since 1877.[2] It helped to define for generations of Dutch children how the world looked, a world that included their country's overseas possessions – not only the Dutch East Indies (present-day Indonesia) but also the Dutch West Indies and Surinam. Of these possessions, by far the largest and economically most important was the Dutch East Indies. It is revealing to consider the way in which this possession – where Almayer, Willems, Jim and Heyst are largely portrayed, and where much of Conrad's Malay fiction is set or partly set – was represented in the 1887 edition of the Atlas (*Bos' schoolatlas* 1887), a date that fell in the period when Conrad was present in South East Asia.

Almayer's declaration of residency – 'I believe I am the only white man on the east coast that is a settled resident' – appears to be a claim of a successfully transnational migrant. But such transnationalism is problematized in various ways in *Almayer's Folly*, as it is elsewhere in the Malay fiction. If we consider this problematization first in political terms, although Almayer may consider himself 'settled' it is in the context of a certain political indeterminacy, something that Conrad is at pains to show regarding Dutch rule, and not only in *Almayer's Folly*. In the *Schoolatlas* the main map (XXXIX) of 'De oostindische archipel' (the Eastern, or Malay, Archipelago) is a political map, primarily of colonial possession, the Archipelago being shown as entirely under British, Dutch, Portuguese and Spanish sovereignty.[3] This, however, is illusory, for during most of the period of the Dutch presence in Indonesia considerable parts of the Archipelago were not in fact in their possession, but were still independent states. Dain's father, for example, is 'the independent Rajah of Bali' (Conrad [1895] 1923: 81), and part of what was shown as Dutch in map XXXIX was only within what the Dutch considered to be their sphere of influence in the Archipelago.[4] In the latter part of the nineteenth century the Netherlands was still in the process of acquiring more of the Archipelago as well as consolidating its control over some of the parts over which it exercised suzerainty, all of which was part of a long process of trade and occupation that had begun in the seventeenth century.[5] In the case of the eastern part of Dutch Borneo in which Berau is situated (the setting for Sambir in *Almayer's Folly* and *An Outcast of the Islands* and of Patusan in *Lord Jim*, albeit Patusan is located geographically in north-west Sumatra) the states had signed treaties of fealty with the Dutch East Indies government and had Dutch administrative officials in place. These states were, however, self-governing, something that is mentioned in *Lord Jim* in connection with Brown's arrival: 'perhaps he had heard of Patusan – or perhaps he just only happened to see the name written in small letters on the chart – probably that of a largish village up a river in a native state' (Conrad [1900] 1923: 357). The political situation thus resists any simple interpretation of what it is to be 'settled' in, or to belong to, the settlement of Sambir or of Patusan, Almayer's reference to 'the east coast' being apolitical, suggesting perhaps statehood in limbo. Conrad's faithful portrayal of this political reality includes, for example, 'the news of Acheen war and of the unsuccessful Dutch expedition' (Conrad [1895] 1923: 48), and the fact that 'the hostilities between Dutch and Malays threatened to spread from Sumatra over the whole archipelago' (81). Almayer reinforces this when he complains to the visiting Dutch naval officers about east Borneo, saying that they 'have no grip on this country' (138), 'country' itself being apolitical terminology, in addition to which sovereignty over the Berau area is uncertain since 'the establishment of the British Borneo Company affected even the sluggish flow of the Pantai life. Great changes were expected; annexation was talked of; the Arabs grew civil' (33).

Almayer's apparent settledness is problematized, secondly, by the language of his assertion. To be 'resident' means to have a permanent home somewhere, but the word 'settled' serves to unsettle this notion by recalling the inevitable earlier place of residence of a migrant, thereby also attaching a degree of impermanence to the latest place of residence. This is decidedly the case with Almayer: from his childhood and youth as the son of discontented Dutch migrants to Java, where his father worked for the Government 'Botanical Gardens of Buitenzorg' (Conrad [1895] 1923: 5), Almayer became a clerk in Hudig's godowns in Macassar, and then migrated to Borneo to marry Lingard's adopted Sulu daughter. It is an unsettledness that is emphasized by a chain of longing down the generations to be in a truer abode, one in the Netherlands itself. Almayer's mother 'from the depths of her long easy-chair bewailed the lost glories of Amsterdam, where she had been brought up' (5), and Almayer imagines 'the big mansion in Amsterdam, that earthly paradise of his dreams' (10). And in another sense, no resident could be more unsettled than Almayer in Sambir, for not only is he against those among whom he lives, but his relationship with his wife – with whom love might have suggested the possibility of a transnational relationship – is as poor as might have been expected from his regarding her from the outset as 'a slave, after all', a view derived from his having, ironically, an 'Eastern mind' (11), a mind of colonial Indies formation.

A third aspect problematizes Almayer's apparent settledness. When his wife sharply reminds him that her marriage to him brings her within 'Blanda law' ('your own Christian wife after your own Blanda law!' (40)), i.e. the law of the Dutch in the East Indies, this reminds us not only that they are both subject to a legal system derived from another nation, but that because of Almayer's European status they are in a different legal category of citizenship from nearly all their neighbours in their region, her European status conferred by her marriage. The system also confirms Almayer as a legally defined outsider, a 'European'. In the 1880s there were four legally defined categories of *Burgelijke Stand* (civil status) in the Dutch East Indies: Europeans, Chinese, Other Foreign Asians and Natives (Boomgaard 1991: 67–9). To record the legal separateness and rights of Europeans, a register was published annually: *Naamlijst der Europeesche Inwoners van het Mannelijk Geslacht in Nederlandsch-Indië en Opgave omtrent hun Burgerlijken Stand* (Register of the European Inhabitants of the Male Gender in the Dutch East Indies and Showing Their Civil Status). In the volume for 1888 the first part (1888: 1–220) is the alphabetical list for the whole Dutch East Indies, by administrative area and name, of all permanent male residents aged sixteen or over. In the section for '*Zuider- en Oosterafdeeling van Borneo*' (South and East Division of Borneo) (198–202), the region in which Berau is situated, we find under 'Goenoeng Taboer' (202) the names of 'Olmeijer, C., Veer, C.H. de, and Williams, C.', and under Boeloengan on the same page 'Lingard jr., J.' (van Marle 2005: 2).[6] The prototypes of Almayer, as well as of Jim Lingard and the alcoholic Carel de Veer, are therefore firmly enmeshed in the bureaucratic evidential machinery of ethnic distinction, small numbers of individuals whose civil status indicates not so much a belonging as an externally imposed category of citizenship.[7]

Almayer thus resides in the Dutch East Indies on the colonist's favourable terms. He might have been expected to describe his situation in terms such as 'I have lived here for twenty years', but this more normal mode of expression is denied to him; he can see his living in Sambir only in terms of his unusualness and difference. His term 'settled resident' communicates the fact that his status is in both colonial and wider cultural terms that of someone whose residence is defined by the nature of its beginning, a definition that, with the additional colonial perspective, marks him out as having effectively appropriated his residency. It is a function of Almayer's failure to exist transnationally that he is denied a true place in the community he has supposedly adopted, a denial that Conrad makes evident too in the normal linguistic territory of 'settled' being withheld from him.

Many Ethnic Groups: Difference and Separateness

In those of Conrad's works set against a colonial background it is not unusual for critics to focus primarily in cultural terms on the issues that stem from colonialism; indeed, postcolonial studies have encouraged such a focus, resulting sometimes in an impoverished simplification of what is a more complex portrayal by Conrad of ethnicity and society (see Francis 2014). In his Asian fiction, Conrad frequently refers to races (or ethnic groups as we would now generally term them) other than the colonial and European, and he does not simply refer to any homogeneous indigenous ethnic group, a fact highlighted by Robert Hampson when he points out that in *Almayer's Folly* and *Lord Jim* 'the background is full of the political life of the Bugis and the Malays' (Hampson 2000: 142–3). Indeed, Sambir is described as having 'settlers of various races' (Conrad [1896] 1923: 50). Conrad's reference to other ethnic groups additionally includes Arabs and Chinese – such as Jim-Eng who 'settled here a couple of years ago' (181) – as well as less frequent references to groups such as Dayaks, Eurasians and 'half-castes' (as they are termed in Conrad), 'Bugis and Sulu, Bajow and Illanun' (Moore 2005: vii). But in writing of such a range of ethnic groups it is difference, separateness and sometimes violence rather than any transnational convergence that emerge, the transnational coming powerfully to the fore by virtue of its absence, a feature that enlarges Conrad's transnational reach beyond the colonial or the national alone.

Examples could be given from across Conrad's Malay, and Asian, fiction of the separateness of individual ethnic groups, including, for all their apparent common heritage, Malay ethnic groups. Indeed, Hampson's differentiation between Malay and Bugis is an important example, given the significant cultural differences between the many different ethnic groups in the Archipelago who could otherwise all too simply be termed 'Malay'. Hugh Clifford, reviewing anonymously Conrad's *An Outcast of the Islands*, *Tales of Unrest*, and *The Nigger of the 'Narcissus'*, famously claimed that Conrad's writing showed his lack of understanding of Malays ('The Trail', 1898: 142). The Indonesian scholar G. J. Resink, however, convincingly claimed that Clifford was mistaken, since the 'Malays' portrayed by Conrad were, in fact, 'Buginezen, Mandarezen en Makassaren' (Buginese, Mandarese and Makassars) and that Conrad's representation was reliable (Resink 1965: 42). It is not unreasonable to consider Resink's validation of Conrad's portrayal of the Bugis as supporting Conrad's wider ethnic awareness.

If we consider the migrational background in the settings of *Almayer's Folly*, *An Outcast of the Islands* and *Lord Jim*, the starting point can be taken as the fact that Sambir and Patusan are both described as settlements, places that are of relatively recent establishment, the populations therefore having arrived largely as migrants. The complexity of ethnic groups in this part of Borneo, as well as in other parts of the Dutch East Indies, can be gauged from another map in the *Bos-Niermeyer schoolatlas*, from the 1956 edition: map A of '*Landaarden van Borneo (Kalimantan) en Celebes (Sulawesi)*' (Ethnographic maps of Borneo (Kalimantan) and Celebes [Sulawesi]) is of former Dutch East Borneo, and shows the ethnic composition of the population (Bos-Niermeyer 1956: sheet 36a, scale 1:6,000,000). The interior of eastern Borneo is shown as populated by Dayaks, five sub-groups of whom are identified. Stretching north-south and some 50–60 miles from east to west is a coastal strip settled by Malays. Within that band there are four areas of Bugis settlers, clustered around the mouths of the four main rivers, one of which is the River Pantai on which Conrad's Berau is situated.[8] This mapping is in line with Conrad's description of Sambir and Patusan in *Almayer's Folly* and *Lord Jim* respectively as thirty miles up-river from a river's mouth, and in a place with both Malay and Bugis settlers. Over a period of centuries the Archipelago had seen Malays and Bugis emigrating from the places from where they originally derived: Malays from the west of Sumatra, the Malay Peninsula and north-west Borneo, and Bugis from south-west Sulawesi following war in the seventeenth century.

Arabs had also emigrated over a period of centuries from the Persian Gulf, particularly from the Hadhramaut. They were known as traders, diplomats and religious figures, activities evident in Conrad's writing. With Arab women staying in Arabia, Arab emigrants married local women, as did the Chinese, who were present in Batavia from a very early stage of the town's establishment, where they were renowned, as throughout the Archipelago, as men of business. They married local women in the widespread settlements from which they operated, something that in turn strengthened their network for trade.[9]

Such a long history of emigration might be imagined as having led to societies that we could term transnational, but the tendency of the individual cultures was to associate with their own, a separateness also evident in Conrad. In Sambir and Patusan homes of the different ethnic groups are associated with stockades, compounds and enclosures, the violence of the ethnic composition evident in Marlow's recounting that 'there wasn't a week without some fight in Patusan at that time' (Conrad [1900] 1923: 255). This spatial separateness was reinforced by colonial law. In the Dutch East Indies Arabs were classified as *Vreemde Oosterlingen* (foreign orientals), which resulted in restrictions on which schools they could attend, where they could travel and where they could live, Arabs often living in a *kampung Arab* (Arab village or area). Such Arab and Chinese communities had their own leaders, responsible for maintaining law and order.[10] In the case of Singapore and other Straits Settlements this separateness was emphasized in colonial town planning, which provided for various areas dedicated to individual ethnic groups. An example of this can be seen in the 'Plan of the Town of Singapore by Lieut. Jackson', which provided for separate Arab, Bugis, Chinese, Chuliah (immigrants from the Indian subcontinent), European and Malay areas.[11]

Eurasians and 'half-castes' are reserved for particular scorn by characters in the Malay fiction, marked out as separate and substandard whether from the viewpoint of European or other ethnic groups.[12] The merging of two such groups might seem to offer the possibility of a loosening of identity relating to a single ethnic group, a step on a possible route to a transnational identity. What Conrad portrays, however, is an underlying ethnic rejection by and of these ethnic groups. Willems considers Joanna's family 'those degenerate descendants of Portuguese conquerors' (Conrad [1896] 1923: 4), a group who have not taken on a new ethnic identity that can be valued by other ethnic groups, but seen only as having suffered a racial decline registered as degeneracy. The family in their turn regard themselves as superior and European: 'You are a savage. Not at all like we, whites' (28), Leonard tells Willems. In the case of the captain of Stein's brigantine who takes Jim to Patusan, Marlow's disdain is marked, focusing on the small size of the 'dapper little half-caste', his use of English, his 'smirking' (Conrad [1900] 1923: 238) and his 'bursting with importance' (240).[13] Cornelius is another 'half-caste' of Portuguese descent, unsuitably married to Jewel's Eurasian mother, and not truly part of Patusan society. Marlow observes: 'His slow laborious walk resembled the creeping of a repulsive beetle, the legs alone moving with horrid industry while the body glided evenly' (285). Cornelius also asserts his Europeanness: 'I am an Englishman, too. From Malacca' (368). The 'third-class deputy-assistant resident' Marlow meets he describes as 'a big, fat, greasy, blinking fellow of mixed descent' (278). The clerk of Archie Ruthvel, the 'principal shipping-master' (37), is described by one of those who abandoned the *Patna* as 'a cocky half-bred little quill-driver' (48), and by Marlow as an 'obliging little Portuguese half-caste with a miserably skinny neck' (37), whose 'race', significantly, is inescapably 'two races rather' (38).

Marlow's frequent, almost insistent, claims of Jim as being 'one of us' are usually read as reflecting a certain type of Englishness and the brotherhood of the sea. But in the context of Willems's disdain for Leonard, as well as Marlow's for the captain and for the deputy-assistant-resident – and in the face of not only the captain's pride in his use of what he supposes is sophisticated English speech but also the claims to Europeanness, if not Englishness, by those of largely other ethnic origin (Leonard, Cornelius) – Marlow's insistence on Jim's likeness as 'one of us' (Conrad [1900] 1923: 43) seems tinged with a fearful need to proclaim a common identity, a nationalism far from any transnationalism.[14] Marlow's repeated claim seems all the more desperate given Jim's rapid retreat through South East Asia in which his frenzied re-locations and his desire for anonymity seem to admit of the alarming possibility of his submersion in an alien culture. And Jim himself is not above a slightly patronizing attitude to the foreigner and immigrant Stein for his use of 'war-comrade' (233) and 'vain expense' (236), an ironic stance given that Jim inarticulately 'tacked on the words "old man" to some half-uttered expression of gratitude' (241) in speaking to Marlow.

Belonging: Personal possessions and the transnationalism of things

In considering transnationalism, Conrad's characters can also be revealing in terms of their possessions or what they built or lived in, objects voiceless but not expressionless. Almayer's claim about the uniqueness of his residing on the east coast is rendered the more strange when seen alongside another of his claims, regarding his possessions, that his are 'the only geese on the east coast' (Conrad [1895] 1923: 122) (despite the 'adverse climatic conditions' (Conrad [1912] 1923: 87) of Borneo the – historical – geese must endure). Almayer's claims in identical terms for himself and his geese underline the bizarreness of both his and the geese being there. Similarly, the historical Almayer of *A Personal Record* is rendered the more out-of-place by his 'importing a pony', a creature that mirrors the importation of Almayer into Sambir by Lingard. There is no purpose for this pony, since Almayer, 'aiming at the grandiose', 'could not ride it', and in the settlement 'there was only one path that was practicable for a pony: a quarter of a mile at most, hedged in by hundreds of square leagues of virgin forest' (76); pony and master alike communicate their inappropriateness in this setting.

Hotels feature in important ways in Conrad to indicate the separateness of colonial incomers, these buildings marking out proprietary territory that could be regarded as extraterritorial. Lower-class boarding houses segregate ethnic groups, as for Pedro in *Victory*.[15] For Lingard's flirting with 'half-caste girls' (Conrad [1895]

1923: 7) at the Sunda Hotel in Macassar, the hotel becomes a location available to Western notions of morality within a wider culture with quite different moral values. In the case of houses, while the title *Almayer's Folly* refers to Almayer's own folly, it also resonates with the name conferred by the Dutch 'lighthearted seamen' (37) on the new house Almayer has had built: 'Almayer's Folly' (37). This building has been constructed by Almayer 'for the use of the future engineers, agents, or settlers of the new Company' (33) since he had imagined that the British North Borneo Company would obtain control of the area in which Sambir is situated, only then for him to find that 'the claim to that part of the East Coast was abandoned, leaving the Pantai river under the nominal power of Holland' (34). It is a house designed to be a new start for Almayer, in which he wishes to obtain profitable influence with the British, 'who knew how to develop a rich country' (36). Showing the house to the visiting Dutch seamen, Almayer 'stamped his foot to show the solidity of the neatly-fitting floors and expatiated upon the beauties and convenience of the building' (36). Just as Almayer's political loyalties are foreign – Dutch and European – so he is keen to operate what in effect will be a purely European house, where he will welcome European migrants, associates of a chartered company, a corporate colonizer. The design of the house is distinctly European, with features such as stone and intended sash-windows, but it is unfinished: there are 'great empty rooms where the tepid wind entering through the sashless windows whirled gently the dried leaves and the dust of many days of neglect' (35), with 'stones, decaying planks, and half-sawn beams' (12). Almayer's unoccupied and uncertain building contrasts with the lights of the buildings and activities of other inhabitants of the settlement:

> the long line of Malay houses crowding the bank, with here and there a dim light twinkling through bamboo walls, or a smoky torch burning on the platforms built out over the river. [...] Founded solidly on a firm ground with plenty of space, starred by many lights burning strong and white, with a suggestion of paraffin and lamp-glasses, stood the house and the godowns of Abdulla bin Selim, the great trader of Sambir. (14–15)

Indeed, from one perspective *Almayer's Folly* is a history of four houses, all but one of which work against any notion of the transnational. We learn with regard to the Almayers' first house of 'the *Flash* freighted with materials for building a new house' that 'left the harbour of Batavia' (Conrad [1895] 1923: 23), a house built by an outsider of imported, migrated materials. In the office, those business possessions that indicate what is truly behind his wishing to be a 'settled resident' have been neglected, indicating the end of Almayer's *raison d'être*, their moving portrayal showing the lack of even any business record of his life: 'books open with torn pages bestrewed the floor; other books lay about grimy and black, looking as if they had never been opened. Account books' (199).

The house to which Almayer aspires, albeit an imaginary house in Amsterdam, is just as significant as his two houses in Sambir. It is in effect the true home of Almayer, for whom, as we have seen, 'gleamed like a fairy palace the big mansion in Amsterdam, that earthly paradise of his dreams' (10), Sambir only ever having been intended as a place of transit. By contrast the house in which Almayer ends his days is his new house, but renamed by Jim-Eng 'House of heavenly delight', a name transferred from the house in which Jim-Eng previously lived: 'All the same like my house' (205), as he says. The history of these houses is thus completed by the irony of Almayer living with a Chinese man who has transferred the house into his own, foreign, culture, a transnational approximation that Almayer never previously tolerated. The sequence of these houses is poignantly reflected in *An Outcast of the Islands*, in the house of cards built by Lingard for Almayer's little daughter Nina, who says, 'I want a house, and another house on the roof, and another on the roof – high. High! Like the places where they dwell – my brothers – in the land where the sun sleeps'; 'the white men are my brothers' (Conrad [1896] 1923: 194). Lingard duly builds three houses, but when he attempts the fourth the entire structure collapses, the dream, like Almayer's own, dissolved.

Transnationalism and the dead

We may well feel, if we visit old Christian cemeteries in parts of South East Asia (see Figures 1–4), places that are somehow misplaced survivors of a different culture, that it is only in death that some permanent, albeit mournful, alliance can finally, even if then, take place between one ethnic group and the homeland of another. It is in this foreign homeland that the main characters in the Malay fiction face death, all of them outcasts of a sort: Almayer, Heyst, Jim and Willems. Whether recording the multiple deaths in families from tropical illness, or the many who died during shorter transit, such as Elizabeth Gray in Singapore in Figure 4, the wife of a Master Mariner, the tombstones generally record no compelling sense of residence, as also in Penang in Figure 1. In the ruined St. Paul's Church in Melaka (Figure 3), accretions of Portuguese and then Dutch tombstones line the walls; the Dutch Graveyard (Figure 2) succeeds it with Dutch and British graves; and the Dutch, and later British, Christ Church Melaka concludes it. The migrants rest where it is 'crowded yet empty, like an

Figure 1 Kawasan Perkuburan Kristian (The Christian Cemetery, Penang) (Andrew Francis, 19 August 2010).

Figure 2 Kubur Belanda (The Dutch Graveyard), Melaka (Malacca) (Andrew Francis, 13 February 2014).

Figure 3 St Paul's Church, Melaka (Malacca) (Andrew Francis, 13 February 2014).

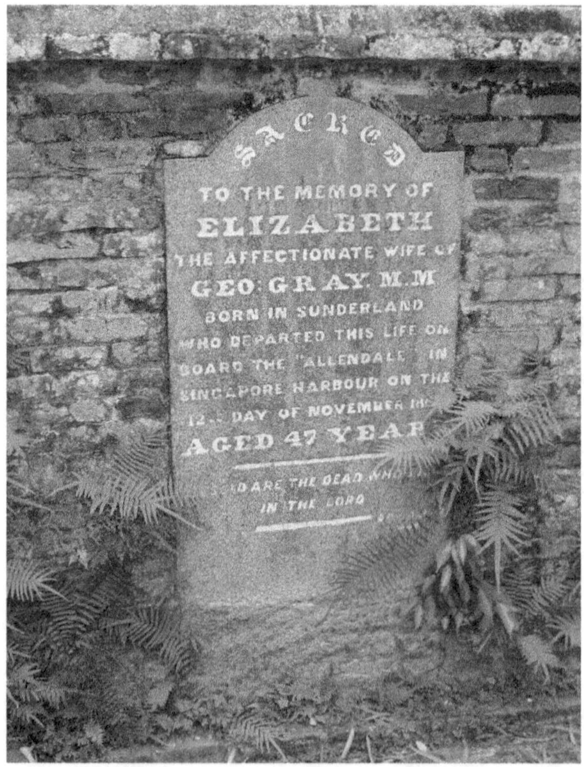

Figure 4 Tombstone of 'Elizabeth' Mrs Gray. Fort Canning Cemetery, Singapore. Died 12 November 1861 (Andrew Francis, 11 February 2014).

old cemetery full of neglected graves' (Conrad [1896] 1923: 282), a hollow end and one marked even in death by spatial separation from other ethnic groups' cemeteries.

Almayer's declaration of being 'the only white man on the east coast that is a settled resident' (Conrad [1895] 1923: 122) is, significantly, repeated when he dies: 'the only white man on the east coast was dead' (208), a statement that defines him in death, as in life, by his whiteness and by the strangeness of his being in Sambir. The repetition works to ironize Almayer's life, seen at its end as definable by his colour and his place of residence, mere externals. The fact of his not belonging is emphasized by his death being couched in terms of Islam and not of the Christianity to which his European heritage links him: 'his soul […] stood now in the presence of Infinite Wisdom' (208), terms that are reinforced by the scene of his death being focalized through Abdullah, who is reminded in his rival Almayer's end of his own death to come. Abdullah's use of his prayer beads is mentioned twice in this final scene, as if invoking 'Allah! The Merciful! The Compassionate!' (208) on behalf of Almayer, resonant words with which the novel ends and which seem to convey an at last newly transnational Almayer, received across cultures. And yet Abdullah only 'glanced coldly' (208) at Almayer's face, something that, taken with Abdullah's focus on his own death and religious practice, as well as Abdullah's seeing Almayer's life in terms of his commercial superiority, seems to serve not as an offer of spiritual comfort for the deceased but to shut the isolated Almayer out from even spiritual inclusion in the land in which he has supposedly settled. Death, as love, might have been expected to provide a transnational sympathy, but Conrad, writing in full awareness of the transnational, suggests that even in death, Almayer's colonial intrusion and migrant's difference of ethnic group remain beyond the scope of any such reconciliation.

We are not told where and with what rites Almayer is buried, as if his status of unsettled 'settled resident' is continued into an uncertain resting-place. Similar doubts and unsettledness surround the deaths of others in the Asian fiction. The case of Willems and Aïssa in *An Outcast of the Islands* is particularly illuminating with regard to transnationalism. Their relationship is the longest and most detailed representation in Conrad's Asian fiction of the possibility of love between different ethnic groups, a love between a troubled white man and a woman who cross their cultural boundaries ('I am like white women' (Conrad [1896] 1923: 184), Aïssa says), a relationship that might seem to promise a possibility of a true ethnic crossing. But its outcome is only that 'hate filled the world, filled the space between them – the hate of race, the hate of hopeless diversity, the hate of blood' (359). It is the same hate as that between Aïssa and another ethnic group, Joanna being called 'A Sirani woman. A woman of a people despised by all', and Joanna regarding Aïssa as a 'heathen savage' (358).

After Aïssa shoots Willems, Lingard sees to it that he is buried beneath a 'granite' (368) gravestone, a burial that might at first seem a peaceful laying to rest, the heavy and solid granite granting perhaps some affirmation of worth after a life of dishonesty and of domineering, racist behaviour. Yet the narrative of this burial is unsettling and unrestful. Just as Almayer's death was unsettled by being focalized through Abdullah, Willems's is similarly, through Almayer's critical account of it to the 'Roumanian, half naturalist, half orchid-hunter for commercial purposes' (360–1). Almayer mocks the 'hundred and twenty dollars thrown away' (364) by Lingard on the gravestone and questions its apparently meaningless inscription: '"Peter Willems, Delivered by the Mercy of God from his Enemy." What enemy – unless Captain Lingard himself? And then it has no sense' (364–5), as if the inscription has been unsuitably selected from a monumental mason's book of examples. And yet, one might interpret that 'Enemy' as being, ironically, a demon within Willems himself, one that set him on his fateful course with Aïssa, of a love between different ethnic groups that in their case could not succeed.

There is a loneliness and defeat to Willems's grave that is underscored by the granite slab being 'imported' (368), a hallmark of difference from local community as it was with the building materials for Almayer's first home, his pony and his geese. Furthermore, Willems's grave is placed not within the community of Sambir, but, appropriately, set apart, at a distance, across the barrier of a river, where Willems lies beneath the 'far-off and invisible slab of imported granite' (368). Almayer has to make a telling effort to discern the grave for the Roumanian, an effort that emphasizes Willems's removal: 'on the top of that hill, there, on the other side of the river' (365).[16] 'Almayer looked for a long time at the clean-cut outline of the summit, as if trying to make out through darkness and distance the shape of that expensive tombstone' (366–7), a tombstone that sees Willems subsumed only on death into the land of Sambir, but even then only into the 'black, rounded mass' (366) of the hill, a resting place that resists any identification of Willems with residence or belonging. Willems felt 'all the hate of his race, of his morality, of his intelligence' (126) for those amongst whom he lived, and Almayer declared that despite living within the community of Sambir he had nevertheless lived his life 'in great solitude' (Conrad [1895] 1923: 122). There can, not surprisingly, be no fitting remembrance in death for either of these colonial representatives: both Willems's grave and the petering out of Almayer's life mournfully affirm the two men's profound disillusionment as well as their failure to live transnationally.

Notes

1 The term 'Malay fiction' here is used to include Conrad's works of Asian fiction, i.e. those set mainly or partly in Asia, but excluding 'Falk' and *The Shadow-Line* as these are largely set in Bangkok.

2 Translations throughout are by the author.

3 Scale 1:12,000,000.

4 For a discussion of the administration and legal status of Dutch East Indies possessions, see Cribb (2010: 123–36), and Francis (2015: 13–15). As Cribb notes, the Dutch East Indies comprised some 280 states.

5 G. J. Resink (1911–97), Professor of Law at the University of Indonesia, whose fascination with Conrad's writing resulted in fourteen essays, and who corresponded with Conrad scholars such as Andrzej Braun, Hans van Marle and Zdzisław Najder, as well as with scholars of Dutch literature and history, including Charles Boxer and Peter King, argued forcefully (Resink: 1979) against the notion that the Netherlands had held sway over the Archipelago from the seventeenth century.

6 This is the volume that Hans van Marle consulted, surprising himself at the ease with which he was able to identify Almayer's historical prototype Olmeijer, though van Marle did not give much in the way of publication details when he described it as 'the official directory of European inhabitants of the Netherlands East Indies for the year 1888' (van Marle 2005: 2).

7 An annual British imperial publication similarly recorded the names of 'Foreign Residents' in Asia (*The Chronicle and Directory* 1888: 21–274b). However, this List includes individuals of various nationalities, not just British, and is not overtly concerned with their civil status. Carel de Veer was a Dutchman who is also known from interviews carried out in Berau by R. Haverschmidt in the 1950s that are referred to in Allen (1967: 224–5).

8 Draper (1904: 16) describes the encouragement of Bugis into eastern Borneo: 'The late Sultan [of Kutai], Mahomad Soleman Chaliphat oel [*sic*] Moeminin, was a very progressive ruler, who foresaw the benefits of closer settlement. He persuaded many thousands of Bugis to leave their native islands and settle in Borneo.'

9 See Cribb (2010: 59) for a summary of immigration into Indonesia.

10 Ibid., 132, for further information about Chinese communities.

11 See Pearson (1973: 150) for the Plan.

12 For further information, see Francis (2015: 58–61).

13 For a fuller analysis of Marlow's attitude to the captain, see Francis (2016: 139–41).

14 Such is the significance of 'one of us' that this phrase concludes the 'Author's Note' following Conrad's resolve 'to seek fit words for [Jim's] meaning' (Conrad [1900] 1923, ix).

15 For a fuller study of hotels in this regard, see Francis (2017).

16 This recalls perhaps the location across the river of the graves of the two Olmeijer children and their mother in Gunung Tabor in a cemetery 'for Europeans and Malays converted to the Christian faith'. See Allen (1967: 195, 220).

Works Cited

Allen, J. (1967), *The Sea Years of Joseph Conrad*, London: Methuen.

Boomgaard, P. and A. J. Gooszen (1991), *Population Trends 1795–96. Changing Economy in Indonesia: A Selection of Statistical Source Material from the Early 19th Century Up to 1940*, 17 vols, vol. 11. ed. P. Boomgaard et al., trans. J. W. F. Arriens, Amsterdam: Royal Tropical Institute: 1975–96.

Bos-Niermeyer schoolatlas der gehele [*sic*] *aarde*. (1956), 39th improved and extended edn, rev. P. Eibergen (Groningen and Djakarta: Wolters, 1956, 2nd impr. 1956), n. pag. *Bos' schoolatlas der geheele* [*sic*] *aarde*. (1887), 8th edn, rev. and enlg'd P.R. Bos, Groningen: J. B. Wolters, n.p.

The Chronicle & Directory for China, Corea, Japan, The Philippines, Cochin-China, Annam, Tonquin, Siam, Borneo, Straits Settlements, Malay States, and c., (with which is incorporated 'The China Directory') for the Year 1888. ([1888(?)]), Hongkong: 'Daily Press' Office.

Conrad, J. ([1895] 1923), *Almayer's Folly*, London: J. M. Dent.

Conrad, J. ([1896] 1923), *An Outcast of the Islands, London*: J. M. Dent.

Conrad, J. ([1900] 1923), *Lord Jim*, London: J. M. Dent.

Conrad, J. ([1912] 1923), *A Personal Record*, London: J. M. Dent.

Cribb, R. (2010), *Historical Atlas of Indonesia*, Richmond, Surrey: Curzon.

Draper, D. ([1904 (?)], *Borneo Pictures*, Johannesburg: Argus.

Francis, A. (2014), 'Postcolonial Conrad', in John Stape (ed.), *The New Cambridge Companion to Joseph Conrad*, 147–59, New York: Cambridge University Press.

Francis, A. (2015), *Culture and Commerce in Conrad's Asian Fiction*, Cambridge: Cambridge University Press.

Francis, A. (2016), 'Languages in Conrad's Malay Fiction', in Katherine Isobel Baxter and Robert Hampson (eds), *Conrad and Language*, 132–50, Edinburgh: Edinburgh University Press.

Francis, A. (2017), 'Accommodating Space, Time, and Culture: Reading across Cultures and Colonialism in the Hotels of Conrad's Asian Fiction', *Transnational Conrad*, Special issue, *L'Époque Conradienne*, 41: 87–97.

Hampson, R. (2000), *Cross-Cultural Encounters in Joseph Conrad's Malay Fiction*, Basingstoke: Palgrave.

Moore, G. M. (2005), 'Introductory' to *A Joseph Conrad Archive* (see van Marle 2005: vii–xi).

Naamlijst der Europeesche Inwoners van het Mannelijk Geslacht in Nederlandsch-Indië en Opgave omtrent hun Burgerlijken Stand (Register of the European Inhabitants of the Male Gender in the Dutch East Indies and Showing their Civil Status). (1888), Batavia: Landsdrukkerij.

Pearson, H. F. (1973), 'Lt. Jackson's Plan of Singapore', in Tan Sri Datuk Mubin Sheppard (ed.), *150th Anniversary of the Founding of Singapore*, M.B.R.A.S. reprints, 1 ([n.p.]: Malaysian Branch of the Royal Asiatic Society: 150–4 (reprinted from the *Journal of the Malayan Branch of the Royal Asiatic Society*, 26 (1): 200–4).

Resink, G. J. (1959), 'De archipel voor Joseph Conrad' (Joseph Conrad's Eastern Archipelago), *Bijdragen tot de Taal-, Land- en Volkenkunde*, 115 (2): 192–208.

Resink, G. J. (1965), 'Conradiaanse interraciale vriendschappen' (Conradian Interracial Friendships), *Forum der Letteren*, 6 (1): 35–47.

'The Trail of the Bookworm: Mr Joseph Conrad at Home and Abroad' (1898), *Singapore Free Press*: 142.

van Marle, H. (2005), '"Joseph Conrad in Indonesia" (An unpublished paper read at the British Council, Münster, Germany, 9 February 1961)', Gene M. Moore (ed.), *A Joseph Conrad Archive: The Letters and Papers of Hans van Marle*, Special issue, *The Conradian*, 30 (2): 1–11.

Part Three

Modernity and the transnational

9

Arab and Muslim transnationalism in Conrad's Malay fiction

Katherine Isobel Baxter
Northumbria University

This chapter examines the mobility between East Asia and the Middle East in Conrad's Malay fiction. This mobility is represented primarily by Arab traders and by Muslim Malays who have undertaken or, in the case of *Lord Jim*, are undertaking Hajj. Much has been said about the transnationalism of Conrad's Malay fiction and the cross-cultural encounters that ensue.[1] Likewise, John Lester has discussed in considerable detail Conrad's representations of Islam in *Conrad and Religion* (1988). Nonetheless, little attention has been given to the particular kinds of transnationalism and migration that enabled the spread of Islam to the Malay Archipelago and that gave rise to particular kinds of 'native' mobility that punctured European colonial boundaries. By situating Conrad's transnational Arab traders and Malay Hajjis in their historical context, I want to argue that their representation animates a complex set of globalized relations that has remained hidden in plain sight in Conrad's Malay fiction. Indeed, the mobilities that Conrad dramatizes through these characters highlight the divergent forms of transnational colonial, non-colonial and anti-colonial activity that were at play across the Indian Ocean during the latter half of the nineteenth century.

In order to explore Conrad's representation of these transnational activities, it is necessary to provide some historical context. In the first part of this chapter, therefore, I will outline why non-white, and more specifically non-British, transnationalism across the regions around the Indian Ocean was of particular concern to British colonial powers during Conrad's lifetime. Following on from this I provide a brief account of the more specific history of movement and migration between the Middle East and East Asia, which increasingly came to be characterized by religious exchange, particularly Hajj. I then turn to consider Conrad's own representations of these mobilities in the context of an established

European literary corpus of Hajj narratives, most famously Richard Burton's *Personal Narrative of a Pilgrimage to El-Medinah and Meccah* (1855–6), which Conrad is known to have consulted. As we shall see, while Conrad's depictions of Arab and Hajji Malays often draw on popular conventions they nonetheless signal and speak to the shifting power dynamics of late British colonialism on the cusp of dramatic change.

Colonial anxieties

During Conrad's lifetime there was a sustained concern amongst colonial powers about the mobility of colonial subjects. The freedom of movement that their subject status granted was legislated for carefully and repeatedly, frequently along racial lines.[2] This is not to say that colonial subjects were unable to travel internationally, rather that colonial authorities attempted to regulate such movement thoroughly. The Indian Rebellion of 1857 and revolutionary uprisings in Egypt in 1882 had left the British, in particular, exceedingly anxious about the possibilities of insurrection in its territories. These British territories had become increasingly varied and far flung as the nineteenth century advanced, including chartered companies such as the British North Borneo Company; dominions like Canada and New Zealand; protectorates such as British Somaliland; and several whose status was ambiguous such as the Aden 'settlement' and the 'veiled protectorate' of Egypt. Movement of subjects meant movement of ideas, and the British wanted to avoid the migration of anti-colonial thinking within and across these regions.

These regions were nonetheless connected by the flow of trade that the British imperial project aimed to serve, as a brief examination of British colonial territories around the Arabian Sea illustrates. Aden, for example, was a crucial coal and trading port at the mouth of the Red Sea, linking the African and Indian continents, as well as the movement of goods and people between Europe and East Asia. The construction of the Suez Canal meant that Egypt was likewise crucial for East–West trade. Further East, India was an important midway point in the passage from the Suez to British territories in the Far East and Pacific. Furthermore, while Aden was technically governed from British India rather than directly from London, British Somaliland was initially governed from Aden and thereby from British India, creating networks not only of trade but also of law. The routes of these networks were nothing new even if British control of them was. What I want to draw attention to at this stage, however, is that the movement that these networks facilitated was both valued as the commercial lifeblood of the empire and feared as its Achilles' heel.

In this context, the prospect of transnational movement operating outside European imperial control or transgressing the borders of that control was perceived as a threat. In the Far East such movement was embodied primarily by the Chinese and Arabs, and the threat posed by the Arab presence in the Malay Archipelago was particularly troubling.[3] Firstly, since the Malays shared their Muslim faith with the Arabs there was a concern that they would ally with each other rather than with an 'infidel' European administration. Secondly, Arab traders were often involved in the transportation of pilgrims on Hajj from the Malay Archipelago and thus enabled the mass movement of subjects to and through regions in the Arabian Peninsula beyond the reach of the colonial authorities. Thirdly, as communities identified by religion and ethnicity rather than by a clearly defined nationality, Arabs did not fit into the regulatory frameworks of political statehood that European powers were using increasingly to map (ideologically and cartographically) the world and its inhabitants. Furthermore, larger anxieties about pan-Islamic uprisings fed suspicion of Arab migration to and movement within the Far East.

This anxiety was not unfounded. In 1881 anti-European feeling erupted in the 'Urabi revolution in Egypt. This 'proto-nationalist display of anger at foreign incursion' led to riots in European-dominated Alexandria in 1882 (Ulrichsen 2014: 21). The prospect of increased Egyptian political autonomy was particularly alarming given the strategic importance of the Suez for European trade, and Britain's response was to set up Egypt as a protectorate in all but name.[4] In the same period Abdul Hamid II, Sultan of the Ottoman Empire and consequently Caliph of Mecca, adopted a policy of pan-Islamism in an attempt to bind the increasingly disparate constituent parts of the empire in resistance to Western influence. The limited effect of Hamid's policy is evident in the Mahdi uprising in Sudan of the same period. Sudan was ruled from Egypt as part of the Ottoman Empire. In 1881 the religious leader Muhammad Ahmad declared himself the 'Mahdi' (the messiah of Islam) and led a long transnational rebellion in Sudan and Abyssinia (now Ethiopia). Ahmad's rebellion drew upon resentment not only of excessive taxation by the Egyptian authorities and of a clampdown on slave trading, but also of a perceived laxness in religious observance amongst Sudan's Egyptian and Ottoman rulers. The rebellion was put down by the British military in their role as unofficial colonial power in Egypt. Thus while in some areas of Egypt there was revolt against European imperialism, elsewhere in North East Africa there was revolt against Ottoman-Egyptian imperialism, which prompted collaboration between British and Egyptian administrations in its suppression.

Both the Mahdi rebellion and Britain's increasing influence over Egypt were symptoms of the decline of the Ottoman Empire over the nineteenth century. This decline led to increased instability in the Muslim world, with rival religious and political leaders vying for control of different regions and the key religious sites of pilgrimage, Mecca and Medina. These sites are located in the Hejaz, in the west of the Arabian Peninsula along the eastern shore of the Red Sea. It was thus a matter of concern to the British who controlled the Hejaz, as much as who controlled Aden at the southern tip of the Red Sea or Egypt and Sudan on the western shores, since it was through this sea that British trade passed to enter the Arabian Sea. It is not surprising then that the crumbling Ottoman Empire and Hamid II's pan-Islamic ideals presented attractive opportunities to Germany as it sought to invigorate its status outside Europe. Kris K. Manjapra notes that in 1898, on a visit to the Ottoman Empire, Kaiser Wilhelm II 'declared himself a "friend" to the "300 million Moslems of the world" at Damascus, and encouraged rumours in the Turkish press that he would convert to Islam' (2006: 365; quoting Levine 2000: 61). Wilhelm's visit coincided with a growth of German ethnographic interest in the Muslim world amongst both academics and political experts.[5]

Following partition in 1905, the growing extremism of the anti-colonial Swadeshi movement in India excited German orientalists and politicians alike with the hope that the movement might finally bring British rule in India to an end. By 1908 Germany was second only to Britain in shipping traffic to India. The idea of overthrowing British rule in India was therefore not only a strike against a European rival but also a strategic international goal for Germany's own transnational trading interests. Despite the fact that Swadeshi was primarily a Hindu nationalist movement, some German politicians chose to understand it as a Muslim uprising, conflating Swadeshi with a misplaced perception that pan-Islamism was breaking out across the British Empire. Consequently in the years leading up to and during the First World War Germany actively sought to promote pan-Islamic jihad amongst the Asian populations of the British Empire even, in the case of India, if not all those populations were in fact Muslim.[6]

Britain's anxieties about the extent of its own influence in the Levant, Suez, the Red and Arabian Seas, and the Indian Ocean were thus hardly unfounded given the huge importance of these regions to the functioning of the Empire and the real threats posed by rival powers and the transnational spread of anti-colonial movements. The stakes were raised further at the outbreak of the First

World War, when British interests in the oil fields of Mesopotamia and Persia (present-day Iraq and Iran) were sharpened by the navy's adoption in 1912 of oil, rather than coal, to power all new vessels in its fleet.[7] Oil was already becoming a significant commodity for British industry, but its colonial territories were not particularly oil rich.[8] Gaining control of the Persian and Mesopotamian fields, the latter nominally controlled by the Ottomans, was an opportunity to secure British oil supplies for the future. Thus, from the second half of the nineteenth century through the first decade of territorial wrangling following the First World War, the movement of ideas and peoples across and within Muslim world (from North Africa to the Malay Peninsula) was of significant importance to the British Empire.

For my purposes here, what is striking is the coincidence between this period of British interest in the Muslim world and the temporality of Conrad's literary world, that is to say the period in which he was writing and the period(s) in which he sets his fiction. Indeed Conrad's own lifetime coincides relatively precisely with the period I have been outlining, born as he was in 1857, the year of the Indian Rebellion, and dying in 1924, the year that Atatürk led the new Turkish government in abolishing the Caliphate, the last symbol of the old Ottoman regime. From *Punch* cartoons and memoirs, journalism and fiction, Conrad and his readers would have been familiar with the importance of the Suez, the Mahdi uprising, the decline of the Ottoman Empire, nationalist rebellions in India and Egypt, and, following the excited international coverage of the *Jeddah* story (to which we will turn shortly), the significance of Hajj for Muslim Malays in the Far East. With the exception of the *Patna* incident in *Lord Jim* Conrad did not write about these issues directly. Indeed, despite the importance of the Arabian Sea to British maritime commerce Conrad's nautical fiction avoids overt representation of the region. Nonetheless, whether Conrad intended this or not, the Arab and Muslim characters who appear repeatedly in his Malay fiction were likely to have been read by his contemporary public in the light of these larger global politics.

Arab and Malay relations

Arab and Malay relations are thought to predate the Common Era and are well documented from the middle of the first millennium CE.[9] Mohammad Redzuan Othman notes, however, that in that first millennium trade was limited between Arabs and Malays (2009: 84). It was trade with China that motivated Arab migration to the Malay Archipelago in the first instance.

This pattern of trade shifted as European demand for goods from the region increased (Othman lists 'pepper, ginger, cinnamon, sugar, cloves, nutmeg' for both medicinal and culinary uses [2009: 84]). Gradually Melaka emerged as a key node in commercial travel, where Chinese merchants exchanged goods with those from India and the Middle East. Consequently, Arab traders focused their routes on the Indian Ocean, rather than on the China Seas, and developed more extensive trading relations across the Malay and Indonesian Archipelagos (Othman 2009: 85). By the first centuries of the second millennium CE Arab traders were well established in Melaka, both from the Arabian Peninsula and from North Africa. In 1511, however, the Portuguese international wars against Islam reached Melaka and, following its fall to the Portuguese, Arab trading in the region was considerably reduced until the middle of the nineteenth century (Othman 2009: 86).

From early on Arab trade with the Far East was funnelled through Aden. Situated at the point at which the Red Sea, fed by the Gulfs of Aqaba and Suez, meets the Arabian Sea, and not much more than a stone's throw from the Horn of Africa, Aden was particularly well placed as a trading hub between east and west, north and south. From the seventeenth century onwards, Arabian trade with and migration to the Far East came predominantly from Hadhramaut, the southern region of the Arabian Peninsula on whose tip Aden sits. Othman suggests several causes for this predominance: firstly, the Hadhramaut region is climatically inhospitable; secondly, and consequently, Hadhramis 'had a long history of migration' already both regionally and further afield (e.g. East Africa and India) and so were predisposed to migration; finally, the violent expansion of Wahhabism across the central and eastern Arabian Peninsula at the end of the eighteenth century led many to seek exile from persecution (2009: 95).

While trade relations between the Middle East and the Malay Archipelago preceded religious ones, Islam reached the region within fifty years or so of its advent in CE 622 (Othman 2009: 86). Orientalist scholarship has tended to attribute the arrival of Islam to Indian missionaries; however, early Malay accounts clearly indicate the importance of direct Arab influence too (Othman 2009: 89). This influence did not abate and, while the archipelago produced its own Islamic leaders, accounts and records from the nineteenth century demonstrate that scholars and preachers from the Middle East continued to travel to the Far East, supporting Islamic instruction and practice (Othman 2009: 90–1). At the same time, Muslims from the Far East travelled west not only on pilgrimage but also to study in the educational centres of North Africa and the Arabian Peninsula.

Anthony Reid notes that 'as representatives of the pure source of Islam, Arab immigrants commanded a natural respect in nineteenth-century South East Asia, particularly if they were Sayyids' (1967). Sayyids 'claimed that they were descendants of the prophet and traced their genealogy through the line of Isa al-Muhajr' (Othman 2009: 97). In fact, most Hadhrami migrants claimed Sayyidi ancestry and actively preserved this distinctive identity. We see this distinction briefly in *The Shadow-Line* when the narrator notes that his previous berth had been aboard a ship owned by an 'Arab', adding, 'and a Syed at that' (Conrad 1917: 5). Others, who did not claim descent from the Prophet, tended to use the title 'Shaykh' (technically the plural of *mashayikh* meaning scholar or holy man [Othman 2009: 98]). We also find in *Lord Jim* Sherif Ali, whose title 'Sharif' signals descent from the Prophet through a different line from the Sayyids.

The transnational impulses of trade and religion thus brought the Far East and the Middle East into regular contact over many centuries. We see this reflected in the various 'Arabs' of Conrad's fiction, that is to say those who, even if like Abdulla they had been born in the Far East, trace their family tree back to the Arabian Peninsula. We also see it in the many Muslim characters whose ethnicity roots them in the Malay Archipelago but who have undertaken Hajj. Conrad presents a considerable number of pilgrims from all ranks and backgrounds. Famously, of course, the *Patna* is carrying East Asian pilgrims towards Mecca. Less memorable, perhaps, but nonetheless significant is the fact that Reshid in *Almayer's Folly*, both the 'kassab', or storekeeper, and Wasub, the serang, in *The Rescue*, as well as Karain's sword bearer are all Hajjis. In *An Outcast of the Islands* not only is it Patalolo's great desire before he dies to reach Mecca, but we learn that Babalatchi has completed Hajj.

Indeed, despite the costs, dangers and the restrictions imposed by colonial governments, many from the Malay and Indonesian archipelagos made the pilgrimage. Reid suggests that 'in the last three decades of the nineteenth century … [Indonesian pilgrims formed] on average about 15 per cent of the total overseas arrivals in the Hejaz' (1967: 269). Hajj was first and foremost an act of devotion, but it also provided opportunities, however brief, to learn from and network with Arab Muslims and those South East Asians who had migrated ('semipermanently' [Reid 1967: 269]) to Mecca and who fostered an 'international and distinctly anti-colonial outlook' (Reid 1967: 269). Returning home, the title Hajji garnered respect; more than this though the experiences of international travel and worship also gave pilgrims new perspectives and insights.

Writing about Arabs and Hajjis in the Malay Peninsula

Richard Burton was by no means the first but was certainly one of the most celebrated European authors of an account of Hajj, having made the pilgrimage himself in disguise in 1853. His *Personal Narrative* recounting this expedition was an immediate success, going through multiple international editions in the nineteenth and early twentieth centuries. Lester (1988) and Hans van Marle (1985) have explored the influence of Burton on Conrad's presentation of Islam in his Malay fiction. Nonetheless, although Burton notes the presence of '*Jawi* – Java Moslems' in the cosmopolitan environs of Medina, he does not otherwise give much attention to Arabs and Hajjis from the Far East (1858: 275). Thus, while Conrad's representations draw on and would have been read by his contemporary audience in the context of Burton's earlier *Narrative*, it is important to recognize how they intersect with a more specific discourse at the time concerning South East Asian Islam.

In a valuable account of this discourse, Syed Muhd Khairudin Aljunied notes the early influence of the British administrators William Marsden, Thomas Stamford Raffles and John Crawfurd in the development of a narrative that correlated Arabs and Hajjis with anti-colonialism (2004: 162). Aljunied suggests that it was Marsden who established 'a "natural link" between *hajjis* and Arabs', a link that Raffles expanded upon to associate Wahabbist Arab influence on Hajjis with rebellions against colonial rule (2004: 162–3). Crawfurd echoed this sentiment in his *History of the Indian Archipelago* (1820), which was translated into Dutch three years after its English-language publication, cementing an association between Arabs, the transnationalism of Hajj, religious fanaticism and Malay insurrection. This association was perpetuated in Dutch and English language texts throughout the nineteenth century, finding fictional force in novels like Louis Couperus's *De Stille Kracht* (*The Hidden Force*) (1900). Challenges to this association, such as C. Snouck Hurgronje's *Mekka in the Latter Part of the Nineteenth Century* (1888), were influential exceptions that nonetheless proved the rule (Aljunied 2004: 168–9).

Interestingly, while Conrad draws on familiar tropes from this discourse in his representation of migrant and transnational Arabs and Hajjis, the motivations and functions of these characters within Conrad's plots are more varied than the model Aljunied outlines. These characters are present in Conrad's fiction from the outset, and indeed are most frequent in his early fiction (for example *Almayer's Folly*, *An Outcast of the Islands*, *The Rescue* which was begun in 1896, *Lord Jim* and 'Karain'). Conrad's first Hajji, Syed Reshid, is also the most caricatured in his Malay fiction. Reshid embodies the stereotype of the well-to-do pilgrim, privileged enough by the inherited wealth of his Straits Arab uncle, Abdulla, to make the journey at a young age, arrogant in the status it brings him on his return. He rejoices in his 'green jacket and the proud title of Hadji'; yet when he accompanies Abdulla to Almayer's house in pursuit of marriage to Nina he appears 'very rakish and dissipated', affecting 'the greatest indifference … examining his aristocratically small hands with great attention' (Conrad 1995: 35). Nina is to be added to his 'harem' of 'several Malay women', Abdulla explains (Conrad 1995: 36). His suit rejected, he turns first to illicit trade in gunpowder and then plays upon Taminah's broken heart in an attempt to thwart Dain and Nina. Petulant, vain and deceitful, Reshid is thus drawn from stock Orientalist images of the privileged Arab pilgrim whose piety is hypocritical and whose pilgrimage is made in the service of self-aggrandisement.

Babalatchi is painted with more nuance, but Conrad nonetheless attributes an untrustworthiness to his character in keeping with colonial concerns about the influence of Hajj. Thus, in *An Outcast of the Islands*, we are told that Babalatchi had 'gathered wisdom in many lands, and after attaching himself to Omar el Badavi, he *affected* great piety (as became a pilgrim), although unable to read the inspired words of the Prophet' (1975: 50, emphasis added). Here Babalatchi's mobile gathering of wisdom 'in many lands' echoes the anxiety that the British and Dutch powers felt about Malay Hajjis coming into contact with cosmopolitan and anti-colonial ideas while on their pilgrimage. Furthermore, Conrad undercuts Babalatchi's special status as Hajji by denigrating his illiteracy and casting his piety as affectation. In the same novel, Patololo's desire to go to Mecca is painted with similar colours of hypocrisy: not only his own but the hypocrisy of Abdulla and Lakamba who self-servingly support his wishes on the assumption that he will never make it beyond Penang. Thus, in *An Outcast* Hajj is depicted and deployed primarily as a political device. In his first two novels, then, Conrad refuses to entertain the possibility of his characters undertaking Hajj for genuinely pious ends and instead presents his Hajjis as self-serving.

In *The Rescue* this sceptical presentation is modified. Certainly, the Sumatran kassab effects a certain 'comical truculence' to match the 'dignity and ease' of his position as storekeeper and Hajji. By contrast, however, the serang, Wasub, is portrayed quite differently (Conrad 1920: 20). Wasub's status is repeated emphatically at his first appearance when the helmsman entreats him as 'Haji Wasub' three times in the space of a few lines. The third-person narration then repeats the attribution twice more in the next two pages before the kassab picks it up a few pages further on, noting that he is 'Haji, even as I am'. Wasub himself, however, doesn't use the term, although we are told he 'was not insensible to the sound of his rightful title' (Conrad 1920: 22). Instead Wasub invites Lingard to attend to his advice because he is 'a pilgrim' who has 'listened to words of wisdom in many places' (Conrad 1920: 180). Here, Babalatchi's active 'gathering' of wisdom on his travels is made to seem less dangerous in Wasub's more passive 'listening'.

Conrad's repeated use the term 'Haji' early in the novel suggests he expects his readers to understand it, and so we must presume that Wasub's different terminology is intentional. Indeed, Wasub's self-designation as a 'pilgrim' (a term he repeats) places a different emphasis on his character, suggesting to Conrad's English language audience endurance and faithfulness, rather than the self-serving desire used to characterize the kassab and other Hajjis in the earlier fiction. Here the term 'pilgrim' is applied sincerely in contrast with its application to Babalatchi in *An Outcast*, where its irony is signalled by the parenthetical aside in which it appears. Wasub's pious characteristics are borne out in the novel by his devoted service to Lingard: when Lingard collapses, as Jaffir delivers his last message from his deathbed, it is Wasub who catches him (Conrad 1920: 400). This devotion also permits a certain intimate capacity for straight-talking as when he tells a reluctant Lingard forthrightly: 'Tuan, it is necessary that you should hear Jaffir' (Conrad 1920: 398). In turn, it is to Wasub that Lingard entrusts Jaffir's body, 'to bury him decently according to their faith' (Conrad 1920: 401). Distinct from the vanity of the Straits Arab Reshid and the deviousness of Babalatchi, Wasub embodies a positive, if no less romanticized, figure of the Hajji.

Wasub's role as confidant to Lingard finds an interesting parallel in Karain's sword bearer. As Karain explains to Hollis and his companions,

> when I met him [his sword bearer] he was returning from a pilgrimage … he had gone to the holy place with his son, his son's wife, and a little child; and on their return, by the favour of the Most High, they all died … and the old man reached his country alone. He was a pilgrim serene and pious, very wise and very lonely. (Conrad 1898: 58)

As for Wasub, piety and wisdom are brought together under the anglicized title 'pilgrim' rather than the Arabic term 'Hajji' and although in fact no specific faith is mentioned Conrad signals this to us by the apparent fatalism of Karain's phrasing 'by the favour of the Most High', whose contorted translation of *inshallah* 'God's will' estranges (and orientalizes) the sentiment. More subtly, and perhaps unbeknownst to Conrad himself, the sword bearer's use of charms and his ability to 'command a spirit stronger than the unrest of [Karain's] dead friend' suggest that on his long pilgrimage he was exposed to Hadhramauti Islam rather than Wahhabism (1898: 58–9). For whereas Hadhramauti Muslims venerated saints and entertained a broad sphere of spiritual belief, Wahhabists sought to stamp out these practices as a corruption of the pure faith.

The violent zeal of Wahhabism, which swept through the Arabian Peninsula in the latter half of the nineteenth century, was of particular concern to the British and Dutch colonists in the Far East. They feared that Wahhabism would stir up a global pan-Islamist movement to overthrow colonial rule in India, Africa and the Middle East, and that would take control of the Ottoman Empire. This fear was excessive but not wholly without substance, as we have seen, insofar as Germany sought to agitate pan-Islamism against the British Empire before and during the First World War. As Eric Tagliacozzo explains, these anxieties about pan-Islamism led to increasingly tight colonial regulation of movement by Arabs and Muslims in the colonial Far East (2005). Permits to go on Hajj had to be applied for in advance, and both the Dutch and British endeavoured to monitor the movement of Malay and Indonesian pilgrims once they arrived in the Hejaz.

Renisa Mawani's account of the ill-fated voyage of the *Komagata Maru* in 1914 provides further context for these anxieties.[10] The *Komagata Maru* was chartered from its Japanese owners by Gurdit Singh, an Indian businessman in Hong Kong, to transport Indian migrants to Canada. Singh's larger objective was to establish a maritime business in international travel for Indian passengers, since the British restricted Indian travel on British vessels. As Mawani argues, the ship's voyage crystallized long-standing concerns about the mobility of colonized people. While there is, of course, a difference between the migration of Singh's passengers bound for Canada, and the pilgrimage of Hajj, reading the trans-oceanic mobility of Conrad's Arab traders and Hajji Malays against the legal test case of the *Komagata Maru* brings that mobility sharply into focus. Whether as colonial subjects by virtue of their birth in European colonies, like Singh and his passengers, or as international traders nominally outside the apparatus of European rule, the mobility of Arab and Muslim Malays undermined the increasingly cartographical understanding of empire held in Europe, that is to say the idea that empires were defined by geographical borders.

In this context Abdulla's first job, a 'commercial expedition, as his father's representative on board a pilgrim ship chartered by a wealthy Arab to convey a crowd of pious Malays to the Holy Shrine', stands metonymically for the threat he poses to Lingard's supreme control over Sambir (Conrad 1975: 96). Lingard boasts just a few pages earlier: 'The Arabs have been hanging about outside this river for years – and I am still the only trader here; the master here' (Conrad 1975: 83). By the end of the novel, however, Lingard's dominance of Sambir has been undermined by Abdulla's penetration of the river. No longer 'outside the river', Abdulla establishes himself as Lingard's rival for, and successor in, trade with the interior. Abdulla's earlier job aboard the pilgrim ship likewise enacts this penetration of European dominance: the pilgrim ship carries colonial subjects in a non-European 'commercial' enterprise that defies geopolitical borders and control. Abdulla thus reflects larger concerns about Arab–Malay transnationalism and migration that were prevalent in the second half of the nineteenth century.

While this reference to Abdulla's youthful employment is Conrad's earliest representation of the commerce of Hajj, his most famous, of course, is found in *Lord Jim*. The *Patna* incident is based on the abandonment of a real pilgrim ship, the *Jeddah*, in 1880. The *Jeddah* had been built in Dumbarton specifically for the transportation of pilgrims. Syed Mahomed bin Alsagoff, the ship's owner, was a member of the influential Straits Arab Alsagoff family who had come to Singapore from the Hadhramaut in 1824. On its fateful sailing its captain and officers were European, but many of the crew were not and its passengers were picked up from Singapore and Penang. Like the *Komagata Maru*, moreover, the incident prompted wrangling about international legal jurisdiction. Following the Court of Inquiry at Aden (governed from India), the Legislative Council of Singapore debated whether they could bring the captain to trial on the basis that 'the Merchant Shipping Act extends to all parts of Her Majesty's dominions and colonies' (Proceedings 1880).[11]

Conrad reconstructs and elaborates on the international character of the *Jeddah* affair. The *Patna* is 'owned by a Chinaman, chartered by an Arab, and commanded by a sort of renegade New South Wales German' (Conrad 1923: 14). Following their desertion, the crew are rescued by French sailors who take them to Bombay (present-day Mumbai) while the ship is towed to Aden.[12] Meanwhile, the diversity of the pilgrims is presented with poetic flourish:

> coming from north and south and from the outskirts of the East, after treading the jungle paths, descending the rivers, coasting in praus along the shallows, crossing in small canoes from island to island … from solitary huts in the wilderness, from populous campongs, from villages by the sea. (Conrad 1923: 14)

And like Abdulla in *An Outcast*, and Syed Mahomed bin Alsagoff's nephew, who had been aboard the *Jeddah*, an 'Arab' accompanies the *Patna*'s Hajjis as their 'leader' (Conrad 1923: 15).

The transnationalism of the *Patna* incident is in keeping with the multinational Indian Ocean maritime world represented in the first part of *Lord Jim*, where Italian, Dutch, South Asian, Greek and Portuguese characters appear more or less fleetingly. Conrad's decision to dramatize Jim's debasement aboard a pilgrim ship, however, draws our attention to a particular kind of transnationalism that transgresses European colonial control. For, even though pilgrim ships were regulated in their ports of origin (e.g. in terms of the number of lifeboats to be carried), the pilgrims and their Arab leaders were traveling into regions of the Arabian Peninsula that were beyond the reach of European colonial authorities. Moreover, their journey represented a movement governed by faith that bore little relation to the commercially driven European mobilities of the period. The larger geopolitical implications of Arab–Malay relations that Hajj encompassed at the turn of the century remain latent in *Lord Jim*. Nonetheless, in focusing less on individuals like Abdulla and Karain's sword bearer, as the earlier fiction had, and instead on the practicalities of mass pilgrimage itself, *Lord Jim* makes visible alternative and powerful forms of transnationalism and globalization that cut across European narratives of empire.

Conclusion

Andrew Francis usefully draws our attention to the fact that while *Almayer's Folly* and *An Outcast of the Islands* dramatize the ascension of Arab trade at the expense of European alliances, in reality the influence of Arab trade was on the wane both in the period Conrad represents and in the years he was writing (2015: 62). Nonetheless, as Tagliacozzo and others demonstrate, in this same period large numbers were travelling from the Far East on Hajj and at the same time Islamic schooling in the Malay Archipelago was expanding, supported by migrant scholars from the Middle East (Tagliacozzo 2013: 181, Aljunied 2004: 166, Othman 2009: 90–1). The relationship between the increasingly commercial business of international travel and the transnational circulation of religious ideas is reflected and refracted in Conrad's various Arab traders and his Hajji Malays. Moreover, whether by presenting a story of Arab supremacy at odds with the history of commerce in the region or by returning repeatedly to the trope of Hajj, Conrad's fiction taps into larger European fears of pan-Islamic anti-colonial movements, which located danger in the long-established migratory, familial and religious networks, which criss-crossed the Indian Ocean in defiance of bureaucratic colonial borders.

Notes

1 See, for example, Robert Hampson (2000); Norman Sherry (1966); Heliéna Krenn (1990).
2 For an example of the legislative debates around the rights to international free movement of colonial subjects see Renisa Mawani's discussion of the *Komagata Maru* case in 1914 (2018).
3 I have reflected on the challenge posed by transnational Chinese traders in Conrad's fiction elsewhere (2010 and 2020). See also Heliéna Krenn (1995), and Agnes Yeow (2004).
4 Egypt was already controlled to a large extent by France and Britain following their agreement to bail out the country's debt (Ulrichsen 2014: 17).
5 For example Max von Oppenheim, who became German general consul in 1896, published several books at the turn of the century on Muslim culture, which demonstrate his fascination with Islamic fanaticism (Manjapra 2006: 368–9).
6 For a fuller account of Germany's conflation of Swadeshi with jihad, and its consequences, see Manjapra.
7 This adoption came after trials with HMS *Spiteful*, which had been adapted to run on oil in 1904.
8 Although prospecting began early in the twentieth century, oil was not found in Nigeria until the 1950s.
9 See G. R. Tibbetts, cited in Othman (2009).
10 See Mawani (2018).
11 In the end the Council did not pursue legal action against the captain because, whilst all held him responsible and reprehensible, it was not thought that a successful prosecution could be made.
12 The crew and passengers of the *Jeddah* were found by British sailors and all were taken to Aden.

Works Cited

Aljunied, S. M. K. (2004), 'Edward Said and Southeast Asian Islam: Western Representations of Meccan Pilgrims (Hajjis) in the Dutch East Indies, 1800–1900', *Journal of Commonwealth and Postcolonial Studies*, 11 (1–2): 159–75.

Baxter, K. (2010), *Joseph Conrad and the Swan Song of Romance*, Farnham: Ashgate.

Baxter, K. (2017), 'Geography and Law in *Almayer's Folly*', *Conradiana* 49 (2–3): 67–84.

Burton, R. (1858), *Personal Narrative of a Pilgrimage to El-Medinah and Meccah*, Boston: Shepard, Clark and Brown.

Conrad, J. (1898), 'Karain', in *Tales of Unrest*, London: Fisher Unwin.

Conrad, J. (1917), *The Shadow-Line*, New York: Doubleday, Page and Co.

Conrad, J. (1920), *The Rescue*, London: Dent.

Conrad, J. (1923), *Lord Jim*, London: Dent.

Conrad, J. (1975), *An Outcast of the Islands*, London: Penguin.

Conrad, J. (1995), *Almayer's Folly*, Cambridge: Cambridge University Press.

Francis, A. (2015), *Culture and Commerce in Conrad's Asian Fiction*, Cambridge: Cambridge University Press.

Hampson, R. (2000), *Cross-Cultural Encounters in Joseph Conrad's Malay Fiction*, Basingstoke: Palgrave.

Krenn, H. (1990), *Conrad's Lingard Trilogy: Empire, Race, and Women in the Malay Novels*, New York: Garland Press.

Krenn, H. (1995), 'China and the Chinese in the Works of Joseph Conrad', *Conradiana*, 27 (2): 83–96.

Lester, J. (1988), *Conrad and Religion*, Basingstoke: Palgrave Macmillan.

Levine, I. D., ed. (2000), *Letters from the Kaiser to the Czar*, New York: F. A. Stokes.

Manjapra, K. K. (2006), 'The Illusions of Encounter: Muslim "minds" and Hindu Revolutionaries in First World War Germany and After', *Journal of Global History*, 1: 363–82.

Marle, H. v. (1985), 'Conrad and Richard Burton on Islam', *Conradiana*, 17: 137–42.

Mawani, R. (2018), *Across Oceans of Law: The* Komagata Maru *and Jurisdiction in the Time of Empire*, Durham, NC: Duke University Press.

Moore, G. (2003), 'Newspaper Accounts of the *Jeddah* Affair', in A. Simmons and J. H. Stape (eds), *Lord Jim: Centennial Essays*, 104–39, Amsterdam: Rodopi.

Othman, M. R. (2009): 'The Origins and Contributions of Early Arabs in Malaya', in E. Tagliacozzo (ed.), *Southeast Asia and the Middle East: Islam, Movement, and the Longue Durée*, 83–107, Stanford, CA: Stanford University Press.

'Proceedings of the Legislative Council of Singapore, 14 September 1880' (1880), in the *Straits Times Overland Journal*, 20 September: 2–3.

Reid, A. (1967), 'Nineteenth Century Pan-Islam in Indonesia and Malaysia', *Journal of Asian Studies*, 26 (2): 267–83.

Sherry, N. (1966), *Conrad's Eastern World*, Cambridge: Cambridge University Press.

Tagliacozzo, E. (2005), *Secret Trades, Porous Borders: Smuggling and States Along a Southeast Asian Frontier, 1965–1915*, New Haven, CT: Yale University Press.

Tagliacozzo, E. (2013), *The Longest Journey: Southeast Asians and the Pilgrimage to Mecca*, Oxford: Oxford University Press.

Ulrichsen, K. C. (2014), *The First World War in the Middle East*, London: Hurst and Co.

Yeow, A. (2004), 'Conrad and The Straits Chinese: The Politics of Chinese Enterprise and Identity in the Colonial State', *The Conradian*, 29 (1): 84–98.

'Amy Foster', *Amerika* and *After Bread*: Modernism, technology and the immigrant

Yael Levin
Hebrew University of Jerusalem

> London is the world town, not because of its vastness; it is vast because of its assimilative powers, because it destroys all race characteristics, insensibly and, as it were, anaesthetically … London will do all this imperceptibly. And, in externals, that is the high-water mark of achievement of the Modern Spirit. (Hueffer 1905: 12–13)

Joseph Conrad's 'Amy Foster' presents a series of frustrations: the misleading focus of its title, Yanko's failed absorption in his new home, the encounter with an inhospitable culture. This chapter will read the story against the backdrop of the fiction of immigration to the new world in order to tease out a generically determined frustration that merits consideration. My claim is that in bringing his protagonist back to the familiar and reassuring spaces of agricultural life, the author deliberately rejects the conventions of the fiction of immigration that were definitive of the age.[1] The story offers a glimpse of these conventions in the abrupt and fast-paced shifts that accompany Yanko's journey through the modern and industrial West. The sinking of Yanko's ship, however, spells the abandonment of this plot trajectory. In place of the sensory confusion associated with the experience of a late-nineteenth-century port and the metropolis that it feeds, Yanko and the narrative are led to a small rural town in Kent. This jarring turn confronts the reader with an economic and cultural xenophobia that cannot be marginalized by the alienations of the dizzying and distracting experience of modern life.

Work on this chapter was supported by the Israel Science Foundation (grant no. 468/17).

Conrad's story undercuts the 'assimilative powers' (Hueffer 1905: 12) to which Ford Madox Hueffer alludes in *The Soul of London* and returns to a more traditional exploration of cultural encounter. The omission of the modern-city tropes may be read as Conrad's deliberate decision to eschew what Ford describes as the anesthetizing effects of technology, its razing of cultural and national nuances. 'Amy Foster' (1901) Franz Kafka's *Amerika* (1927) and Henryk Sienkiewicz's *After Bread* (1880) are read here side by side in order to show how modernist writing anticipates recent debates on the role of technology in the creation of blind spots to cultural difference.[2] The representation of attention, pace and memory will be used to demonstrate where modernism is complicit in the marginalization of cultural difference and where it demands, stages or resists the reconfiguration of immigrant subjectivity. Such an investigation will serve not only to test tensions within modernist thought, but as a counterpoint to similar tensions in recent critical debates on migrant subjectivity, between universalizing gestures and the emphasis on difference, between the position that all subjects are created in movement and the critique of such abstractions due to their cancellation of cultural and ethnic specificities.[3] By returning to difference and upsetting generic expectations, Conrad's writing serves as a warning against ideologically motivated generalizations both modernist and contemporary.

Failed assimilation: Memory and the scene of temptation in *After Bread*

In *The Soul of London,* Ford Madox Hueffer remarks on the assimilative powers of the modern metropolis:

> If in its tolerance it finds a place for all eccentricities of physiognomy, of costume, of cult, it does so because it crushes out and floods over the significance of those eccentricities … In its innumerable passages and crannies it swallows up Mormon and Mussulman, Benedictine and Agapemonite, Jew and Malay, Russian and Neapolitan. It assimilates and slowly digests them, converting them, with the most potent of all juices, into the singular and inevitable product that is the Londoner—that is, in fact, the Modern. (1905: 11–12)

Ford describes the city's powers of assimilation as the blurring of cultural and religious boundaries. Much of the fiction of the age appears to bear out this ideology of the 'Modern' in its intimation that the demands of modern life do not lie in cultural adaptation but in the radical reconfiguration of subjectivity.

The greatest obstacles to a successful absorption in the new world relate to the transformation of one's cognitive and perceptual modes of engagement with reality. The migrant subject's cultural and religious loyalties are of no interest to the city – it is how he responds to sensory overload that will determine the success of his absorption.

Two forms of response to the challenges of the new are explored in Henryk Sienkiewicz's *After Bread*.[4] The first is anchored in memory; the second in modes of perception. Economic ruin drives Lorenz and his daughter Mary from their Polish home of Lipintse. Their voyage to the new world repeatedly evokes memories of the people and vistas left behind. Mary compares all the young men she encounters to the fiancé she was forced to abandon. Her reluctance to betray his memory, in defiance of her father's command that she 'put him out of [her] head' (Sienkiewicz 1897: 13), is just one expression of the two characters' method of experiencing the present through the past. The narrator repeatedly reminds the readers that their loyalties and sentiments remain grounded in Lipintse: 'When they saw the "beloved sun" they felt more easy in their hearts, for it looked to them *exactly as it did in Lipintse*. All to them was new and strange, and only this disk of the sun, bright and radiant, appeared like an old friend and guardian' (12, my emphasis). The new is repeatedly framed by the old; sensory input is mitigated through the power of memory: 'The sea-breezes sang in [Lorenz's] ears and kept repeating, "Lipintse! Lipintse!" Sometimes it whistled like a Polish flute' (19).

Where Mary's and Lorenz's voyage is grounded in the familiar, Yanko's experience of his new home hinges on difference:

> There was nothing here the same as in his country! The earth and the water were different; there were no images of the Redeemer by the roadside. The very grass was different, and the trees. All the trees but the three old Norway pines on the bit of lawn before Swaffer's house, and these reminded him of his country. He had been detected once, after dusk, with his forehead against the trunk of one of them, sobbing, and talking to himself. They had been like brothers to him at that time, he affirmed. Everything else was strange. (Conrad 1950: 129)

Though the distinction between these two responses is significant, both scenes show that immigrant subjectivity is grounded in memory. The insight works against post-structural and materialist critiques of a fixed or disembodied definition of migrant subjectivity. Where such critiques attach the self to movement and flux, our characters' identities are fixed.[5] In these scenes all three characters filter the present through their sense of the past.

As they near New York, Lorenz's reaction assumes new form:

> The ship came nearer and nearer—the beautiful city arose as if from the water. Lorenz, who was filled with astonishment and joy, took off his cap, opened wide his mouth and looked … Lorenz not only wondered, but he *coveted.* Seeing the green shores on both sides of the bay, the darker green of the uplands, the cultivated lawns and grounds, he spoke again … 'In Poland *I was a peasant*, but here I shall be *a large land-owner.*' (Sienkiewicz 1897: 44–5, my emphases)

The scene depicts a turn from memory to the new-world tropes of amazement and spectatorship. This is also linked to a change in tense from an emphasis on the past (what was) to the future (what will be). The excerpt might thus serve as a turning point from the nostalgic sea voyage and its insinuation of a fixed subject position to a more receptive and changeable one. The moralizing overtones characterizing the language, however, do not allow us to see this transformation as an 'achievement' (Hueffer 1905: 13), to revert to Ford's term. We read the scene not as a rebirth but as a prelude to disillusionment. Suggestive of a scene of temptation, the longing that the new generates is morally suspect. Lorenz *covets.*

A tension arises between these two models of response and the two warring definitions of subjectivity to which they are attached: one anchored in the past, the other fashioned in an immersion in the sensory flux associated with the present. An openness to the new is key to their survival, but it is also a marker of moral failing. The new world and its figurative expressions in technology, the crowd, filth and noise are seen as hell-on-earth, 'a human Gehenna' (Sienkiewicz 1897: 58); the old pastoral life is a boon, a refuge; it is associated with Christian values and a nurturing family life. This moral marker of difference between the old and the new, between rural life and technological progress, is evident from the start. During their sea voyage, the propeller 'churned the water more violently and the smokestack sent forth great clouds of smoke, and these two were like some evil spirits who carried [Lorenz] farther and farther from Lipintse' (19).

The scene of temptation evidenced on arrival resonates with a Faustian motif that is introduced during the voyage: 'At moments he was apprehensive that perhaps these "heathen" as he called his fellow-travelers, would cast him into the sea or command him to change his religion, or to sign some paper, perhaps, even a "*cyrograf!*"—to sell his soul to the devil' (18).[6] Lorenz's fear finds its historical correlate in the widespread late-nineteenth-century suspicion of the travel agents who capitalized on immigration and encouraged Eastern European subjects to leave their home countries. The fear is similarly emphasized in 'Amy

Foster' where Yanko is pictured as a 'victim' of 'scoundrels' 'in league with the local usurers' (a clear reference to Jews) whose object is 'to get hold of the poor ignorant people's homesteads' (Conrad 1950: 121).[7]

The late years of the nineteenth century saw widespread debates on the implications of emigration. In *The Great Departure*, Tara Zahra writes that

> in the eyes of many emigration reformers, particularly religious officials, emigration posed a mortal threat to the traditional family structure. Emigration separated parents and children and husbands and wives, and isolated couples from extended kin. It catapulted peasants from tight-knit rural villages to anonymous cities, exposing them to new forms of temptation and vice. Social reformers and theorists constantly bemoaned the allegedly destructive effects of migration on family life and gender roles, and sought ways to keep transnational families and "traditional" values intact. (2016: 81)

Such fears were fed by public trials against travel agents, one of which was the famous 1889 trial at Wadowice.[8] Sixty-five defendants (Jewish travel agents) 'were accused of seducing migrants into abandoning their homeland with false promises of an American El Dorado' only to deliver them 'into hard labor in American factories, mines, and brothels' (Zahra 2016: 23). Zahra explains that 'the trial at Wadowice reflected and promoted the conviction that agents were to blame for mass emigration. The anti-Semitic *Deutsche Volksblatt* declared, "There is no doubt that this massive emigration … was not the consequence of overpopulation or economic conditions in the province, but that it was artificially nourished by the propaganda of agents"' (2016: 43).

To view the mass migration of the nineteenth century as a product of a nefarious conspiracy is to recast it as a moral threat to the ideals, faith and norms of traditional life, a suspicion that is confirmed in Sienkiewicz's novel. Lorenz and his daughter are not only physically but also mentally and spiritually undone by the experience. The arrival in New York upsets Lorenz's meek nature and rapidly unhinges him. Thomas Gladsky claims the novel 'emphasizes the pressures of urban environment, natural disaster, and human depravity (American depravity in this case)'; and, standing 'as an admonition to would-be immigrants', it shows that the 'peasant is ill-prepared for the "promised land"' (1992: 41).

After Bread offers a poignant challenging of Ford's celebration of the modern city's ability to 'insensibly' create uniformity.[9] In Lipintse Lorenz and Mary knew they could rely on the charity of their neighbours. New York offers no such consolations:

> But in this great city, that hummed like a mighty engine, everybody rushed onward and looked only ahead, so that they could not see the suffering of others. The head swam here, the arms drooped, the eyes were bewildered with the many sights, and the thoughts chased each other; everything was so strange and repelling, whirling at full speed, so that they who did not know how to revolve in this wheel were cast out and broken like an earthen jar. (Sienkiewicz 1897: 61)

This is a cautionary tale on the dangers of immigration, on the impossible demands the city places on the immigrant's perceptive abilities. If Lorenz's and Mary's identities are anchored in memory, to be tossed and turned and stripped of their past is to be broken. Moreover, we cannot view the inability to adapt as a failing, as the new-world values have been coloured by a set of damning figurative associations from the start. The insistence on the new world's inhuman realities allows us to read their tragic deaths as a form of moral resistance or an abiding innocence. Such resistance has its scopic expressions. Eyes that were initially marvelling and receptive are, by the end of their life in the city, 'bewildered', 'large and vacant' (61). The ability to marvel and see is restored only once they are outside the dirty, confused and crowded city and on the road, where 'there were fields and pastures and forests in the far distance, and houses shaded by trees, and immense stretches of young green crops were everywhere just as in Poland' (106). Finally co-opted in the service of memory, the motif of sight in *After Bread* suggests that Mary and Lorenz can only see (at) home.

Seeing through glass: Refracting the new

Where the first part of *After Bread* establishes its characters' fixity in memory, Kafka's unfinished novel begins by breaking with the past: 'As he entered New York Harbor on the now slow-moving ship, Karl Rossmann, a seventeen-year-old youth who had been sent to America by his poor parents because a servant girl had seduced him and borne a child by him, saw the Statue of Liberty, which he had been observing for some time, as if in a sudden burst of sunlight.' Home is here imagined as a place of seduction and poverty rather than the seat of family life and Christian values; New York is cast as a symbol of liberty and light. The freedoms it promises are associated with a symbolic severance. In Kafka's imagination, the statue no longer holds a torch: 'The arm with the sword now reached aloft, and about her figure blew the free winds' (Kafka 2008: 3). We can view this sword as the modernist demand for a break with history; the call to make it new. Karl quickly learns that memory will be of little use to him here. Where Lorenz and Mary are never free of the sounds of Lipintse, Karl finds that his home-town melodies have been rendered ineffective:

> In his first days there Karl had hoped to accomplish a great deal through his piano playing and was not ashamed—at least just before falling asleep—to imagine that his playing might *directly* affect his situation in America. It certainly sounded strange whenever he stood in front of windows opening out onto the noisy street, playing an old soldier's song from his homeland, which the soldiers, who used to lie by the barrack windows at night looking down at the dark square, would sing from one window to the next – but then when he looked down on the street he could see that it had not changed at all and merely formed one small part of a great cycle that one could not actually bring to a halt unless one were aware of all of the forces operating in the circle. (39–40, my emphasis)

The passage is demonstrative of the evacuation of the emotional resonance described by Georg Simmel in 'The Metropolis and Mental Life': 'the reaction of the metropolitan person to those events is moved to a sphere of mental activity which is least sensitive and which is furthest removed from the depths of the personality' (1971: 326). Tying the reconfiguration of subjectivity to a certain emotional flattening that occurs in the transition from rural to urban life, Simmel suggests that the metropolitan type finds security in the rational. The assessment links, in his essay, to the law of the market, the monetizing of value and the replacement of quality for quantity. We may relate Simmel's account of the emotional insulations associated with the market to a more generalized emphasis on mediation and circuitry. This is evident in the recurrence of the imagery of glass, a material that is not only ingrained in new-world architecture, but one that doubles as mediation and transparency – the sense of seeing, but seeing through a distorting or diffusing lens:

> In the morning and in the evening and at night in his dreams, this street was filled with constantly bustling traffic, which seen from above seemed like a continually self-replenishing mixture of distorted human figures and of the roofs of all sorts of vehicles, constantly scattered by new arrivals, out of which there arose a new, stronger, wilder mixture of noise, dust, and smells, and, catching and penetrating it all, a powerful light that was continually dispersed, carried away, and avidly refracted by the mass of objects that made such a physical impression on one's dazzled eye that it seemed as if a glass pane, hanging over the street and covering everything, were being smashed again and again with the utmost force. (Kafka 2008: 36)

The imagery of refraction, mediation and glass accommodates the moral and perceptual lessons offered by Karl's guardian. Karl is instructed that he should not 'become seriously engaged in anything', 'he should not let anything beguile him'. Newcomers to the city who do so become 'lost sheep'. Though this would appear to reinvoke the fear of temptation explored in *After Bread*, here the danger of such depth-perception is a confusion that departs from the connotations of sin explored in the earlier novel. Taught that 'gazing down at the street' is nothing short of calamitous, Karl quickly learns to avoid the balcony and its dangerous vistas. If there is a morality at work here it is of a capitalist nature – the danger is of becoming ineffectual, lost, unproductive. What is to be avoided is 'all that solitary idleness, that wasteful staring out on a bustling New York day' (36).

Counter-intuitively, perhaps, mediation serves to save time and money. One takes detours to avoid traffic; the telephone and telegraph compress time and distance. Even the nature of his uncle's business contributes to the motif: intermediary trading bypasses the inefficiency of direct human contact. The very configuration of the human subject undergoes a cubist-like fragmentation. The broken jar imagery of *After Bread* has transformed into a new model for identity in *Amerika*. An employee in the telephone room is described 'with his head tucked into a steel band that pressed the earpieces up against his ears. His right arm lay on a small table as if were a heavy burden, and only the fingers holding a pencil twitched at a rapid and inhumanly regular pace' (43). Head, ear, arm, fingers work side by side in a disjointed fashion, each autonomous, each appearing to be physically separate from the others. Unity gives way to utility and to the maximization of effect; each organ contributes autonomously to the line of production. A similar scene emerges in the description of the porter's lodge where the clerks dispensing information to the hotel's guests have to contend with 'at least ten inquiring faces standing at the window before them'. The scene depicts 'a confusion of tongues among the ten questioners, who changed continually, as if each had been dispatched from a different country' (173). The production line imagery again disperses the human into faces and tongues, so that the tower of babel imagery is literalized in a confusion of limbs and organs. Humans become parts in an assembly line – they not only serve it in disassembled fashion but also tend to others as an assemblage of organs rather than as unique and whole individuals.

The scene also highlights a stark contrast between the invisibility of the protagonists in Sienkiewicz's city and the painful exposure evident here: 'There did not even seem to be a corner anywhere in the porter's lodge where one could hide from the eyes of those people. For all their rushing about—they sought to advance, arms extended, heads lowered, eyes peering, luggage raised in the air—hardly any of them failed to glance into the porter's lodge' (172). The experience combines a stream of visual stimuli and a panopticon-like sense of being watched. The implication is that, despite the emphasis on mediated experience, the transparency of glass produces the sensation that 'one stood in their midst' (172). The distance may offer a sense of isolation, but not privacy. One is not removed from the spatio-temporal present.

Though the motif of sight serves the novel's exploration of a new mode of perception and being in the world, here too it emerges as a battleground of resistance. Where Mary and Lorenz could not see beyond their memories of home, Karl battles with his captors in the only way he can – through the independent use of his eyes.[10] His captor Brunelda turns to him as they stand on a balcony to view a parade on the street:

> 'Don't you want to look through the glasses?' …
> 'I can see well enough', said Karl.
> 'Do try them', she said, 'you'll see better.'
> 'I've good eyes', Karl answered, 'I can see everything.'
>
> When she brought the glasses close to his eyes, he felt that this was not so much kindness as an intrusion on her part, and indeed she said only one word, 'Here!' in a melodious but also rather threatening manner. Karl already held the glasses to his eyes and could not in fact see anything. (222–3)

With the help of the opera glasses Karl is finally able to see 'everything, if only indistinctly' (223). The idea that things should not be seen too distinctly is thus reiterated here.

In 1907 Conrad had already presented a conflation of similar motifs in *The Secret Agent*. Here, the hazards of looking too closely are explored against the backdrop of a dark, corrupt metropolis. The novel places Stevie and Winnie on two sides of a continuum of perceptive tendencies. Christina Britzolakis notes that 'Stevie's "peculiar" nature manifests itself as an extreme sensitivity to stimuli; he seems to lack the "protective shield" that Freud proposes in *Beyond the Pleasure Principle*' (2005: 10). Simmel's 'protective organ' (1971: 326) may offer a more apposite notation here, but the point recalls the demands on the subject's perceptive abilities we see in *After Bread* and *Amerika*. More in keeping with Simmel's idea of the rational faculty as a protection against emotional excitation, Winnie's tendency to avoid looking too closely into things is noted throughout in a kind of foreboding leitmotif. When Winnie finally sheds these protections the novel comes to its tragic conclusion. We find a better likeness to Ford's picture of

London and the depictions in Kafka's and Sienkiewicz's novels in the images of the Strand in the concluding pages of 'Karain'. Here, 'innumerable eyes stared straight in front, feet moved hurriedly, blank faces flowed, arms swung' (Conrad 1947: 53). Conrad demonstrates his awareness of the oppressions of the metropolis in both works. The first provides the corrupt moral backdrop for the action, the second the distractions of an 'unreal city'. That Conrad chooses the setting of a rural community for those same lessons on moral decay and the erosion of values in 'Amy Foster' is telling. The moral condemnation is no longer levelled at the anonymous, utilitarian and technological face of what Ford dubs the modern spirit, but at the parochial xenophobia of a familiar old-world community.[11]

Immigrant subjectivity: Old and new

From the outset, 'Amy Foster' is associated with a number of motifs that offer a striking contrast to the urban and fast-paced settings of the modern metropolis. The repetition of 'country' and 'slow' in the first paragraphs draws attention to this difference. Doctor Kennedy is a renowned scientist who, after travelling through 'continents with unexplored interiors', has decided to 'come to a country practice—from choice' (Conrad 1950: 106). The suggestion is that one comes to Colebrook to retire. And the intimation that both narrators arrive by choice or invitation grates against Yanko's lack of agency. On the latter's passage to Colebrook Kennedy recalls, 'we mustn't forget he had been taken out of his knowledge, that he had been sea-sick and battened down below for four days, that he had no general notion of a ship or of the sea, and therefore could have no definite idea of what was happening to him' (123–4). Mary, Lorenz and Yanko are all said to suffer the manipulations of nefarious travel agents, but Yanko's lack of agency is heightened in that his destination is left to chance. It is not by intention that he arrives in Kent.

Unlike the fast-paced life in the metropolis, movement in Colebrook conforms to the pace of walking or a ride in a dogcart. Kennedy's horse is a 'tired chestnut' whose trot soon slows down to a walk. A passing by waggon rolls by 'gently' (108). The space makes no demands on the senses. Amy's life shows each day to be the same as the last:

> New Barns is an isolated farmhouse a mile away from the road, and she was content to look day after day at the same fields, hollows, rises; at the trees and the hedgerows; at the faces of the four men about the farm, always the same—day after day, month after month, year after year. (109–10)

The lack of stimulation works its way into the inhabitants' mode of perception. No one sees. Amy's eyes are 'slow' (107); the townspeople have 'slow' 'downcast eyes' (110). These are all in contrast to Kennedy's 'attentive eyes' (106) and Yanko's 'quick, far-reaching eyes' (130). But we cannot distinguish the two modes of perception on the basis of urban and rural life, the new and the old world. That the community does not see cannot be relegated to the transiency, anonymity and superficiality of an urban setting.[12] Yanko is himself a symbol of that slow world that is encountered here, and he *sees*.

Where the motif of sight can nevertheless be read with the other novels is that here, too, it is a symbol for life and freedom. Through her relationship with Yanko, Amy enjoys a brief lifting of her myopia, a brief freedom, as it were. Her previous slowness is replaced by 'unblinking, fascinated eyes' (136) that anticipate Yanko on the road. But her love for her husband wanes – as does his own life-force. Once he is settled and is awarded Swaffer's gift of land, he too loses the quickness of his eye. Touched, perhaps, by the same curse that, as Kennedy reflects, weighs down the townspeople, he, too, no longer sees. His initiation into the community may be sanctioned by marriage, but it is accompanied by the symbolically meaningful gift of a 'black eye' offered by an intolerant congregation at the tap-room (133). The ritual is dubbed 'an ejection' (133), but it renders Yanko more rather than less like them. In keeping with the company he now keeps, he becomes 'less keen of eye' and 'looks at the sea with indifferent, unseeing eyes' (137). Amy herself reverts to a vision that is 'blurred', 'shortsighted' and 'dumb' (138). At the time of Yanko's illness Kennedy reflects that she seems 'to see nothing at all' (139). Where utility, materialism and the modern spirit serve to oppress Karl, Lorenz and Mary, Conrad suggests that the Christian, rural values of an old-world community produce a similar effect. In the metropolis the offenders are anonymous, the products of a rapidly advancing materialistic, technological world. Yanko, however, suffers at the hands of named characters who experience no urban, technological distractions. The community Yanko encounters is just as inhumane as the one Lorenz and Mary meet in New York. Yanko's insight on the different cultural norms recall Lorenz's. As he tells Kennedy, 'in his country, even if they gave nothing, they spoke gently to beggars. The children in his country were not taught to throw stones at those who asked for compassion. Smith's strategy overcame him completely. The wood-lodge presented the horrible aspect of a dungeon' (124). The incarcerations and subservience we encounter in Kafka's *Amerika* are encased in steel and glass, signposts of the new world. Here, the weapons of oppression conform to old-world materials – stones and wood. Conrad reminds his readers that the familiar old-world abuses live on in the twentieth century.

The choice of setting is briefly interrupted by the description of Yanko's journey and its evocation of some of the tropes of the modern spirit: 'There was a roof over him, which seemed made of glass … Steam-machines rolled in at one end and out at the other … He could not give [Kennedy] an idea of how large and lofty and full of noise and smoke and gloom, and clang of iron, the place was, but someone had told [Yanko] it was called Berlin' (114–15). The attributes of a new, technological world recall both the modern spirit as explored by Kafka and the moral denunciations offered in *After Bread.* The scope, speed and architectural motifs of steel and glass recall the former, but the association of technology with the agents of temptation recalls the latter. Yanko relates that the three Jews 'kept a cunning telegraph machine, through which they could talk to the Emperor of America' (116).

Yanko's travels are fragmented; his experience unfolds in a sequence of abrupt shifts allowing no coherent view of the changing landscape. He is constantly in the dark – first in the wagon, then the train carriage and then the ship's hold; the passage reads as a series of cultural shocks that render his environment unfamiliar, isolating and hostile. Sitting in a train carriage, Yanko 'looked out of the window, which had a wonderfully clear glass in it, and the trees, the houses, the fields, and the long roads seemed to fly round and round about him till his head swam' (114). Where Mary's and Lorenz's passage to the new world allows them to take cognizance of the growing distance from home and identify familiar anchors with which to work through the experience, Yanko is deprived of the sense of duration and distance. Wolfgang Schivelbusch suggests that, 'compared to the eotechnical space-time relationship, the one created by the railroad appears abstract and disorientating' because it does 'not appear embedded in the space of the landscape the way coach and highway are' but seems to rather 'strike through it' (2014: 37).

Todd Presner unpacks the experiential differences between new and old modes of transportation, between the train and automobile on the one hand, and ships and carriages on the other. The latter, he argues, ensure the distance of the subject from the perceived world and foster the illusion of continuity and insularity of mind regardless of the changing landscape. Such modes of travel are associated with 'an episteme in which experience and expectation are never broken apart and world spectatorship is made possible by the absolute distinction between the knowing subject and the object known' (Presner 2012: 67). By speeding up movement and upsetting the illusion of fixity from which the subject views the world, the train and automobile undo this separation. They produce a temporal and spatial confusion. The compression of space-time yields a sense of an ongoing spatio-temporal present. Ford describes the frustrations of train travel as owing to the upending of the expectation of seeing effects through – the glimpses of life given are always incomplete: 'the constant succession of much smaller happenings that one sees, and that one never sees completed, gives to looking out of train windows a touch of pathos and of dissatisfaction. It is akin to the sentiment ingrained in humanity of liking a story to have an end' (1905: 61). Yanko's passage offers a similar sense of fragmentation, one that anticipates Karl's experience in *Amerika*. It is thus all the more jarring when it concludes in Colebrook. The sudden deceleration does away with the spatio-temporal compressions encountered along the way and once again allows the reader, and Yanko, to glimpse the unmediated truths of cultural encounter.

Conclusion

Read with Henryk Sienkiewicz's *After Bread* and Franz Kafka's *Amerika*, Joseph Conrad's 'Amy Foster' emerges as a cultural and philosophical study of the clashing of two complementary discourses on the evolution of the human subject. Both are fundamental to the modernist project. The first is glimpsed in the sentiments expressed by Ford in *The Soul of London*, where he records the transformation of human experience in response to the technological and material evolution of the city. Such sentiment is expressed in more aggressively radical terms in Filippo Tommaso Marinetti's 'Manifesto of Futurism' (1909) and its celebration of velocity as 'eternal and omnipresent' (51). In the 'Technical Manifesto of Futurist Literature' published three years later, Marinetti calls for the replacement of what he views as a calcified conceptualization of the human subject with one inspired by speed, urbanization, machine and sensory flux.

The second finds inspiration in the unique position of the immigrant. In *Exiles and Emigres: Studies in Modern Literature*, Terry Eagleton famously notes that 'the seven most significant writers of twentieth-century English literature have been a Pole, three Americans, two Irishmen and an Englishman' (1970: 9). Whether it is the futurist subject or the exile, both show modernism to be propelled by figures of movement and displacement, a subject that is permeable and fluid and is no longer accommodated by the principles of cohesion and stability we associate with the Cartesian *cogito*.

'Amy Foster' draws attention to the tension between the technological and migratory frameworks for the rethinking of subjectivity. The first unfolds in a universalizing gesture. The city homogenizes difference; it undoes cultural, ethnic and racial human variety. The second calls attention to and cements difference. Offering a viewpoint that is uniquely other, the immigrant perspective effects a much-needed defamiliarization of a world to which we have become habituated. If the first plays out in an ongoing present of constant sensory stimuli, the second hangs on the tension between past and present, between memory and perception. The first encapsulates all in one, the second hinges on a division between a nation left and a nation adopted. It recalls Conrad's famous self-assessment as *homo duplex*.

Recent critical thought on the migrant subject brings the universalizing gesture of the first to bear on the second. In his analysis of the decentred dynamics of Kafka's *Amerika*, Presner describes how the transformed immigrant subject is denied the possibility of orienting 'his body in the space observed'; there is no longer 'any organizing logic inherent to the geography'. The notion of a divided consciousness is removed. The new subject 'is neither the master nor the center of the coordinate system'. He 'has no history and cannot be placed in a narrative of before and after, "no longer" and "not yet," because it has no temporal extension: it is pure event' (Presner 2012: 97–8). We see a glimpse of this in Yanko's passage to the new world, a passage that, to follow Presner's definition, reads as 'pure event'. The fluid subjectivity tied to such experience is nevertheless abandoned once Yanko arrives in the slow, country town of Colebrook. His experience of displacement is no longer the product of the distractions of an ongoing present but is once again anchored in the past, in a repository of memory. The return is suggestive of Conrad's resistance to the anaesthetizing effects of the metropolis, its razing of racial and cultural difference. Such resistance is meaningful both as a commentary on tensions within modernist thought and in anticipating critiques of the universalizing gestures of more recent reformulations of migrant and techno-subjectivity.[13] The story returns us to traditional forms of human encounter in order to remind us that subjectivity is not always a product of slippage, that certain forms of foreignness have 'a peculiar and indelible stamp' (Conrad 1950: 131–2) that cannot be insensibly erased. Subjects may be created in a flux of movement and context, in the unfolding of pure event; but they also contain fixities and divisions that will not yield to the forces of assimilation.

Notes

1 In this I depart from other generic framings of the story. Richard Ruppel, for example, reads the story with colonial fiction in teasing out ironies owing to its stylization as a 'colonialist story in reverse' (1996: 126).
2 The belief in technology's contribution to the obfuscation of geopolitical differences is still evident today. Though more than a century separates the two writers, Philip Leonard's recent commentary on the digital revolution recalls Ford's description of the way in which the modern city destroys racial and cultural divisions: 'The web's second incarnation has allowed it to graduate to greater heights of collaboration and interactivity, with online networks allowing groups to traverse the confines of space that have traditionally shaped social association. *Citizen Cyborg* (Hughes 2004), *The Cyborg Self and the Networked City* (Mitchell 2004), *The World is Flat* (Friedman 2006): such titles speak of the new *habitus* that transcends the imagined space of the nation-state, a digital (non-)place that can finally fulfil the promise of participatory citizenship because it is *globally* inclusive' (2010: 251).
3 Such universalizations occur when the migrant is transformed into a figure for 'the long concealed truth of human nature, exposing how movement is the norm rather than the exception, and how we are fundamentally creatures of movement rather than settlement' (Moslund 2010: 2). My analysis touches on immigrant (as opposed to migrant) subjectivity in gesturing to a point of departure and destination – as opposed to a life of ongoing movement. The distinction may well point to diverging critical interests across moments in history, but I would nevertheless like to draw attention to the difference between the two in thinking what is lost in the creation of the more inclusive category of the migrant.
4 Critics have noted Conrad's familiarity with and indebtedness to Henryk Sienkiewicz. Andrzej Busza was first to cite *After Bread* as an antecedent to 'Amy Foster' (see 1966: 224–8).
5 Thomas Nail is exemplary in offering such a contemporary redefinition of the migrant subject. He argues that 'the first problem is that the migrant has been predominantly understood from the perspective of *stasis* and perceived as a secondary or derivative figure with respect to place-bound social membership. Place-bound membership in a society is assumed as primary; secondary is the movement back and forth between social points' (2015: 3). The examples offered above are better accommodated by the hierarchy that Nail questions.
6 *Cyrograf* is the Polish word for pledge.
7 I address Conrad's treatment of his Jewish characters in greater detail in 'The Spatialization of Moral Judgement: Borders in "Amy Foster", *Heart of Darkness* and *Under Western Eyes*'. Though it is beyond the scope of the analysis here, I would like to draw attention to the way in which 'Amy Foster' and *After Bread* both highlight

the roles of Jewish agents in bringing about the protagonists' plans to emigrate. Lorenz recalls the events precipitating the moment of departure:

> At the inn he met a German, who pretended to be a flax-buyer, but who was in reality an emigrant steamship agent. This German expatiated on the wonders and marvels of America. He promised him for nothing more land than the largest farm in Lipintse—together with woods and pasture lands, so that the peasant's eyes beamed with anticipation. He believed, yet doubted, but the Jew milk-merchant, who accompanied the German, said that the American government gave to everybody as much land as they could use. The Jew had been so informed by his nephew… They tempted the peasant till they secured him. (Sienkiewicz 1897: 16)

8 Zahra notes that 'the complete trial records of the Wadowice trial appear to be missing. Local, regional, and imperial newspapers all sent reporters to Galicia, however, and published daily updates, commentary, and transcripts of the proceedings' (2016: 42).

9 Though Ford celebrates London, many of the qualities he ascribes to it are likewise present in Sienkiewicz's description of New York. Ford writes: 'we, who are not made for strong impressions, are ourselves inclined to shudder. Or one may grow bewildered to the point of losing hold of one's identity amid the crash and charge of goods trucks' (1905: 56–7). The impressions are similar to those expressed in *After Bread,* but the sentiments attached to them are not. Ford sees this as a romantic, hopeful and joyful trajectory to the future; Sienkiewicz associates this with suffering and moral decay.

10 One of the greatest ironies in the novel is that America proves to be a place of incarceration and enslavement; Karl's adventures lead him from one mode of subservience to another.

11 Yanko also encounters acts of kindness in Colebrook. To follow the moral binary presented in *After Bread,* however, these may well be expected in such a setting. Though this will not be the focus of the discussion, it is important to note that even these acts of kindness offer further evidence of Conrad's wariness of the violence of assimilation. Though Amy is initially attracted to Yanko's otherness, she is finally unnerved by it. The Swaffer family's attempts to transform Yanko into a local suggest they too are unable to accept difference. Swaffer regards Yanko initially as 'quite a curiosity' (Conrad 1950: 126). And though he employs him and offers him the reward of a cottage and land, his regard for the younger man remains, in Dr Kennedy's words, 'curiously feudal' (136). Yanko may grow to view him as a father figure, but the sentiment (the repetition of the word 'curious' is telling) is not reciprocated.

12 The indifference we might encounter in a city is not malicious – it is faceless. Nels Anderson defines the 'urbanized man' as one who 'remains oriented in the

crowd. He is not disturbed by the coming and going of people, hence he is always making new acquaintances and forgetting the old ones; *transiency* is one of his characteristics. He cannot know all persons about him well and he may not wish to. Thus, again to use a term from Wirth, interpersonal relations are marked by *superficiality*. Since the urbanized man cannot know all people, and may not wish to, he acquires the ability to move in the crowd without caring who the people are about him, and he does not invite their approaches; *anonymity* is still a third characteristic' (2007: 1).

13 As Leonard explains, the 'narratives of cultural inclusivity and social progress' that are associated with the digital platform and the democratization of information 'are deeply flawed. Reasserting a stubbornly colonial ethic, liberal – and libertarian – accounts of transnational participation have repeatedly assumed their right to universal representation by conjuring away any attachment to space and culture, celebrating the nation-state's transcendence while continuing to find a home in regions and nations whose authority is built on a colonial legacy. Too often, the "we" invoked in discourses of cultural representation and political participation either excludes groups who do not identify with the new inclusivity, or tolerates those groups only at the margins of social life' (2010: 251–2). Leonard further notes that 'the persistence of a technological divide is becoming increasingly apparent, with what might variously (and problematically) be termed first world, developed, or industrial nations continuing to benefit from the uneven distribution of information (and other) technologies' (252).

Works Cited

Anderson, N. (2007), *The Urban Community: A World Perspective*, Oxon: Routledge.

Britzolakis, C. (2005), 'Pathologies of the Imperial Metropolis: Impressionism as Traumatic Afterimage in Conrad and Ford', *Journal of Modern Literature*, 29 (1): 1–20.

Budrewicz-Beratan, A. (2010), 'American Travel Books of Charles Dickens and Henryk Sienkiewicz', in J. Sztachelska and M. Grzegorz (eds), *Metamorphoses of Travel Writing: Across Theories, Genres, Centuries and Literary Traditions*, 88–103, Cambridge: Cambridge Scholars Publishing.

Busza, A. (1966), 'Conrad's Polish Literary Background and Some Illustrations of Polish Literature on His Work', *Antemurale*, 10: 109–255.

Conrad, J. (1947), 'Karain', in *Almayer's Folly and Tales of Unrest*, 3–55, London: J. M. Dent.

Conrad, J. (1950), 'Amy Foster', in *The Nigger of the 'Narcissus,' Typhoon and Other Stories*, 105–42, London: J. M. Dent.

Eagleton, T. (1970), *Exiles and Émigrés: Studies in Modern Literature*, London: Chatto and Windus.

Gladsky, T. S. (1992), *Princes, Peasants, and Other Polish Selves: Ethnicity in American Literature*, Amherst: The University of Massachusetts Press.

Hueffer, F. M. (1905), *The Soul of London: A Survey of a Modern City*, London: Alston Rivers.

Kafka, F. (2008), *Amerika: The Missing Person*, trans. Mark Harman, New York: Schocken Books.

Leonard, P. (2010), 'Virtually Postcolonial?', in P. Patton and S. Bignall (eds), *Deleuze and the Postcolonial*, 251–71, Edinburgh: Edinburgh University Press.

Levin, Y. (2017), 'The Spatialization of Moral Judgement: Borders in 'Amy Foster', *Heart of Darkness* and *Under Western Eyes*', *Conradiana*, 49 2–3 (2018): 85–102. [Published 2/2021].

Marinetti, F. T. (2009), 'The Founding and Manifesto of Futurism', trans. L. Rainey, in L. Rainey, C. Poggi and L. Wittman (eds), *Futurism: An Anthology*, 49–54, New Haven: Yale University Press.

Marinetti, F. T. (2009), 'Technical Manifesto of Futurist Literature', trans L. Rainey, in L. Rainey, C. Poggi and L. Wittman (eds), *Futurism: An Anthology*, 119–24, New Haven: Yale University Press.

Moslund, S. M. (2010), *Migration Literature and Hybridity: The Different Speeds of Transcultural Change*, New York: Palgrave Macmillan.

Nail, T. (2015), *The Figure of the Migrant*, Stanford: Stanford University Press.

Presner, T. S. (2012), *Mobile Modernity: Germans, Jews, Trains*, Columbia: Columbia University Press.

Ruppel, R. (1996), 'Yanko Goorall in The Heart of Darkness: "Amy Foster" as Colonialist Text', *Conradiana*, 28 (2): 126–32.

Schivelbusch, W. (2014), *The Railway Journey: The Industrialization of Time and Space in the Nineteenth Century*, Oakland: University of California Press.

Sienkiewicz, H. (1897), *After Bread*, trans. Vatslaf A. Hlasko and Thomas H. Bullick, New York: R. F. Fenno.

Simmel, G. (1971), 'The Metropolis and Mental Life', in Donald N. Levine (ed), *On Individuality and Social Forms*, 324–39, Chicago: University of Chicago Press.

Zahra, T. (2016), *The Great Departure: Mass Migration from Eastern Europe and the Making of the Free World*, Chicago: Turabian.

11

Four exiles in three volumes: W. G. Sebald, Ewa Kuryluk, Juan Gabriel Vásquez and Joseph Conrad

Laurence Davies
King's College London

In fond memory of Alois and Eva Krušina.[1]

To begin with

This is a study of Conrad as a vivid presence in three books: W. G. Sebald's *The Rings of Saturn*, Ewa Kuryluk's *Century 21* and Juan Gabriel Vásquez's *The Secret History of Costaguana*.[2] These authors invoke Conrad's legacy in transnational texts sounding out the life and works of their transnational predecessor. Born in Bavaria, Sebald (1944–2001) spent the last three decades of his life teaching German literature at the University of East Anglia. Writing in German, he explored the borderlands of fiction, history, memoir and memory, visiting and revisiting nineteenth- and twentieth-century imperialism, both world wars, and the pre- and post-war diasporas. *Vertigo* (*Schwindel.Gefühle*), *The Emigrants* (*Die Ausgewanderten*) and *Austerlitz* are other examples of his involvement with exile, memory and recuperation. Ewa Kuryluk was born in Kraków in 1946 and had her secondary education in Vienna while her father was Polish ambassador there. Her family of artists, writers, scientists and musicians is honoured among the Righteous at Yad Vashem. Returning to Poland, she began her career as an artist, but left in 1981 just before the imposition of martial law. She lived first in New York and then in San Diego. At the end of the decade, during the collapse of the Communist regime and the lifting of artistic censorship, she returned to Poland. Kuryluk is a prolific painter, photographer, textile artist, poet, distinguished art historian and experimental novelist who has collaborated on artistic projects all over the world. Born in Colombia, Juan Gabriel Vásquez (1973) has now returned to Bogotá after living in France, Belgium and Catalonia; he has dual Spanish and Colombian nationality. As he told a fellow Colombian who had moved to New York, his original decision to leave Colombia for Paris was partly a reaction to the violence of his native land, and partly a vision of Paris as the ideal city for Latin American writers (Paternostro 2010: 76–7). Among his other works are the novel *The Informers* (*Los informantes*, 2004), which concerns the plight of Jewish refugees in Colombia, and two volumes as yet untranslated: a short biography, *Joseph Conrad: El hombre de ninguna parte* (2004) and *El arte de la distorsión y otros ensayos* (2009), a collection of essays, among them one on Sebald and three partly or wholly devoted to Conrad.[3]

The novels are at least as varied in geography and literary strategy as the lives of their creators. Indeed, to class them all as novels needs a generously loose fit. *The Rings of Saturn*, for instance, might be described as a memoir, novel, extended essay – or all three. It bears out a comment by Wai Chee Dimock: 'What genre is dealing with is a volatile body of material, still developing, still in transit, and always on the verge of taking flight, in some unknown and unpredictable direction' (Dimock 2006: 74). The armature of Sebald's book is an atmospherically detailed and therapeutic walk across the interior and littoral of East Anglia (specifically the county of Suffolk), described in the subtitle of the original German edition as 'Eine englische Wallfahrt' (An English Pilgrimage), but its many strands and points of reference include Belgium, the Belgian Congo, Poland and imperial China. Among other cities and countries, *Century 21* brings in Venice, Trieste, Afghanistan, Poland, Japan, Singapore, Canada, Mexico, California and New York. One of the wonderfully disorienting photographs at the end of the book is a shot of Kuryluk (called in the narration Ann Kar or Moon Scholar) as a young girl skiing in 'Moonomalaya' early in the fourth millennium CE. Another photograph, dating from the third century BCE, shows us Berenice, Ptolemaic Queen of Gaza, in conversation with the Umbrian poet Propertius, who lived in the first century BCE and wears a duckbill cap back to front. The climax of *The Secret History of Costaguana* is reached in London, but the blood-stained stories the narrator José Altamirano has told us, and throughout a marathon night told Conrad, are set against a background of nineteenth-century Colombian civil wars, the struggle for power over the Isthmus of Panama and the American-engineered secession of Panama from Colombia. To say the least, these three books differ drastically, being in their notably idiosyncratic ways experimental, visionary, provocative. What they do have in common are care and imagination in the treatment of violence, a willingness to jump generic fences, and an astounding fluidity of movement through space and time.

As transnational fictions, essays or memoirs they have multiple existences (or, to use a stronger phrase, ontological positions). They reflect their authors' experiences of migration, whether by volition or by force of circumstance. They tell stories of dispossession, distance, difference, dislocation, loss, but also, in some instances, curiosity, hunger for the new, joy at escaping from the old. They feel affinities with Conrad, they read him in fresh ways, they set him in new frames, just as Conrad did himself they find the words they need.[4] By extension, they not only pass on this freshness to their readers, they set up the possibility of conversations among themselves. Whether or not in translation, they enrich the literatures of Poland, Germany and Colombia (not to mention the Spanish-speaking world in general), and English literature too. Wai Chee Dimock's vision of American literature through time and space retains its power elsewhere: 'Rather than being a discrete entity, it is better seen as a crisscrossing set of pathways, open-ended and ever multiplying, weaving in and out of other geographies, other languages and cultures' (Dimock 2006: 3).

The Rings of Saturn

Conrad appears in the fifth chapter of *The Rings of Saturn*. He is far from the only author to figure in Sebald's labyrinth. Sir Thomas Browne, the seventeenth-century physician, scientist, antiquarian, masterly prose stylist, and Christian apologist,[5] is the principal figure in the first and last chapters, beginning with the fate of his skull and rounding off with the custom of draping black silk ribbons over the mirrors of a house of mourning, 'so that the soul, as it left the body, would not be distracted on its final journey, either by a reflection of itself or by a last glimpse of the land now being lost for ever' (Sebald 1998: 296). In a later chapter, we find the contemporary poet, translator and critic Michael Hamburger, whose family left Berlin for London in 1933. Sebald visits his friend and Anne, his wife, quotes extensively from Hamburger's memoirs, and describes an almost surreal state of memory, dream and hallucination common to all three. Other key authors are Edward FitzGerald, a religious sceptic well known for his rendering of *The Rubaiyat of Omar Khayyam*, and François-René, vicomte de Chateaubriand, the diplomat, memoirist, author of novels with exotic settings, and another Christian apologist. Besides these aesthetic and biographical anatomies, Sebald refers to Borges's heterocosmic story 'Tlön, Uqbar, Orbis Tertius' and, in a divagation to Belgium in the Conrad chapter, recalls the scene in Stendhal's *The Charterhouse of Parma* (*La Chartreuse de Parme*), where the anti-hero Fabrice del Dongo stumbles onto the battlefield of Waterloo unable to fathom the horror or the meaning of what is going on.

These are authors who see the world from international as well as domestic perspectives. Browne, for example, had a lifelong fascination with rare knowledge from every known quarter or the world and had studied medicine in Padua, Montpellier and Leyden, where he took his doctorate. In France and Italy, this resolute Anglican acknowledged that there was 'a Geography of Religions as well as Lands' and admitted that 'There are questionlesse both in Greek, Roman, and African Churches, solemneties, and ceremonies, whereof the wiser zeales do make a Christian use' (Browne 1977: 61, 63) – this at a time when the religious hatreds of the Thirty Years War were ravaging north and central Europe. Breton by origin, Chateaubriand had visited the post-Revolutionary United States and written (somewhat fancifully) about its First Nations; later he travelled in North Africa and West Asia, and turned *Paradise Lost* into French prose. Although as an adult FitzGerald scarcely ever budged from East Anglia, he rendered into English prose or verse not only Persian poetry and Ancient Greek tragedies, but eight Golden Age Spanish plays by Pedro Calderón de la Barca. The works of authors like these, Borges and Stendhal of course included, and Sebald too, give the lie to the crass sophism that a citizen of the world is a citizen of nowhere.[6]

Sebald knew East Anglia well, its history, its industries, its farms, its politics, its ecosystems, its land and seascapes, its inhabitants poor and rich, its curiosities, its visitors, its paths and highways, its ruins, its traces of former glory. Sir Thomas Browne practised medicine in Norwich for over forty years. Edward FitzGerald lived in Woodbridge, Suffolk, and spent part of his summers sailing a herring lugger out of Lowestoft. In exile from Revolutionary France, Chateaubriand lived mostly in a London garret, but spent some time in Bungay, Suffolk, reading French and Italian literature with Charlotte Ives, the fifteen-year-old daughter of a rural clergyman. In Sebald's words (characteristically lacking in quotation marks), 'With some dismay, as he later wrote in his *Mémoires d'outre-tombe*, I could foresee the moment at which I would be obliged to leave' (Sebald 1998: 252). In the course of *The Rings of Saturn*, Sebald finds his way to FitzGerald's grave and the remote church of Ilketshall St Margaret, 'whose souls number no more today than in the Middle Ages' (250), and whose rector had once been the Revd Ives. En route to the church, Sebald is confused by 'the labyrinthine system of footpaths and the many places where a right of way marked on the map had been ploughed up or was now overgrown' (250). One of the resonances of the *Wallfahrt* in the book's German subtitle is that of the literary pilgrimage, as favoured by Victorian travellers. One of the others is the ironic pilgrimage of indirection and uncertainty as seen by Conrad in the Congo watershed.[7]

Several threads lead to Conrad's appearance. In the second chapter, Sebald has written on the decline of the once great fishing port and seaside resort of Lowestoft, where Conrad made his first landfall in England. In the fourth chapter, Sebald has been describing frightful atrocities in the First and Second World Wars, culminating in a passage about atrocities in Croatia so dreadful that even Nazis were appalled. As so often in his work, Sebald uses grainy or otherwise defaced photographs which, paradoxically, suggest both distance in time and space and a rough immediacy. On his second night in a seaside hotel, Sebald watches a BBC documentary about Sir Roger Casement's life as a champion of human rights in Africa and South America and later as an Irish nationalist martyr and victim of Black propaganda executed as a traitor to the British state. This presentation of Casement brackets the presentation of Conrad, whom he had known in Africa. Sebald's vision of Conrad's life has three aspects: the child and youth in captive Poland, the sailor in the making and the witness to the horrors of King Albert's Congo.

For his sources, Sebald uses biographies, letters (mainly those to Conrad's 'Aunt' Marguerite Poradowska), *Heart of Darkness* and *A Personal Record.* He often mingles direct quotation with commentary, paraphrase and extra detail without any indication of shifts in genre, or mode or point of view. There is no point in complaining about his scholarship (which in any case was formidable); it's more rewarding to notice the fullness of what he does. Here is an example, based on a passage in the Author's Note added to *A Personal Record* in 1919 Sebald refers briefly to the story of Conrad's father burning his manuscripts (Conrad 2008: 6).[8] Sebald adds: 'At times, when he did so, a weightless flake of soot ash like a scrap of black silk would drift through the room, borne up on the air, before sinking to the floor somewhere or dissolving into the dark' (Sebald 1998: 108). This is not just a picturesque detail. In the network of motif and allusion that characterizes his work, it connects with both the motif of silk that runs all through the volume and the tradition of Polish women, in defiance of the occupying forces, wearing black silk in mourning for the suffering and deaths in the two uprisings (105). The burning fragments also have their existence in an atmosphere of literary fragility and mutability.

Sebald's account of Conrad's visits to Lowestoft between June and September 1878 (punctuated by three coastal voyages in the *Skimmer of the Seas*) speculates about the gaps in chronology, some of which have since been filled (e.g. Najder 2007: 70–3). What is striking, however, is his research into Conrad's newspaper reading at the time.[9] As one might expect, he finds no mention of Conrad, but what catches his attention are the *faits divers*, the reports in a few lines of gossip, crime, rebellion, accident and horror from around the world. For instance:

> an explosion in a mine in Wigan cost two hundred lives; in Rumelia there was a Mohammedan uprising; in South Africa the kaffir unrest had to be suppressed; Lord Grenville expatiated on the education of the fair sex ... the young Queen of Spain was growing weaker by the day; work on the fortifications of Hong Kong, where two thousand coolies were slaving, was approaching completion. (Sebald 1998: 114)

In one way, these miniature global narrations have an affinity with Sebald's own writing, with its peripatetic standpoints and disconcerting juxtapositions; in another, they differ by being so transitory, by seeming at first so gory yet so trivial. As Walter Benjamin argued in 1936: 'Every morning brings us the news of the globe, and yet we are poor in noteworthy stories ... In other words, by now almost nothing that happens benefits story telling; almost everything benefits information' (Benjamin 1969: 89). Yet when taken as part of the warp and weft of Sebald's text, the fugitive effect is woven among his major topics, high among them the brutalities of imperialism. In this particular chapter, we have the oppression of partitioned Poland, the plight of Ireland and the monstrous exploitation of indigenous labour in the Congo and Peru.

Two pages after the glimpse of the toiling coolies, Sebald turns to Conrad's experiences with the Société Anonyme Belge pour le Commerce du Haut-Congo. Even on the voyage out, 'the madness of the whole colonial enterprise was gradually borne in upon Korzeniowski' (Sebald 1998: 117). Covering this crisis in Conrad's life, there are extensive quotations from *Heart of Darkness* and from letters. Again and again in this chapter there is an emphasis on complicity. Sebald speaks of the ruthless enslavement and 'legendary profits' of the Upper Congo company, 'sanctioned by all the shareholders and all the Europeans contracted to work in the new colony' (118). He reminds us that between 1890 and 1900, an estimated half a million Congolese people died each year. Over the same period, the price of a share in the railway company of the so-called Free State rose from 320 to 2,850 Belgian francs (119). When Sebald goes on to describe Casement's exposure of the tortures and massacres perpetrated by the plantation bosses of the Peruvian Amazon Company, he is careful to note that the company's head office was in the City of London (128). This whole chapter shows an alertness to what R. B. Cunninghame Graham liked to call 'latitudinal influence':[10] that is to say the shucking off of responsibilities and restraints when crossing the gap from metropolis to colony. That 'influence' is, of course, a powerful presence in *Heart of Darkness*. For Casement, the gap stretched not only from Brussels to the Congo and London to Putumayo but, after his conversion to Irish nationalism, from London to Ireland. Another example of moral distancing is the appearance of Kafka's uncle Joseph Loewy, who had been a manager on the failed project to dig a sea-level canal across the Isthmus of Panama that took the lives of many workers.[11] Very soon after Conrad left the Congo basin, Loewy arrived there, ready to supervise the construction of the railway about which Conrad is so scathing. Loewy's sanguinary work earned him the gold medal of the Order of the Lion, awarded in person by Leopold II, King of the Belgians (121–2).[12]

At a literal level, of course, this is a ramshackle coincidence. As Juan Gabriel Vásquez puts it: 'Coincidence – insignificant coincidence if it comes to that – is one of Sebald's favourite tendencies, that collector of *objets trouvés*' (Vásquez 2009).[13] There are plenty of other unsettling juxtapositions in Sebald. Recalling his first visit to Brussels, he sees a ubiquity of 'African trophies, and pot plants, some of which were quite enormous'; among them, of course, are rubber plants, awful reminders of the Congo (Sebald 1998: 123). The chapter following the accounts of Conrad and Casement grows out of a tradition among local historians in Suffolk that the rolling stock on a local branch line was originally built to ferry the Emperor of China between summer and winter palaces, and still bore painted traces of the imperial dragon. Starting from that observation, the narrative brings up a whole catalogue of strife, greed and bloodshed: the Opium Wars, the sacking of the Summer Palace and the Taiping rebellion, a series of battles between the Qing dynasty and the followers of Hong Xiuquan, who believed he was Jesus Christ's younger brother. The suppression of the rebellion took many millions of lives.[14]

Sebald's is an art of a myriad intersections. It also embraces an impressive range of knowledges. No wonder Sir Thomas Browne appears so frequently, as if Sebald is restitching the dissociation of sensibility that T. S. Eliot saw as such a deplorable process in late-seventeenth-century culture. But what of Conrad? He is there in *The Rings of Saturn* as a witness, and what is more, a witness whose outlook was drastically modified by what he saw and heard in the Congo. Prior to that, when young, he witnessed the hardship and indignities inflicted on Poland and Ukraine by two great land empires, Russian and Austro-Hungarian. (Contiguous imperialism is sometimes passed over, not least in the present day, by those who take overseas imperialism as the primary model for understanding cultural, economic and political colonialism.)[15] Moreover, he was a polyglot who had lived many lives in many places and whose writings, particularly in the letters, show traces of Italian, German, Spanish, Latin, Arabic and Malay, as well as his principal languages, Polish, French and English.

Thinking about his friendship with Michael Hamburger, Sebald asks, 'Across what distances in time do the elective affinities and correspondences connect. How is it that one perceives oneself in another human being, or, if not oneself, then one's own precursor?' (Sebald 1998: 182).[16] Between Sebald and the authors figuring in *The Rings of Saturn*, powerful elective affinities are at work, not least with Conrad. In temperament, the two of them are children of Saturn, prone to melancholia. The opening sentence of Sebald's narrative runs as follows: 'In August 1992, when the dog days were drawing to an end, I set off to walk the county of Suffolk, in the hope of dispelling the emptiness that takes hold of me whenever I have completed a long stint of work' (3). No wonder Anderson refers to 'Sebald's realm of chronic depressives' (Anderson 2003: 113). After his disillusioning experiences up river, 'Korzeniowski was so sick in body and in soul that he longed for death. But it was to be another three months before this man, whose protracted bouts of despair were henceforth to alternate with his writing, was able to depart homeward from Boma' (121). They were both acutely aware of scale, of the affinities and tensions between the very large and the very small, the very brief and the extremely long. We might think, for example, of Marlow's description of the river, with its contrast between the tiny steamer and the vast primeval forests (Davies 2018: passim). In dealing with what she calls 'The problem of scale', Wai Chee Dimock uses the language of fractal geometry: 'For it is only when the scale gets smaller and the details get finer that previously hidden dimensions can come swirling out. Scalar opposites here generate a dialectic that makes the global an effect of the grainy' (Dimock 2006: 77). Sebald quotes with much respect the words of a colleague at the University of East Anglia, Janine Dakyns, a Flaubertian: 'In a grain of sand in the hem of Emma Bovary's winter gown, said Janine, Flaubert saw the whole of the Sahara. For him, every speck of dust weighed as heavy as the Atlas mountains' (Sebald 1998: 8). While waiting for a taxi from the Hamburgers' house in the country, 'I saw, with a shudder that went to the roots of my hair a beetle rowing across the surface of the water, from one dark shore to the other' (190). On the other hand at Dunwich, a town that has been slipping under the waves since the thirteenth century, 'If you look out from the cliff-top across the sea towards where the town must once have been, you can sense the immense power of emptiness' (159). That power of emptiness is akin, for instance, to storms and doldrums in 'The Secret Sharer' and *The Shadow-Line*. A remark to T. Fisher Unwin, Conrad's first publisher, speaks for both authors, with their strange connections and unpredictable events: 'Our captivity within the incomprehensible logic of accident is the only fact of the universe' (Conrad *CL* 1: 302).

Century 21

Among the photographs at the back of the volume, there is an unfamiliar portrait of Conrad. It was taken in the Singapore Botanical Gardens by Teresa Polska-Ingeneral, a glamorous patron of the arts. Conrad returned the compliment with a portrait of Mme Polska-Ingeneral taken at the Sea Saga Studio. Yet surely there is something out of kilter here? The rains of Singapore can be flatteningly intense, but who in her or his right mind, particularly a sailor, would wear a heavy trench-coat and a trilby hat in an equatorial downpour? The figure of the man himself is not at all like Conrad – lanky rather than stocky, almost ephebic. Moreover the back of the park-bench carries an advertisement for one of the 7,000 businesses franchised by Century 21, a global company based in New Jersey. Many of the photographs, including the ones by or of Conrad, were taken in San Diego, with fellow artists and writers standing in for the great and more or less good of literature and philosophy. Among the other images, we can find, besides the picture of Propertius with Queen Berenice already noted, Propertius in Venice dressed as a gondolier, and Propertius in Beijing looking remarkably like Ezra Pound; then there are Simone de Beauvoir and Jean-Paul Sartre at a café table in Venice with Anna Karenina in the foreground, Djuna Barnes in Kyoto, an ageing Italo Svevo in Trieste, Goethe with one of his Charlottes, and the philosopher and Christian mystic Simone Weil sharing a book with Moses Maimonides. Perhaps the volume is his *Guide for the Perplexed*?

The narrative of *Century 21* is as vertiginous as those photographs. For simplicity's sake, I shall limit myself to the rendering of Conrad. His name comes up in the very first paragraph, associated with an imaginary town on the Persian Gulf where there are shrines dedicated to Conrad and to Malcolm Lowry. A couple of pages later, Conrad and Lowry are in an apartment on the Upper West Side of Manhattan, where Simone Weil holds forth at a symposium on *Antigone*. 'Proust had an asthma attack and couldn't come, but he left a message on Simone's machine' (Kuryluk 1992: 7). In, let us call it, biographical time, Lowry was born in 1909, while Conrad was at work on 'Razumov' (the first version of *Under Western Eyes*) and died in 1957 of barbiturate and alcohol poisoning a hundred years after Conrad's birth. Starting with Albert Guerard and Muriel Bradbook, scholars have long acknowledged Conrad's influence on Lowry's fiction, especially in the first and maritime novel *Ultramarine* (1933). In Kuryluk World, however, causality is topsy-turvy. 'Conrad bites his pencil, doodles, scribbles, tears page after page, and around 3:00 A.M. groans: God! Punish me for plagiarizing Malcolm, make me write on my own' (107). Lowry is equally disturbed by Conrad: 'Why do I oscillate between classifying him as a fake, and giving him the credit of being a genius? … A Pole, he insists on penetrating into the heart of darkness. But unlike most of his country-men, good at going under, he's spared – shielded from malaria and stopped from hitting the bottle by a curious charm: the English language' (88). Later on, amid the wider group of authors, Conrad associates *Heart of Darkness* with the Soviet invasion of Afghanistan (147). Lowry dies, but persists in Conrad's imagination, sharing a shack by the ocean, playing *id* to Conrad's *superego*: 'that fiend of mine who was my best friend. My twin, my secret sharer, he doesn't leave me. I learn his texts by heart and they mix with my own stuff' (208). By the time we reach the book's coda, however, Conrad has recovered sufficiently to go on cruises round the world with Svevo (310).

Whatever's going on here? Conrad and Lowry's *odi et amo* friendship is just one of many narrative strands, as woven together by a textile artist and scholar of iconic veils such as the Veronica and the Mandylion of Edessa (Kuryluk 1991). One should also emphasize that although gloriously witty and bursting with marvellous incongruities, this novel could hardly be accused of post-modernist flippancy. The Afghanistan section, for example, is heartrending in its description of a children's hospital with no medicines, and the various alternative biographies are overshadowed by the Holocaust. To move away for a moment from *Century 21* her review essay of Claude Lanzmann's film *Shoah* for the *New Criterion* shows a notably sensitive, judicious and deeply moral mind at work (Kuryluk 1985).

Conrad's presence in the novel allows for an element of satire, even mockery in its rendering of Polish culture. There is a blending here of many elements: Polish surrealism in cinema, theatre, visual art and fiction (Bruno Schulz was a family friend), Menippean satire, Aristophanic satire, the dialogues of the dead as imagined by Lucian of Samosata. It is also tempting to see in the strange literary genealogies of this volume reversals of cause and effect analogous to quantum uncertainty as imagined by a polymathic author.

Another approach to the world of this novel would be to see it as a blissful evocation of freedom from simple narratives of artistic progress, like T. S. Eliot's vision of a corpus of literature existing outside teleological or otherwise historicized versions of the canon, or Pound's assertion that all literature is synchronous,[17] or Bakhtin's vision of a timeless community of carnival, as proposed in *Problems of Dostoevsky's Poetics*. Yet for all the blissfulness and freeing-up, there's much here to shock – and to freshen our experiences of reading, hearing, writing. Borges says of 'Pierre Menard Author of the *Quixote*' that he has, 'perhaps unwittingly', invented a 'technique of deliberate anachronism and fallacious attribution. That technique … encourages us to read the *Odyssey* as though it came after the *Aeneid*. … This technique fills the calmest books with adventure. Attributing the *Imitatio Christi* to Louis Ferdinand Céline or James Joyce–is that not sufficient renovation of those faint spiritual admonitions?' (Borges 1999: 95).

The Secret History of Costaguana

The date is 7 August 1924. Colombians are celebrating the national holiday on the anniversary of the Battle of Boyacá, the turning point in 1819 of Bolívar's campaign to drive imperial Spanish forces out of northern South America. It is also the day of Conrad's funeral. José Altamirano, a Colombian journalist now living in London, has been one of the mourners in Canterbury. His grief, however, is for himself, and not for Conrad, 'the man who robbed me' (Vásquez 2010: 4). His imaginary readers are variously theatre-goers, 'Readers of the Jury', or just his daughter Eloísa, whom he has left behind in Panama, but he will not yet tell any of them the how, when and where of this robbery. If, as soon appears, his life has fallen victim to all kinds of mishap, 'the disagreeable business of destiny has its share of responsibility in all this. Conrad and I, who were born countless meridians apart, our lives marked by the difference of the hemispheres, had a common future.' Thanks to 'the incomprehensible logic of accident', they have become unwitting *Doppelgänger*. In 1876 there was a near miss in what was then the Colombian province of Panamá, when the barque *Saint-Antoine* docked at the port of Colón with a secret cargo of Chassepot rifles, while Altamirano wandered the streets searching for his father and marvelling at the raunchiness of local life. Presenting the events of 1890, Altamirano becomes the 'Historian of Parallel Lines', so that at the turn of every month he keeps track of both lives. In November 1903 there was an actual (and 'fateful' encounter) 'in the chaotic, imperial and decadent city of London' (5). In terms of Conrad's life, the first event is a remote possibility; the other, a pure fiction and the crux of Vásquez's strategy.[18]

Perhaps surprisingly to readers who expect a postcolonial trouncing, Vásquez thinks highly of Conrad, suggesting that *Heart of Darkness*, *Lord Jim*, and *Nostromo* demanded a new way of reading fiction, seeing him as clearly an antecedent of the Latin American Boom in fiction and ranking him with Tolstoy and Cortázar (Vásquez 2009: 154, 147, De Maesener et al. 2013: 213).[19]

José Altamirano starts his monologue with the birth of his father, Don Miguel, 'known to his friends as the last Renaissance Man', a few months after the birth of the 'Republic of Colombia – schizophrenic country that will later be called New Granada or the United States of Colombia or even That Shit Hole' (7). Don Miguel had a degree in law and a clandestine knowledge of surgery. Two malign forces influenced his early career: the Mallarino-Bidlack Treaty with the United States (1846), which marked the beginning of US hegemony over the Isthmus of Panama, and the fierce hostility between Liberals and Conservatives, which resulted throughout the century and long beyond in a series of murderous civil wars triggered partly by conflicts over land tenure and the siting of political power and partly by the conflict between secularism and traditional Catholicism. As a radical secularist, Don Miguel used his powers of oratory and polemic to attack the Church. He was the author, for instance, of the pamphlet *Hell Hath No Fury Like a Jesuit Scorned* (11). Later on, he uses those powers on behalf of the unsuccessful French plan to build a sea-level canal across the isthmus. In this cause Don Miguel moves to Colón, leaving his Ecuadoran wife Antonia de Nárvaez behind and, after the French scheme has been exposed as a swindle, dies of exhaustion, caused perhaps by logorrhoea. José Altamirano's monologue is a mixture of confession, apologia, self-pity, personal and public history – and revenge. He has overheard an American colonel lie to two Colombian generals in order to get them out of the way of a US takeover, but, 'I kept quiet with the most silent of silences that had ever been, the most damaging and most malicious. Because Colombia had ruined my life, because I wanted revenge on my country and its meddling, despotic, murderous history' (267). It is this history that he will offer Conrad very soon after. The setting for pouring out José's memories and revelations is the home of Santiago Pérez Triana in St John's Wood, London. Triana was the son of the Radical Liberal President Santiago Pérez de Manosalbas, and had escaped a hostile government in Bogotá by canoe. He was a powerful advocate for Latin American freedom from US interference and a friend of Cunninghame Graham, who shared his low opinion of *norteño* imperialists, and wrote a preface to *Down the Orinoco in a Canoe* (Triana 1902).[20] As he appears in the *Secret History*, Pérez Triana says to Altamirano: 'I congratulate you. You are now part of the memory of mankind' (294). In the

New Year, the first instalment of *Nostromo* appears in serial. Altamirano's canals are the equivalent of the Gould Concession, and Panama is now Sulaco: 'the land was another, it had another name, and I had been removed from it, erased like an unmentionable sin, obliterated without pity like a dangerous witness' (298–9).

One might count among the many ironies of José Altamirano's unhappy life the quality of his voice. He is a much better writer than his father, who purveys a numbing mixture of dogmatism and efflorescence, and as time goes by gets better and better at flattery and whitewashing. According to José, he is not so much a liar as a man governed by refraction. 'Panamanian reality entered his eyes as if from a stick for measuring water depth from the shore: it folded, it bent, folded at the beginning and bent afterwards or vice versa' (104). José has a bitter wit, a mastery of telling detail and a vulture's eye for corruption. There has been much discussion of Vásquez's amicable rejection of magical realism (Vásquez 2009: 63–72). The only magic in the book is José's ability to swoop through time and space, enabling his familiarity with Klee's monoprint *Angelus Novus* (1920), which Benjamin acquired the following year and discussed, *inter alia*, in 'On the Concept of History' (1940). That very angel has a way of turning up in Colombia, for instance, during the Thousand Days' War (1899–1902). 'The Angel of History's modus operandi was basically the same as usual. The Angel is a brilliant serial killer: once he has found a good way to get men to kill each other he never gives it up, he clings to it with the faith and obstinacy of a St Bernard' (Vásquez 2009: 210). In that war, over 100,000 Colombians died.

As with *The Rings of Saturn* and *Century 21*, there is a good deal of generic instability in this novel. Vásquez has said of it: 'My *Secret History of Costaguana* tells Colombian history in the key of parody or farce' (Vásquez 2009: 43).[21] Elsewhere, he speaks of telling history in the keys both of tragedy and of comedy (Freire 2012: 206–7). The comedy is dark indeed, but so is *The Secret Agent*. Yet the tales of dislocated lives and hard deaths have more than a twinge of sadness. Then, to make the mixture even richer, there is a strain of playfulness in the very idea of turning literary history inside out: in substituting for the courtly Pérez Triana as the informant on Colombian affairs the half-mad Altamirano; in making Colón the scene of the putative gunrunning episode; in ignoring Conrad's other sources from Paraguay, Venezuela, Mexico and Argentina. The Author's note at the back of the volume credits as a source Don José Avellanos's *History of Fifty Years of Misrule* (its pages last seen fluttering across the streets and plazas of Sulaco) just as Borges does in his story 'Guayaquil' (Borges 1999: 390–6). A favourite word in Vásquez's critical vocabulary is *distorsión* (distortion), an art of the unfamiliar and the unexpected viewpoint, a throwing out of kilter.

As he says in an English-language interview: 'What we call the past, public or private, is just a fixed narrative told for the first time by someone with certain interests, prejudices, and biases. Novels remind us of that; there's not one truth, one history, one past' (Paternostro 2010: 78). One could say the same of all three volumes and all four authors.

Notes

1 Before and after the Second World War, Alois Krušina taught at the Charles University in Prague; during the war he was on the staff of the Czechoslovak State Secondary School in Llanwrtyd Wells, mid-Wales. Eva, his wife, had come to the UK as an eighteen-year-old chaperone on a Kindertransport. After the war, she found out that her parents had been imprisoned at Terezin and killed at Auschwitz.
2 Sebald's volume was originally published in German as *Die Ringe des Saturn* in 1995; the English translation by Michael Hulse appeared in 1998. Vásquez's *Historia secreta de Costaguana* appeared in 2007 and Anne Mclean's English translation in 2010. Kuryluk's *Century 21* was written in English and published in the United States in 1992; a Polish translation came out in 1996 as *Wiek 21*.
3 Quotations from these two volumes, interviews with Vásquez, reviews and other critical commentaries were translated by Laurence Davies.
4 Cf. the title of Marie Cardinal's autobiographical and transnational novel, *Les mots pour le dire* (1976); in English as *The Words to Say It* (1983).
5 In its traditional sense of an author who defends a cause rather than an author who expresses regret or shame.
6 For helpful discussions of Sebald, Germany and German literature, see Anderson (2003) and Morgan (2009).
7 Another pilgrim motif appears as one of two epigraphs to the volume. It comes from a letter to Mme Poradowska of 23–25 March 1890 (Conrad *CL* 1, 42–4) and preaches forgiveness to 'pilgrims' who skirt the riverbank without engaging with either joy or horror.
8 Conrad himself records that in 1914 he was shown several hundred folios of his father's manuscripts at the Jagiellonian University Library (Conrad [1911] 2008: 7). Perhaps Apollo Korzeniowski was destroying correspondence that might endanger his comrades.
9 Several biographers of Conrad quote a letter of 1911 to the Belgian scholar Joseph de Smet in which he says that 'his first English reading was the *Standard* newspaper' (Conrad *CL* 4: 409), sometimes adding the *Lowestoft Journal* and/or assuming that the *Standard* was a Lowestoft paper. Sebald echoes these assumptions. In fact the *Lowestoft Standard*, a weekly, began publishing in 1882, so Conrad must have

meant the London daily, which he often cites in his letters. The weekly *Lowestoft Journal and Yarmouth and County Record*, however, did exist in 1878.

10 Cunninghame Graham (1890: 7).

11 The French and American canals are at the heart of *The Secret History of Costaguana*.

12 For a discussion of Conrad, Kafka and Loewy in this context, see Fothergill (2007: 151–2). The third section of *Vertigo* concerns a 'Dr K', who is treated at an Italian sanatorium and writes Kafka's story 'The Hunter Gracchus'.

13 'La coincidencia – la coincidencia insignificante, si vamos a eso – ese coleccionista de objets trouvé'. Coincidences breed coincidences. Long passages of *The Secret History of Costaguana* describe the shambles on the isthmus. The artist Tacita Dean's essay on Sebald reveals that it was her great-great-uncle Sir Rufus Isaacs, who donned the traditional black cap and pronounced sentence of death on Roger Casement (Dean 2003: 128).

14 Remarkably, some cultural critics have dismissed Sebald's work as 'sentimental, arty and conservative', e.g. Martin Stewart in *Radical Philosophy*, quoted by Pearson (Pearson 2008, 262). It is hard to see Sebald's treatment of the Taiping rebellion, exploitation in the Congo 'Free State', the fire raids on German cities or the behaviour of Ustashe in the 'Independent State' of wartime Croatia as having any such weaknesses.

15 Two qualifications: as far as we know, Conrad did not visit the Prussian sector of Poland until immediately before the First World War; the distinction between overseas and contiguous imperialism does not apply in the case of Russia, which embodied both.

16 The concept of 'elective affinity' originated in chemistry. It is defined in the OED as 'the tendency of a substance to combine with certain particular substances in preference to others'. Figuratively, it is most familiar as the title of a novel by Goethe, *Die Wahlverwandtschaften*.

17 'Whoever has approved this idea of order… will not find it preposterous that the past should be altered by the present as much as the present is directed by the past' (Eliot 1932, 15). 'All ages are contemporaneous. … This is especially true of literature, where the real time is independent of the apparent' (Pound 1910: vi).

18 Between 1874 and 1876, Conrad made two voyages to the Caribbean in the *Mont-Blanc* and one in the *Saint-Antoine*. In letters and conversations later in life, he remembered visiting the port of Cartagena in Colombia, and two ports in Venezuela, Puerto Cabello and La Guaira. The chronology is complicated because to reach any of those ports, he would have had to travel in other vessels. (For a discussion, see Najder 207: 50–6.) The claim that one such voyage delivered guns (presumably for conservatives fighting the liberal government's plans for secular education in *la guerra de las escuelas* – the War of the Schools) is flimsier, though

a fascination with gunrunning shows up in such works as 'Karain', *The Rescue* and *The Arrow of Gold*. Vásquez's brief biography suggests that in the Marseille period, Conrad was something of a Jekyll and Hyde, oscillating between salon formality and rough portside adventures (Vásquez [2004] 2007: 24). In any case there is no evidence of a visit to Colón, and Conrad was at Pent Farm in November 1903, not in London.

19 For a sympathetic contextual reading of *Nostromo* in terms of both its historical moment in Latin American politics and culture and its reception among twentieth-century Latin American authors, see French 2008, particularly the discussion of Conrad's influence on the great left-wing Paraguayan novelist and political exile Augusto Roa Bastos and the passage on the Argentinian author and critic Ricardo Piglia, who saw Conrad as a Borderland writer (256–62).

20 The Spanish original, *De Bogotá al Atlántico: por de la vía de los ríos Meta, Vichada, y Orinoco*, first appeared in Paris in 1897, published by Imprenta Sudamericana.

21 'Mi *Historia secreta de Costaguana* cuenta la historia colombiana en clave de parodia o de farsa'.

Works Cited

Anderson, M. M. (2003), 'The Edge of Darkness: On W. G. Sebald', *October*, 106 (Autumn), 102–21.

Benjamin, W. (1969), *Illuminations*, ed. Hannah Arendt, trans. Harry Zohn, New York: Schocken.

Borges, J. L. (1999), *Collected Fictions*, trans. Andrew Hurley, London: Penguin.

Browne, Sir Thomas. (1977), *The Major Works*, ed. C. A. Patrides, Harmondsworth: Penguin English Library.

Conrad, J. ([1921] 2004), *Notes on Life and Letters*, ed. J. H. Stape, assisted by Andrew Busza. Cambridge University Press.

Conrad, J. ([1911 as *Some Reminiscences*, 1916] 2008), *A Personal Record*, ed. Zdzisław Najder and J. H. Stape, Cambridge: Cambridge University Press.

Davies, L. (2018), '"With All that Multitude of Celestial Bodies": Conrad's Sense of Scale', *The Conradian*, 43 (1), 99–120.

Dean, T. (2003), 'W. G. Sebald', *October*, 106 (Autumn), 122–36.

De Maesener et al. (2013), 'Un fósforo en la oscuridad: Conversación con Juan Gabriel Vásquez', *Confluencia*, 28 (2), 209–16.

Dimock, W. C. (2006), *Through Other Continents: American Literature across Deep Time*, Princeton, NJ: Princeton University Press.

Eliot, T. S. ([1917] 1932), 'Tradition and the Individual Talent', *Selected Essays*, London: Faber and Faber, 13–22.

Fothergill, A. (2007), 'Reading Conrad: Melancholy in the Shadow of the Swastika', *Polish Yearbook of Conrad Studies*, 3, 149–64.

Freire, R. R. (2012), 'Literatura y distorsión: entrevista a Juan Gabriel Vásquez', *Nuevo Texto Crítico*, 24/25 (47/48): 203–9.

French, J. L. (2008), 'Martin Decoud in the Afterlife: A Dialogue with Latin American Authors', *Conradiana*, 40 (3), 247–65.

Graham, R. B. Cunninghame (1890), 'Latitudinal Influence', *The People's Press*, 4 October, 7.

Kuryluk, E. (1985), 'Memory and Responsibility: Claude Lanzmann's *Shoah*', *New Criterion*, 1 November, 14–20.

Kuryluk, E. (1991), *Veronica and Her Cloth*, New York: Basil Blackwell.

Kuryluk, E. (1992), *Century 21*, Dalkey Archive: Chicago, 1992.

Morgan, P. (2009), '"Your Story Is Now My Story": The Ethics of Narration in Grass and Sebald', *Monatshefte*, 101 (2), 186–206.

Najder, Z. (2007), *Joseph Conrad: A Life*, trans. Halina Najder, Rochester NY: Camden House.

Paternostro, S. (2010), Interview with Juán Gabriel Vásquez, *Bomb*, 110, 74–9.

Pearson, A. (2008), '"Remembrance… Is Nothing Other than a Quotation": The Intertextual Fictions of W. G. Sebald', *Comparative Literature*, 60 (3), 261–78.

Pound, E. (1910), *The Spirit of Romance*, London: Dent.

Sebald, W. G. (1996), *The Emigrants*, trans. Michael Hulse, London: Vintage.

Sebald, W. G. (1998), *The Rings of Saturn*, trans. Michael Hulse, London: Harvill.

Sebald, W. G. (2001), *Austerlitz*, trans. Anthea Bell, London: Penguin.

Triana, S. Pérez. (1902), *Down the Orinoco in a Canoe*, London: Heinemann.

Vásquez, J. Gabriel. ([2004] 2007), *Joseph Conrad, el hombre de ninguna parte*, Bogotá: Belacqva.

Vásquez, J. Gabriel. ([2007] 2010), *The Secret History of Costaguana*, trans. Anne McLean, London: Bloomsbury.

Vásquez, J. Gabriel. (2009), *El arte de la distorsión y otros ensayos*, Madrid: Alfaguara.

Afterword: How Black lives matter for Conrad's personal record of migration and transnationalism

Chris GoGwilt
Fordham University, New York

The current volume of essays offers a kaleidoscope of different perspectives on two central themes in the work of Joseph Conrad, *migration* and *transnationalism*. Again and again the essayists remind us how life and letters, for Conrad, are premised on migration. They keep returning, with varying kinds of emphasis, to the following facets of Conrad's life experience as migrant: his emigration from Poland; his turn to the sea; his immigration into Britain as a naturalized citizen and the myriad pattern of wanderings throughout his career, including return trips to Poland (while writing his first novel and later at the outbreak of the First World War). Conrad's varied experiences of migration are marked as transnational almost by definition. For someone born on the borderland between nations (ukraine, as Atkinson discusses, means frontier/borderland), the concept of nation was both fundamental and ephemeral – a given, in the form of Polish nationalism; and something always already taken away, partitioned, scored over and over by frontiers and borders. Exiled from birth to an experience of diasporic transnationalism, Conrad's status as migrant was also susceptible to the changing definition of transnationalism – most notably (as Capoferro and Zulli remind us) in the charge levelled against him by the critic Robert Lynd in 1908 that he was 'a man without either country or language…, a cosmopolitan,… a homeless person' (Conrad *CL* 1990: 107–8).

The biographical facts of migration in Conrad's 'cosmopolitan' life are complicated enough. The complications increase exponentially when refracted through the fiction. This collection of essays emphasizes the extent to which Conrad's fiction is populated by many different kinds of migrants. There are sailors, of course, but also migrant labourers and company workers, pilgrims, asylum seekers and refugees, not to mention White colonial settlers like the title-character of Conrad's first novel, *Almayer's Folly*, whose paradoxically 'settled' migrant status as a White man is brilliantly condensed, as Andrew Francis notes, in the ironic description 'settled resident'. Although Conrad's life experience as migrant might at first suggest some fundamental pattern underlying the fiction, no single pattern encompasses all these figures. Robert Hampson begins his essay with the distinction between 'landfall' and 'departure' and floats the possibility of contrasting a pattern of the migrant's arrival (rites of entry, with a focus on Conrad's own naturalization) with that of return (rites of return, with a focus on Conrad's return to Poland late in life). Yet he goes on to show there is no such simple pattern of contrasts underlying the fiction. There is indeed a 'long paper trail' of migration throughout Conrad, but what Hampson actually documents is an array of different, perhaps even incommensurable, migrant experiences – some documented, others undocumented. Many of the essays anchor the experiences of migration and transnationalism in particular texts, the last essay, by Laurence Davies, turning to consider Conrad's appearance in Polish, German and Spanish works by Kuryluk, Sebald and Gabriel Vásquez. One especially important text proves to be *A Personal Record*, the work written at least partly in response to the charge of Conrad's being 'cosmopolitan, a man without either country or language'. Yet Conrad's experiences (his own as well as those recorded in his fiction) defy easy classification. There are many striking recurrences in the patterns of migration, border crossings and transnational aspirations and betrayals traced by these essays; but there is no one master-pattern defining them all. There may only ever be a kaleidoscopic shuffling of perspectives. This volume's kaleidoscope of perspectives is surely enhanced by the transnational profile of its American, British, Israeli, Italian and Polish contributors.

To this kaleidoscope of perspectives I feel bound to add another, no doubt inflected by my own migrant Scottish American perspective, but influenced by a question that imposes itself, in part, because of the time and place in which I happen to be writing these remarks, in New York in June of 2020 at an extraordinary moment in the convergence of two crises – the Covid-19 pandemic and the mass 'Black Lives Matter' demonstrations sparked by the police killing of George Floyd.[1] Do Black lives matter in Conrad? Do Black lives matter for a reading of 'migration' and 'transnationalism' in Conrad? The convergence of two epidemics (the novel coronavirus and the long history of anti-Black racism enforced by police brutality) has called for many reckonings locally, nationally and internationally. I am not at all wanting to claim that this volume can or should provide such a reckoning. Yet the question imposes itself nonetheless: how do Black lives matter for Conrad?

Some of Conrad's readers, from the very beginning, have answered this question negatively: Black lives *don't* seem to matter for Conrad. This is what led Chinua Achebe, in 1975, to denounce Conrad as a racist and to challenge readers of Conrad to come to terms with that racism. Before Achebe, we might consider how W. E. B. DuBois, writing about the Belgian Congo in his 1912 essay 'The Souls of White Folk', suggestively re-signifies Conrad's *Heart of Darkness* without ever naming Conrad (see Mallios, 203ff). Most recently, we might consider Michael Eric Dyson's recommendation that *Heart of Darkness* be struck from the canon (*New York Times*, 4 June 2020). The present moment may forcefully remind us of those readings that find Conrad's texts negating the lives of their Black characters. It may also remind us that those very same readings show how much Black lives matter all the more for understanding Conrad's texts. Because the racism many of us find in some of Conrad's works seems to turn on a disavowal of the way Black lives matter, this fact that is denied – the 'fact of blackness' (in Fanon's formulation[2]) – may turn out to be among the most important determining features generating the narrative insights of his work. Just as Black lives matter for American history (from the middle passage, through slavery, emancipation, Jim Crow, the new Jim Crow and in the current crisis of 2020) – and just as the historical 'fact of blackness' matters for transnational, global history; so, too, Black lives matter for Conrad and the way Conrad has always been read.

All the essays in this volume call attention to problems of race and racism shaping the experiences of migration and transnationalism throughout Conrad's life and work. Indeed, one of the striking features of this volume is just how many variations on the theme of racialized exclusion, discrimination and stereotyping are registered in Conrad's fiction. The volume's kaleidoscopic vision overall is premised, though, on the fact that each essay can only focus on two or three such variations. The value of each essay depends on the selective focus of its attention: whether the particular convergence of peoples on the coastal Borneo region that gives resonance to that phrase 'settled resident' in Francis's essay; or the relevance of the Hajj for all those Arab and Muslim characters Katherine Baxter explores; and perhaps emblematic of all (and a recurrent figure in many of the essays from Hampson to Tania Zulli to Yael Levin) the case of Yanko Goorall, 'a poor emigrant from Central Europe bound to America and washed ashore here' (Conrad, *Typhoon and Other Stories* 1926: 111). Yet while affirming the particularity of migrant crossings each essay seeks to make visible, it is important, too, to note a rather striking absence. None of these essays considers the way Conrad's fiction documents the migrant labour or the transnational significance of Black lives. There is one exception and it comes in a supplemental reading following Hampson's fascinating discussion of the rites that form and dissolve the ship's community in Conrad's *The Nigger of the 'Narcissus'*. While calling attention to marginal figures overlooked by critics (for example, the figure of the prostitute at the end of that narrative), Hampson avoids until the end of his analysis a discussion of that representative migrant figure, James Wait, whose Blackness is precisely the fact around which the migration and transnationalism of all the other characters and figures revolve.

James Wait provides a striking example of the way Black lives do and don't matter for Conrad. The problem, of course, is the way he is singled out – first, and above all, by the racist epithet in the novella's title; and then also by the way his deteriorating health and then death focalizes the crew's simultaneous resentments and sympathies. Wait epitomizes the transnational experience of migrant labour in the British merchant marine. He offers the most vivid, if also problematic, Conradian example of the pan-African networks of communication, trade, and labour aboard ships that gave shape to what Paul Gilroy has called the Black Atlantic 'counterculture of modernity'. Hampson offers an intriguing glimpse of the way Wait's Black Atlantic experience epitomizes the cosmopolitan London life of Britain's merchant sailors' (6). Yet Wait is only an absent presence in the final rites of the crew's collective disintegration on the return to St. Katherine's Dock. Standing in contrast to the rather striking presence of Wait's first appearance in the ship's rollcall for the crew in the beginning, his absence in the end suggests how that collective identity has been defined – all along – through negation. It is, throughout, from the erasure of that Black experience that the complexity of the crew's collective identity emerges:

> He was unique, and as fascinating as only something inhuman could be; he seemed to shout his denials already from beyond the awful border. He was becoming immaterial like an apparition … Through him we were becoming highly humanised, tender, complex, excessively decadent: we understood the subtlety of his fear, sympathised with all his repulsions, shrinkings, evasions, delusions—as though we had been over-civilised, and rotten, and without any knowledge of the meaning of life. We had the air of being initiated in some infamous mysteries; we had the profound grimaces of conspirators, exchanged meaning glances, significant short words. We were inexpressibly vile and very much pleased with ourselves. (Conrad 1926: 139)

Such passages (and there are many such passages) have always made for uncomfortable reading. They offer all at once a grotesque instance of anti-Black racism and an unrelenting dissection of the anti-Black construction of White identity. I confess that I have myself long shied away from reckoning with the full difficulty of reading such passages. Now is not the time to indulge in White hand-wringing, White excuses – all of that would amount to a mimicry of what Conrad's text rehearses as 'the profound grimaces of conspirators, exchanged meaning glances, significant short words'. And yet the question still needs to be asked: in what sense do Black lives matter for Conrad?

James Wait may not be a central figure for any of the essays in this volume, but the experience of migration and transnationalism his character embodies has an important bearing nonetheless on the range of different perspectives each essay analyses. Most of the essays focus on patterns of migration and transnational crossings rather distant from the experience of a James Wait. They tend to focus on the South East Asian settings of Conrad's early fiction (*Almayer's Folly* above all), the European settings of Conrad's autobiographical work (the Polish reminiscences in *A Personal Record* and in 'Poland Revisited'), or the English settings of *The Secret Agent* and 'Amy Foster'. The migrant figures in these border crossings (with the notable exception of the London setting of *The Secret Agent*) may not typically be related to the transnational circuits of communication, trade and culture associated with Gilroy's 'Black Atlantic'. But is this Black Atlantic experience merely absent from Conrad's work as a whole, or is it part of the blind spot of his vision, part of an erasure of Black lives from that experience of migration and transnationalism so central for every other part of his work?

Richard Niland's essay, discussing Conrad's first short story collection, *Tales of Unrest*, and noting how that volume anticipates the geographical range of crossings characteristic of the work to come, makes a striking observation about the underlying and universal pattern of migration evoked by the 'unrest' of the collection's title: 'In particular, unrest comes through the pervasive spectre of death as the ultimate migration.' It is a striking observation in the context of this essay's compelling analysis of the trope of the 'danse macabre' that threads its way through so much of Conrad's fiction. By focusing on the significance of Brittany as a historical epicentre for the cultural images of death and disease, Niland adjusts our view of the kaleidoscope of migrant perspectives in Conrad to recognize an iconography of death figures in all the landscapes of Conrad's fiction – the 'merry dance of death and trade' (Conrad 1926: 62) in *Heart of Darkness*, for example, or the 'picture of a massacre or a pestilence' (Conrad

1926: 67) in describing the dying workers a little later in the same text. Niland briefly discusses the 'danse macabre' in 'An Outpost of Progress', in which the station men are traded for ivory, although there is surely more to be said about the significance of the man who presides over that 'ritualistic dance of death', the cosmopolitan figure of the accountant Henry Price (also called Makola), a migrant company worker from Sierra Leone.[3] Niland might also have drawn from descriptions of James Wait – whose head is figured as a kind of *memento mori* in a sentence excised from the passage I cited above: 'He was becoming immaterial like an apparition; his cheekbones rose, the forehead slanted more; the face was all hollows, patches of shade; and the fleshless head resembled a disinterred black skull, fitted with two restless globes of silver in the sockets of eyes' (Conrad, *Narcissus* 1926: 139). This sentence reproduces the iconography Niland traces back to the Breton culture and iconography of death. The convergence of pestilence, disease and dying Black bodies makes the spectres of Conrad's fiction the uncanny echo of the present moment. I cannot help but read in counterpoint to the 'apparition' of James Wait's head, the now-iconic image of George Floyd's profile – recalling the fact that he had recovered from Covid-19 in the weeks before he was brutally murdered, his has become an emblematic profile of Black lives enduring the twin epidemics of coronavirus and police brutality.

To see 'death' as the 'ultimate migration', as Niland so expressively puts it, is to position the death of Conrad's Black characters at the very heart of those narrative accounts of migration and transnationalism that may at first appear to be distant, geographically and culturally. Black lives matter for Conrad because Black characters are the iconic figures for this 'ultimate migration'. At the centre of *Heart of Darkness*, it is the account of the death of the helmsman that structures the most extensive revelation of Kurtz's character. Although Kurtz's dying words ('The horror! The horror!') become the lens through which successive readers are bound to read the novella's grasp of the genocidal violence of the Belgian exploitation of the Congo, the force of those words emerges in counterpoint to the 'brooding, and menacing expression' of the 'black death-mask' (Conrad 1926: 113) whose unutterable death sentence more strikingly than for Kurtz captures the point Niland emphasizes when he has us consider 'death' as the 'ultimate migration'.

Heart of Darkness may be the text that most clearly links the geography and politics of migration and transnationalism in Conrad to the fate of Black lives. Not many of the essays in this volume directly address this text, but we might want to add to those migrant and transnational figures discussed here, in addition to the figure of James Wait and Henry Price, also the figure of the helmsman. The helmsman is a migrant worker, too, although by contrast to Wait and Henry Price his place of origin isn't specified – he is described simply as 'belonging to some coast tribe' (Conrad 1926: 199). Steering is perhaps the most valued work in all of Conrad, giving heightened symbolic value to the 'ultimate migration' of his death. It is a steamship this helmsman steers, to be sure, not a sailing ship; but Conrad's own rite of passage into the profession, as Atkinson points out in his discussion of the *Record*'s account, is a rite of passage marked by the shift from sail to steam. In this sense the helmsman might be considered a secret sharer of Conrad's own seafaring profession. We might need to qualify Atkinson's claim that the sea is a place to which anyone and everyone has the right of entry; but Atkinson's point underscores the difference and slippage between 'rites' of passage and 'rights' of passage. He poses a question that might fruitfully be applied to every essay; but one we might want to articulate through the lens of Niland's insight – measuring all of those 'rites' and 'rights' (and indeed 'routes' too) against the 'ultimate migration' – the rite of passage into death. Again, all three of these senses converge in the example of James Wait.

Heart of Darkness is paradoxically all at once absolutely central for understanding the interrelated themes of migration and transnationalism and curiously peripheral. It is central because Conrad's own experience in the Congo was so decisive, psychologically, politically and in the shaping of his sense of his own writing career. It is at the same time peripheral, however, in the geographical and cultural significance of those migratory routes and transnational crossings that are more characteristic of his fiction – the Malay settings; the European settings and the English setting. From Conrad's Congo experience only two stories emerge: the shorter 'An Outpost of Progress' (the centrepiece to *Tales of Unrest*) and *Heart of Darkness*. Apart from the pattern of the 'danse macabre' Niland traces from *Tales of Unrest* through all of Conrad's work, it is not clear how the migratory routes running through each of these stories connect with the various trading networks, pilgrimages or emigration routes of the other stories. Henry Price, James Wait and the helmsman of *Heart of Darkness* figure very different kinds of Black migrant experience, underscoring perhaps the incommensurability of discrepant migrant and transnational perspectives throughout Conrad's fiction. To draw attention to these characters may help emphasize how Black lives matter for Conrad; and yet it is important to note, too, how this leaves other Black lives in the shadow – other migrant and transnational characters like Henry Price's Loandan wife, or Kurtz's mistress.

If there is one key text that might explain what links all the various patterns of migration and transnationalism in Conrad, that text might be *A Personal Record*, so often cited by biographers and critics, though less often examined for the complexity of its narrative structure. This autobiographical set of 'Some Reminiscences' was published in the *English Review* from 1908 to 1909 and issued in book form in 1912 as *A Personal Record*. A number of the essays refer to this text, but for different reasons. Hampson and Atkinson cite it for its account of Conrad's passing the professional examinations for the British merchant marine, Hampson emphasizing the way it 'tidied up' this key moment in the rite of passage into British naturalization, Atkinson noting that Conrad's exams inducted him into a profession (sailing) that had been eclipsed (by the steamship).

Two essays (by Capoferro and Adamowicz-Pośpiech) pay closer attention to the narrative complexity of the *Record* linking it to the underlying patterns of migration and transnationalism in Conrad's work overall. Riccardo Capoferro, also focusing on Conrad's account of passing his certificate examinations, finds here a more revealing and deliberative 'self-fashioning' of a 'transnational aesthetic'. His argument draws attention to the self-defensive features of Conrad's account of the process of naturalization, noting how the autobiography aligns the two professions (seafaring and writing) and the process of choosing English and becoming a British citizen. The force of the word 'cosmopolitan' is telling in this regard. Capoferro argues that Conrad fashions an affirmative, positive 'transnational' connotation in the *Record*; but it is important not to forget the pejorative sense of the word in Lynd's original accusation that Conrad's was the 'vision of a cosmopolitan, a man without either country or language'. This seems to evoke the sort of narrow-minded English parochialism that has returned with a vengeance in the sorry spectacle of Brexit.[4] Although the word 'cosmopolitan' in Conrad's time also carried positive connotations (as suggested by the title of the monthly review *Cosmopolis* where Conrad published 'An Outpost of Progress'), it signalled above all a set of pejorative anti-Semitic associations (which still persist today). Following Capoferro's lead, we might see Conrad's reaction against the narrow-minded nationalism, racism and bigotry of this anti-Semitic use of the term 'cosmopolitan' leading in *A Personal Record* to a counter-vision of transnational identification across borders. It is evasive, nonetheless, and the kind of embrace of English it projects suggests more of an avoidance strategy than an affirmation of any one migrant narrative. The *Record*, in this respect, may explain why there can only ever be a kaleidoscope of changing migrant narratives: because Conrad is caught *between* such narratives.

The *Record*'s opening gesture seems to emphasize this evasion of migrant narrative recounting the idleness of Conrad's waiting for an Atlantic passage that would never take place, the 'last employment of my calling' (Conrad, *Record* 1926: 6) for a company intended 'for the transport of French emigrants to Canada' (Conrad, *Record* 1926: 10). The emphasis here is clearly on the shift from one career (seafaring) to another (writing) and what makes the *Record* so memorable is the story it tells not of Conrad's experience but of his first manuscript. In making that shift, however, Conrad goes out of his way to claim one kind of sea passage his career never included – namely, an Atlantic crossing:

> It may be that it was simply the fulfilment of a fate, of that written word on my forehead which apparently forbade me, through all my sea wanderings, ever to achieve the crossing of the Western Ocean – using the words in that special sense in which sailors speak of Western Ocean trade, of Western Ocean packets, of Western Ocean hard cases. (Conrad, *Record* 1926: 10–11)

Conrad seems to be forgetting the experience of his voyages to the Caribbean in the 1870s. Nonetheless, if one considers Conrad's 'transnational aesthetic' as premised on the *evasion* of stereotyped patterns of migration, this marked emphasis on the Atlantic crossing Conrad never took might loom larger in significance. Is this 'Western Ocean' crossing the blind spot around which Conrad's patterns of migration turn? If so, this may explain the force of two kinds of Atlantic seafaring experiences whose absence plays a formative role in the shaping of Conrad's narrative. The first is the one discussed by Yael Levin in her reading of 'Amy Foster' as a kind of counter-narrative telling of the pattern of Eastern European migration to America. Yanko Goorall, after all, though 'bound to America' (in a formulation so well analysed by Nico Israel [35ff]) finds himself instead in the bewildering location of Kent, England. The second is the Black Atlantic experience so famously outlined by Paul Gilroy – and so intriguingly absent, perhaps evasively displaced, in such works as *The Nigger of the 'Narcissus'*, *Heart of Darkness* and *Nostromo*.

Agnieszka Adamowicz-Pośpiech's essay, the second essay to focus on the *Record*, offers a somewhat different perspective. Drawing inspiration from Kenneth White's notion of 'geo-poetics', she describes the *Record* as an 'auto-bio-atlas' coordinating real and imaginary geographies of migration into a singular narrative pattern. Her argument is especially rewarding for drawing attention to the significance of the Polish periodical *Wędrowiec* (*The Wanderer*). She cites one especially revealing moment in the *Record* where Conrad presents what might be described as an abbreviated sketch of the entire 'auto-bio-atlas', presenting in one sentence all the journeys (real and imaginary) framed by the opening and closing passages of his first novel:

> Between its opening exclamation calling Almayer to his dinner in his wife's voice and Abdullah's (his enemy) mental reference to the God of Islam—'The Merciful, the Compassionate'—which closes the book, there were to come several long sea passages, a visit (to use the elevated phraseology suitable to the occasion) to the scenes (some of them) of my childhood and the realization of childhood's vain words, expressing a light-hearted and romantic whim. (Conrad, *Record* 1926: 13)

This one key sentence offers simultaneously a description of his first book, an account of the travels of his first book to Africa and to [the] Ukraine, and a glimpse of a logic linking disparate experiences of migration and border crossings. The 'light-hearted and romantic whim' to go to Central Africa, echoing Marlow's 'hankering' after Africa in *Heart of Darkness*, leads to a rewriting of Marlow's famous map-pointing scene that, for Adamowicz-Pośpiech's argument, points to the influence of the Polish periodical *Wędrowiec*. The passage is premised on the crossing over of widely divergent migratory crossings: Conrad's real voyage to Africa and his home 'visit' (to Ukraine); and all the various migrations converging on the imaginary Borneo setting of *Almayer's Folly* (Arab, Bugis, Sulu, Malay, Balinese, Dutch, English and Romanian). Bringing together African, Malay, European and English perspectives, momentarily at least, into a single sentence, it juxtaposes real and imaginary journeys combining vastly different experiences of migration into a single vision.

The kaleidoscope of discrepant migrant experiences captured in this one 'auto-bio-atlas' picture also offers a condensed rehearsal of almost all the various diasporic movements traced by other essays in this volume. Contrasting the 'folly' of Almayer's White settler assumptions about his own 'settled resident' status (as explored by Francis) with the pious Islamic exclamation of Abdulla (evoking the religious, mercantile and political networks of the Hajj explored by Baxter), the passage also evokes that 'ultimate migration' Niland discusses (rehearsed here around the deathbed of Almayer, whose significance Francis's essay also discusses). The fact that it's the map of Africa that organizes this 'auto-bio-atlas' vignette stands as a reminder that one central pivot around which all those other patterns of migration turn is a transnational migrant Black experience. It's not clear how the Black lives of Conrad's fiction (say, for example, the lives of Henry Price, James Wait and Marlow's helmsman) might illuminate all those patterns of migration converging on this vignette. Notoriously, of course, it is a 'blank space' on the map. This is the negative image of Africa Achebe argues Conrad's racism sets up as a foil for Europe. Nonetheless, those Black migrant experiences condensed and displaced in this image very much matter for the geography and politics of Conrad's vision.

In its reference to the 'opening exclamation calling Almayer to his dinner in his wife's voice', this passage from the *Record* recalls a shared interest on the part of the editors in the significance of food as a mark of migratory crossing and transnational exchange. Both Kim Salmons and Tania Zulli in their essays refer to Conrad's famous first words, the opening shout – 'Kaspar! Makan!' – and develop fascinating, if also contrasting, readings, the one (Salmons) focused more on the object of food itself, the other (Zulli) focused more on the linguistic exchange over food. Salmons argues that food marks either a rite of passage across cultures or a barrier. The opening to *Almayer's Folly* ambiguously suggests both (in its address to the reader as much as in the speaker's address to her husband), although Salmons emphasizes the latter, foregrounding Almayer's inability to appreciate the food he's being invited to eat – Almayer's 'folly', according to Salmons, exemplifies 'the cultural inability of the European to adapt to the local diet as a means of sustenance or wealth, fearing contamination and a dilution of identity' (3). Her essay develops an especially fascinating focus on 'trepang' (the Malay word for sea-cucumber) and birds' nests, suggesting that the Malay trade in these prized Chinese delicacies reveals a nexus of trade and cultural exchange which Almayer ignores. She goes on to compare Almayer's failure to appreciate food in the colonial Malay context with the Assistant Commissioner's all-too-successful ability to assimilate foreign food in the metropolitan London setting of *The Secret Agent.* Food lies at the ambiguous heart of all the cultural crossings and transnational relations in Conrad. Whether in the metropolitan centre or the colonial periphery, food constitutes the nexus of an exchange always at work in the making and unmaking of cultural identities and in the construction and deconstruction of racialized Others. Food may at one moment invite a cultural crossing and in the next (or perhaps even the very same) moment mark a cultural divide.

Salmons refers to an essay by bell hooks that articulates this central ambiguity in the cultural and racial construction of food as exchange, commodity and object of appreciation or appropriation. Towards the end of the essay, summing up the debates she initiated with her students about White people's relation to Black culture, hooks writes: 'The over-riding fear is that cultural, ethnic, and racial differences will be continually commodified and offered up as new dishes to enhance the white palate – that the Other will be eaten, consumed, and forgotten' (hooks, 39). The fear is arguably well grounded in the case of both those White figures (Almayer and the Assistant Commissioner) Salmons discusses. But bell hooks opens up for the possibility of an appreciative, rather than an appropriative desire for the exotic other. Is there room for such a political alliance in Conrad? This remains a key question about each of those instances where food organizes transnational relations and migrant crossings in Conrad's work. One might argue that whereas in *The Secret Agent* the commodification of food has indeed 'eaten, consumed, and forgotten' the Other, in *Almayer's Folly* it is precisely the White man's ignorance that marks a potential for subversion and resistance. Whatever invitation Almayer mishears in his wife's call to dinner, the language itself – Malay – signals a migrant and transnational experience that would give such subversion and resistance the concrete political form of Indonesian anti-colonial nationalism.[5]

Tania Zulli's focus on language ('the language of migration') calls attention to the fundamental ambiguity which underlies, arguably, all forms of dialogic exchange across cultures in Conrad's work. The two primary examples she gives of dialogic exchange also concern food: the opening call to dinner in *Almayer's Folly* and the question Amy Foster asks Yanko Goorall in 'Amy Foster' ('Can you eat this?'). Here it is not primarily the food itself but rather the 'perlocutionary act' of dialogue that matters (the wife's calling Almayer to eat and Amy Foster's signalling an act of kindness). These are dialogic exchanges that position speaker and addressee in certain social relations full of significance in terms of the position of the migrant figure. Zulli describes Almayer as not quite a migrant figure (one might relate this question of Almayer's 'migrant' status to the phrase Francis quotes – 'resident settler' – in order to see how the White settler colonial presence is blind to its own migrant status in relation to others); whereas Yanko Goorall is more 'properly' a migrant – which is to say the Eastern European emigre, immigrant or asylum seeker, whose more typical narrative Yael Levin nonetheless *contrasts* to Yanko Goorall's failed emigration. One might indeed ask: is there any 'proper' migrant, or is the migrant figure not always some distortion of the 'perlocutionary' act by which they are hailed in this or that moment? The call for Almayer to come eat positions the White settler as the privileged man to be served, but also (once one begins to decode the covert plot of the novel) as the hated White colonizer. Amy Foster's question, by contrast, is an act of generosity, although Zulli notes how it positions a potentially deadly gap between host and guest, resident and asylum seeker. It is worth emphasizing that Zulli examines a third important perlocutionary act – the ironic moment at the end of 'Youth' when Marlow is hailed in a language of abuse, mistaken for being another kind of migrant figure altogether – 'I thought you were a shore-boat', the skipper explains later (Conrad, *Youth* 1926: 39). For a fleeting moment Marlow is interpellated by a volley of abuse, put in the position of the subaltern native to whom a whole string of 'unmentionable adjectives' is attached. This third example points to the thoroughly ambivalent grasp of interracial relations around which the whole kaleidoscope of Conrad's migrant and transnational perspectives turns.

As with the word 'cosmopolitan', the term 'migrant' itself (and its cognates 'émigré' 'immigrant') is shot through with the ambivalent language of interracial recognition and racist abuse. In that sense, the end of 'Youth' reveals the ambivalence at the heart of those other two primary examples Zulli analyses – Mrs Almayer's call for Almayer to come 'eat' ('Kaspar! Makan!'); and Amy Foster's invitation to Yanko Goorall ('Can you eat this?') – the one full of resentment and hate (that makes the dinner call almost a form of abuse), the other full of kindness and grace (but, according to Zulli, potentially as deadly as Amy Foster's kindness towards animals). All three examples form complex 'perlocutionary acts' of positioning migrant figures in transnational relations. Between the language of interracial recognition and the language of racist abuse – this is almost always where Conrad positions the experience of migration and transnationalism. We see this in just about every essay in this volume. We see it, too, with James Wait, who is hailed in the most offensive of all racist ways and whose life matters the least and the most in assessing the ambivalent legacy of Conrad's work. Precisely to the extent that Black lives are made to seem *not* to matter for Conrad, Black lives matter all the more. This is why I suggest we add Wait to the rollcall of migrant and transnational figures assembled in this volume's assessment of Conrad's kaleidoscope of migrant and transnational experiences.

Notes

1 For a definitive account of the Black Lives Matter movement, which originated in 2012, see Alicia Garza, 'A Herstory of the #BlackLivesMatter Movement', *The Feminist Wire*, 7 October 2014.

2 The phrase is the title of the first chapter of the English translation of Fanon's *Black Skin, White Masks*. For a discussion of the resonant mistranslation of this chapter see Fred Moten and Julie Beth Napolin.

3 For an especially insightful discussion of this figure see Robert Hampson, 'Joseph Conrad–Postcolonialism and Imperialism', 26–34. The whole essay might be read as an extended answer to the question of how Black lives matter for Conrad's work.

4 It should be noted that Robert Lynd was an Irish nationalist and anti-imperialist, politically opposed to this kind of narrow-minded English parochialism. This makes his accusation, and its effect on Conrad, all the more striking and puzzling. For an account of the complications of Lynd's assessment of Conrad and vice versa, see Richard Niland, '"Who's That Fellow Lynn?": Conrad and Robert Lynd', in *The Conradian*, 33, 1: (Spring 2008): 130–44. Thanks to Laurence Davies for calling my attention to this.

5 Michael North's opening chapter in *The Dialect of Modernism* discusses the significance of the lingua franca Malay for Conrad generally, connecting it more specifically to the force of the racist epithet in the *Narcissus*. In *The Passage of Literature* I further explore the way Conrad's use of Malay coincides with what Pramoedya Ananta Toer calls 'pre-Indonesian'. Julie Beth Napolin's *The Fact of Resonance* extends those and other readings in her first chapter, which offers an extended reading of the opening shout that Salmons and Zulli both discuss here.

Works Cited

Achebe, C. (1989), 'An Image of Africa', in *Hopes and Impediments*. London: Doubleday.

Conrad, J. (1990), *The Collected Letters*, vol. 4, Cambridge: Cambridge University Press.

Conrad, J. (1926), *The Collected Works*, 26 vols, London: Doubleday.

Dyson, M. E. (2020), 'Why Michael Eric Dyson Would Demote "Heart of Darkness" from the Canon', *New York Times*, 4 June.

Fanon, F. (1967), 'The Fact of Blackness', Chapter 5 of *Black Skin, White Masks*, trans. Charles Lam Markmann, Grove.

Garza, A. (2014), 'A Herstory of the #BlackLivesMatter Movement', *The Feminist Wire*, 7 October. Available online: https://thefeministwire.com/2014/10/blacklivesmatter-2/

GoGwilt, C. (2011), *The Passage of Literature: Genealogies of Modernism in Conrad, Rhys, and Pramoedya*, Oxford: Oxford University Press.

Gilroy, Paul. (1993), *The Black Atlantic: Modernity and Double Consciousness*, Harvard: Harvard University Press.

Hampson, R. (March 2011), 'Joseph Conrad – Postcolonialism and Imperialism', *EurAmerica*, 41 (1): 1–46.

hooks, b. (2015), *Black Looks: Race and Representation*, London: Routledge.

Israel, N. (2000), *Outlandish: Writing between Exile and Diaspora*, Stanford: Stanford University Press.

Mallios, P. (2010), *Our Conrad: Constituting American Modernity*, Stanford: Stanford University Press.

Moten, F. (2008), 'The Case of Blackness', *Criticism* 50 (2): 177–218.

Napolin, J. B. (2020), *The Fact of Resonance: Modernist Acoustics and Narrative Form*, New York: Fordham University Press.

Niland, R. (2008), '"Who's That Fellow Lynn?": Conrad and Robert Lynd', *The Conradian*, 33, 1 (Spring 2008).

North, M. (1994), *The Dialect of Modernism: Race, Language & Twentieth-Century Literature*, Oxford: Oxford University Press.

Index of Names

Index of Subjects

www.ingramcontent.com/pod-product-compliance
Lightning Source LLC
Chambersburg PA
CBHW070522100726
47907CB00004B/948

* 9 7 8 1 3 5 0 2 5 5 5 2 4 *